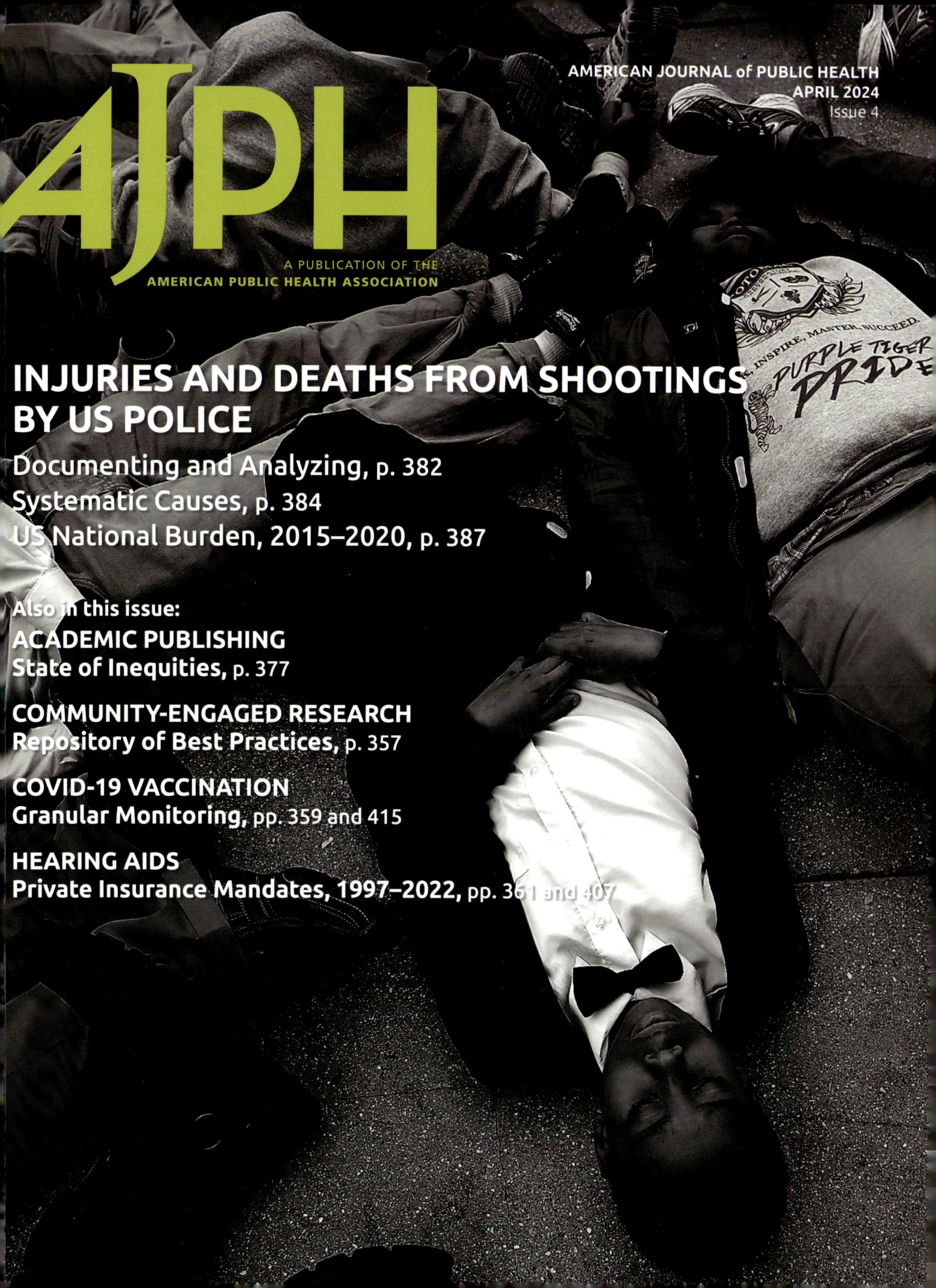


AMERICAN JOURNAL of PUBLIC HEALTH
APRIL 2024
Issue 4

# AJPH

A PUBLICATION OF THE
AMERICAN PUBLIC HEALTH ASSOCIATION

## INJURIES AND DEATHS FROM SHOOTINGS BY US POLICE

Documenting and Analyzing, p. 382
Systematic Causes, p. 384
US National Burden, 2015–2020, p. 387

Also in this issue:

**ACADEMIC PUBLISHING**
**State of Inequities,** p. 377

**COMMUNITY-ENGAGED RESEARCH**
**Repository of Best Practices,** p. 357

**COVID-19 VACCINATION**
**Granular Monitoring,** pp. 359 and 415

**HEARING AIDS**
**Private Insurance Mandates, 1997–2022,** pp. 361 and 407

APHA
AMERICAN PUBLIC HEALTH ASSOCIATION
*For science. For action. For health.*

*AJPH*®, published monthly, is the official Journal of the American Public Health Association®, 800 I St NW, Washington, DC 20001-3710; (202) 777- APHA; TDD (202) 777-2500. APHA is a nongovernmental professional society founded in 1872, representing all disciplines and specialties in public health.



The *American Journal of Public Health*® (*AJPH*) (print ISSN: 0090-0036; electronic ISSN: 1541- 0048), first published in 1911, is the official journal of the American Public Health Association® (APHA). The oldest and largest organization of public health professionals in the world, APHA represents approximately 30 000 members from more than 50 occupations of public health.

**Submissions:** Visit www.editorialmanager.com/ajph or ajph.edmgr.com for online manuscript preparation and submission guidelines. Contributions of original unpublished research, social science analyses, scholarly essays, critical commentaries, departments, and letters to the editor are welcome. Questions? Write ajph.submissions@apha.org or call APHA at (202) 777-2469.

**Print plus online subscriptions:** Institutional price (print copy with online access for a single institution and all authorized users, regardless of geographic location) varies by size of organization and ranges from $993–$1445 for US organizations, and $1073–$1526 for international organizations (air delivery); multiple campuses not permitted without special arrangement. Details of the tiered pricing system at https://subscriptionoffice.com/pages/apha-landing-page. To order, write apha.subscriptions@apha.org.

**Online-only subscriptions:** Institutional price for one institution and its authorized users (regardless of geographic location) is $878–$1307. To order, write apha.subscriptions@apha.org. For academic consortia or multisite corporate subscriptions, contact apha.subscriptions@apha.org.

**Print-only subscriptions:** Institutional price is US $701, $782 international.

**Back print issues:** A limited number of print issues are for sale. Single copies are US $49, $55 international (air delivery). Shipping included; prepay only. To order, write apha.subscriptions@apha.org.

**Reprints:** For prices and ordering information on 50 or more reprints, check the Reprints section at www.ajph.org. To order smaller quantities of reprints (rush delivery), use the "Purchase Article" link on the article site itself.

**Electronic access:** Online articles more than 10 years old are available free for personal use at www.ajph.org. Recent articles are available through pay-per-view: single PDF article for $24, single issue access for 24 hours for $33, or entire site access for 24 hours for $38.

**Postal information:** Periodicals postage paid at Washington, DC, and additional mailing offices. Postmaster: Send address changes to American Journal of Public Health, 800 I St NW, Washington, DC 20001-3710.

**Address changes:** Send to AJPH, Membership Department (members) or AJPH Subscriptions (subscribers), APHA, 800 I St NW, Washington, DC 20001-3710. Or write to membership.mail@apha. org (members) or apha.subscriptions@apha.org (subscribers).

**Advertising:** For pricing and other information, see www.ajph.org. Please write to ashell.alston@apha.org or call (202) 777-2470 for other advertising opportunities. Ask about special exhibit packages and sponsorships. Acceptance of advertising by the *Journal* does not imply endorsement of products.



**Indexes:** Publications that index or abstract articles from AJPH include the following: Ageline, Assia (Applied Social Science Index and Abstracts), Biological Abstracts, Chemical Abstracts, CINAHL, Criminal Justice Abstracts, EMBASE, EMCare, Environmental Abstracts, e-psyche, ERIC, ETOH (Alcohol and Alcohol Problems Science Database), Excerpta Medica, Food Science and Technology, General Science Index, Grateful Med, Hospital Literature Index, Human Resources Abstracts, International Pharmaceutical Abstracts (IPA), Medline, Physical Education Index, Pollution Abstracts, Psychological Abstracts, PsychINFO, Safety Science Abstracts, Sage Family Studies Abstracts, Sage Human Resources Abstracts, Science Citation Index, SCOPUS, SIIC Data Bases, Social Work Research and Abstracts, and Statistical Reference Index (SRI)/LexisNexis.

# AJPH

A PUBLICATION OF THE
**AMERICAN PUBLIC HEALTH ASSOCIATION**

COVER: Schoolchildren from the Potomac Preparatory Charter School take part in a "die-in" during a protest outside the Office of Police Complaints as part of a planned "28 Hours for Mike Brown" protest November 25, 2014, in Washington, DC. Protests took place across the United States in the wake of a Ferguson, MO, grand jury's decision not to indict police officer Darren Wilson in the fatal shooting of 18-year-old Michael Brown.

Cover concept and selection by Aleisha Kropf. Photo by Win McNamee/ Getty Images. Printed with permission.

APHA
AMERICAN PUBLIC HEALTH ASSOCIATION
*For science. For action. For health.*

Promoting public health research, policy, practice, and education is the *AJPH* mission. As we widen our scope to embrace global issues, we also sharpen our focus to support the needs of public health practitioners. We invite contributions of original unpublished research, opinion and commentary, and letters to the editor.

The *Journal* is printed on acid-free recycled paper.

OPEN ACCESS ONLINE ONLY PODCAST DATA SUPPLEMENT AVAILABLE


## EDITOR'S CHOICE

**357** A Repository of Public Health Best Practices From the Heart of the Pandemic
*A. Morabia*

# OPINIONS, IDEAS, & PRACTICE

## EDITORIALS

**359** Novel, Granular Methods to Monitor Vaccine Uptake and Associated Factors Within States
*R. A. Bednarczyk*

**361** State Mandates for Hearing Aid Coverage: An Opportunity for Improving Access to Hearing Health
*E. E. Garcia Morales and N. S. Reed*

**364** Social Justice and Public Health: A Public Health of Consequence, April 2024
*F. Kapadia*

## PERSPECTIVES

**366** Family Child Care Providers' Experience With the Child and Adult Care Food Program During the COVID-19 Pandemic
*B. D. Koester, S. Sloane, K. E. Speirs, E. T. Powers, and R. A. Gordon*

**372** Work Matters: Mainstreaming Worker Health and Safety Is Not Limited to Pandemic Response
*G. R. Wagner and D. Michaels*

**377** Inequities in Academic Publishing: Where Is the Evidence and What Can Be Done?
*M. Loui and S. C. Fiala*

## INJURIES AND DEATHS FROM SHOOTINGS BY POLICE

**382** Unveiling the Unseen: Documenting and Analyzing Nonfatal Shootings by Police
*J. Nix*

**384** Disparities in Policing From Theory to Practice
*H. Zare*

# RESEARCH & ANALYSIS

## INJURIES AND DEATHS FROM SHOOTINGS BY POLICE

**387** National Burden of Injury and Deaths From Shootings by Police in the United States, 2015–2020
*J. A. Ward, J. Cepeda, D. B. Jackson, O. Johnson Jr, D. W. Webster, and C. K. Crifasi*

## CLIMATE CHANGE

**398** Contribution of Cold Versus Climate Change to Mortality in London, UK, 1976–2019
*S. Hajat, D. Gampe, and G. Petrou*

## SURVEILLANCE

**403** Comparing Self-Reported and Aggregated Racial Classification for American Indian/Alaska Native Youths in YRBSS: 2021
*A. Gatewood, A. D. Hendrix-Dicken, and M. Hartwell*

## PRACTICE

**407** Longitudinal Policy Surveillance of Private Insurance Hearing Aid Mandates in the United States: 1997–2022
*M. L. Arnold, B. J. Heslin, M. Dowdy, S. P. Kershner, S. Phillips, B. Lipton, and M. F. Pesko*

**415** County-Level Factors Associated With Influenza and COVID-19 Vaccination in Indiana, 2020–2022
*M. L. Kasting, A. Laily, H. N. Burney, K. J. Head, J. K. Daggy, G. D. Zimet, and L. M. Schwab-Reese*

## OPEN-THEMED RESEARCH

**424** Inequities in Conversion Practice Exposure at the Intersection of Ethnoracial and Gender Identities
*N. K. Tran, E. Lett, A. Flentje, S. Ingram, M. E. Lubensky, Z. Dastur, J. Obedin-Maliver, and M. R. Lunn*

**435** Funding and Delivery of Syringe Services Programs in the United States, 2022
*S. N. Facente, J. L. Humphrey, C. Akiba, S. V. Patel, L. D. Wenger, H. Tookes, R. N. Bluthenthal, P. LaKosky, S. Prohaska, T. Morris, A. H. Kral, and B. H. Lambdin*

# BACKMATTER

## OTHER DEPARTMENTS

**448** Subscription Form

BLACK WOMEN'S REPRODUCTIVE HEALTH & SEXUALITY
A HOLISTIC PUBLIC HEALTH APPROACH

# A Repository of Public Health Best Practices From the Heart of the Pandemic

Alfredo Morabia, MD, PhD
Editor-in-Chief, *AJPH*

The COVID-19 pandemic has been both an opportunity and an accelerator. *AJPH* has now published two supplements (CEAL, https://ajph.aphapublications.org/toc/ajph/114/S1; RADx-UP, https://ajph.aphapublications.org/toc/ajph/112/S9), and three more are being produced. These five supplements comprise a panorama of the public health research that was funded by federal agencies during the COVID-19 pandemic. At the core of these supplements is the community-engaged research and interventions that are now an invaluable component of the tremendous achievements of public health during the pandemic. Reading these documents helps us to understand the key role of public health in getting millions of people tested and millions of vaccine doses from the industry warehouses into people's arms. Federal agencies can be commended for having reacted quickly, efficiently, and appropriately. Hopefully, these *AJPH* supplements will make these achievements also visible to the public at large.

The pandemic surprised us as a society and suddenly upset most of our usual ways of communicating. It also rapidly exacerbated the main dysfunctional aspects of the public health system: minoritized and disenfranchised populations were highly vulnerable to the brutal effects of SARS-CoV-2. Federal agencies opted to fund community-engaged science and interventions targeting the most heavily hit populations. "Unprecedented times combined with striking disparities called for these unprecedented measures" (https://doi.org/10.2105/AJPH.2022.307105), particularly among African American/Black, Hispanic/Latino, American Indian/Alaska Native, Asian, Native Hawaiian, and Pacific Islander populations, as well as socioeconomically disadvantaged populations, underserved rural populations, and sexual and gender minorities.

At the end of the process, some agencies turned to *AJPH* to publish the research conducted using their funds. These projects had not necessarily been led by teams familiar with scientific publications. The editors of *AJPH* have been actively identifying the strongest pieces submitted through Calls for Papers or in other ways, making sure that their content was rigorous and

Continued on page 358...

## HISTORY CORNER

### 6 YEARS AGO

#### The More Things Change, the More Things Stay the Same

Today, it is no longer an issue of being suspected of being a runaway slave; it is just generally being "suspected"—whether while sleeping in a common room in a university dorm, barbequing, walking home while wearing a hoodie, driving, wanting to use the washroom in a coffee shop, and so on. Being non-White is suspect. This reflects and cements a culture in which. . .our chances of being the victim of police homicide are much higher if we are Black or Latino. What can be done? First, better data are critical. . . . If we can document the number of adults who live within a mile of a park and keep counts of workers who get injured or die on the job, we can systematically collect data about injuries and homicides caused by police brutality. We have only recently begun to quantify and qualitatively describe the history of lynching in the United States; we should not wait until we erect monuments decades hence to describe the prevalence of police brutality.

From *AJPH*, September 2018, p. 1128

### 37 YEARS AGO

#### Murder at Work

OSHA [Occupational Safety and Health Administration] has failed to address the serious problem of occupational homicide. With guns met the publication standards of the Journal. Some of our new article formats, such as Notes From the Field, proved to be suitable for capturing local, innovative experiences, in often difficult-to-reach communities. The Journal also established a new format, Qualitative Notes From the Field, to capture voices from local experiences. This format, while not as fully detailed as the traditional research article, provides the information needed for other groups searching for models to know how these were technically performed and to contact the authors for more details. In some cases, the full article may have been published in other, more specialized journals than *AJPH*.

These supplements, altogether, form a catalogue, a repository, and a bank of best community-engaged practices. From this perspective, *AJPH* also takes pride in having featured the experience of thousands of public health professionals and community activists. This anthology of real-time experiences during the pandemic will be of great interest for building a postpandemic public health.

## RAPID ACCELERATION OF DIAGNOSTICS

The National Institutes of Health, through the National Institute on Minority Health and Health Disparities, the National Institute on Aging, and other institutes, launched the Rapid Acceleration of Diagnostics–Underserved Populations (RADx-UP) in April 2020 to support community-engaged research to increase access and uptake of COVID-19 diagnostic tests in underserved and vulnerable populations. To date, 142 RADx-UP projects are a nationwide community of practice comprising multidisciplinary research teams working directly with 409 979 enrolled participants as of February 22, 2024, and using the NIH RADx-UP Common Data Elements. RADx-UP research has implemented and evaluated interventions to, for example, increase testing uptake, reduce vaccine hesitancy in high-risk groups, and promote universal masking in schools.

## COMMUNITY ENGAGEMENT ALLIANCE

The backbone of the Community Engagement Alliance (CEAL) comprises 21 regional research teams geographically dispersed across 21 states, the District of Columbia, and Puerto Rico, and 371 counties, comprising approximately 85 million people. Half of their partners are faith-based, patient advocate, social service, community-based organizations, and other grassroots service-oriented organizations. Their role is to build trust, share science-based knowledge, generate community-engaged mitigation and prevention strategies, and promote participation in COVID-19–related clinical trials.

## OUTLINING A VISION

On May 11, 2023, the US COVID-19 public health emergency declaration expired, but the infrastructure and the methods developed by RADx-UP, CEAL, and programs from the National Institute for Occupational Safety and Health, the Centers for Disease Control and Prevention, and other agencies for which supplements are still in production, need to survive. Beyond COVID-19, the often pioneering approaches can be adapted to chronic diseases. AJPH

DOI: https://doi.org/10.2105/AJPH.2024.307614

## HISTORY CORNER

exceeded only by motor vehicles as a source of fatal injury at work, it is extraordinary that there are no OSHA regulations specifically designed to keep workers from being murdered on the job. Many of the work-related homicides occur in small businesses, yet OSHA gives little attention to workplaces with few employees; those with 10 or fewer are neither inspected by OSHA nor included in mortality estimates by the Bureau of Labor Statistics. . . . [T]here is need for a reporting system that will capture all homicides as well as all work deaths of the self-employed, a sizable group of workers whose safety is largely ignored.

From *AJPH*, October 1987, pp. 1273–1274

# Novel, Granular Methods to Monitor Vaccine Uptake and Associated Factors Within States

Robert A. Bednarczyk, PhD

**ABOUT THE AUTHORS**

*Robert A. Bednarczyk is an associate professor of global health and epidemiology in the Emory University Rollins School of Public Health, a faculty member in the Emory Vaccine Center, and an investigator in the Cancer Prevention and Control Program of the Winship Cancer Institute, Atlanta, GA.*

**See also Kasting et al., p. 415.**

High vaccine coverage is one of the best means of controlling both the transmission and severity of infectious diseases. In the early stages of the COVID-19 pandemic, concerns over a "twindemic" of surging cases of both influenza and COVID-19 during the winter respiratory disease season led to efforts to increase uptake of vaccines against these two diseases.[1] While there have been numerous systems put in place by the US Centers for Disease Control and Prevention (CDC) to assess vaccine uptake, such as the National Immunization Survey (for children aged 19–35 months),[2] National Immunization Survey–Teen (for adolescents aged 13–17 years),[3] and the National Health Information Survey (for adults),[4] these systems are often large enough only to provide very precise estimates of national-level vaccine uptake, with less precise estimates of vaccine coverage at the level of the state or immunization program.

## LIMITATIONS TO CURRENT VACCINE UPTAKE MONITORING SYSTEMS

This limitation is significant, in that it precludes substate analysis of vaccine uptake. Previous research has shown that, within a state, there can be variation in disease incidence based on variation in school entry vaccination requirement exemptions.[5] However, there is not routine reporting of vaccine coverage at granular substate levels. For example, in the 2022 National Immunization Survey–Teen, provider-verified vaccination records were used for analysis for 16 043 adolescents.[3] This provides very precise estimates of national-level vaccine coverage, with 95% confidence interval widths ranging from 2 to 6 percentage points.[3] However, individual state-level estimates had relatively lower precision,[6] owing to state-level sample sizes ranging from 207 to 794, with a median state-level sample size of 274.[7] These sample sizes preclude more granular substate analysis (e.g., at the county level).

## NOVEL METHODS FOR ASSESSING SUBSTATE VACCINE UPTAKE

In this issue of *AJPH*, Kasting et al. (p. 415) utilize two different sources of population-level vaccine uptake data to assess influenza vaccine uptake (using county-level vaccine data from the Centers for Disease Control and Prevention [CDC] FluVaxView Web site) and COVID-19 vaccine uptake (using county-level vaccine data from the Indiana Child and Hoosier Immunization Registry Program, the state immunization information system [IIS]).[8]

Notably, this article highlights county-level variability in vaccine uptake but also provides an assessment of county-level vaccine coverage in the context of county-level sociodemographic data.[8] These analyses help to disentangle factors that may drive vaccine coverage (e.g., health care access, socioeconomic status, insurance coverage, demographics) at the county level.

There are two key takeaways from the findings published by Kasting et al. First, county-level heterogeneity in vaccine coverage is differential by vaccine. For influenza vaccine, there was variability in county-level vaccine coverage, ranging from 33.7% to 53.1%, but this was a much smaller range than that seen for COVID-19 vaccine coverage, which ranged from 31.2% to 87.6%. These types of findings can help establish future research priorities, such as identifying counties where vaccine coverage for both vaccines is either high (potentially indicating consistently higher prevention activities) or low (potentially indicating consistently lower prevention activities), or where there is a split (e.g., high COVID-19 vaccine coverage and low influenza vaccine coverage, or vice versa, which potentially indicates differential manifestations of vaccine hesitance). Being able to make these comparisons can empower local public health and medical professionals to develop and implement more targeted interventions to improve vaccine uptake locally.

Second, using population-level data sources at a more granular substate level can provide an ability to account for socio-demographic differences at these smaller geographies. There were differences in county-level influenza and COVID-19 vaccine uptake, and these county-level sociodemographic characteristic differences provide a greater ability to understand factors that may impact vaccine uptake.

## ADVANCING THE SCIENCE OF VACCINE UPTAKE MEASUREMENT

Combined, these two takeaways show a clear path forward for future vaccine uptake assessments. By using state-level data systems, such as IIS, we can generate more precise estimates of vaccine coverage at very granular substate levels. However, state-level differences in IIS reporting requirements and standards can impact the utility and comparability of these data across states.[8] Similarly, IIS participation is heterogenous across states, and because of population dynamics (e.g., in- and out-migration from individual states, receipt of vaccines at health care facilities in a different state), complete accounting of individual-level vaccine uptake can be difficult.[9]

However, these limitations should not be seen as a reason to not pursue more detailed research activities using IIS data or data from other vaccine reporting sources (e.g., CDC FluVax-View, as used by Kasting et al. in this study), but rather a call to action to identify how best we can use existing data and develop improved data collection and analysis systems to monitor and improve state- and substate-level vaccine coverage.

In summary, the work of Kasting et al. presented here offers a view toward what can be done with more granular and detailed vaccination coverage data. Notably, the authors point out a limitation that ecologic data were used for these analyses. With greater awareness of the potential for more detailed analysis using individual-level vaccination and sociodemographic data, this opens up the opportunity for future studies to look at individual-level data to more completely assess associations between sociodemographics and vaccination status at the county level. AJPH

### CORRESPONDENCE

Correspondence should be sent to Robert A. Bednarczyk, Hubert Department of Global Health, Rollins School of Public Health, Emory University, Mailstop: 1518-002-6CC, RRR 626, 1518 Clifton Rd NE, Atlanta, GA 30322 (e-mail: rbednar@emory.edu). Reprints can be ordered at https://ajph.org by clicking the "Reprints" link.

### PUBLICATION INFORMATION

Full Citation: Bednarczyk RA. Novel, granular methods to monitor vaccine uptake and associated factors within states. *Am J Public Health*. 2024; 114(4):359–360.

Acceptance Date: January 16, 2024.

DOI: https://doi.org/10.2105/AJPH.2024.307594

ORCID iD:
Robert A. Bednarczyk https://orcid.org/0000-0002-6812-0928

### ACKNOWLEDGMENTS

This project was supported in part by National Cancer Institute grant R37CA234119.

### CONFLICTS OF INTEREST

The author has no conflicts of interest to declare.

### REFERENCES

1. Bellizzi S, Panu Napodano CM, Pinto S, Pichierri G. COVID-19 and seasonal influenza: the potential 2021–22 "Twindemic." *Vaccine*. 2022;40(24): 3286–3287. https://doi.org/10.1016/j.vaccine.2022.04.074
2. Hill HA, Yankey D, Elam-Evans LD, Chen M, Singleton JA. Vaccination coverage by age 24 months among children born in 2019 and 2020—National Immunization Survey-Child, United States, 2020–2022. *MMWR Morb Mortal Wkly Rep*. 2023;72(44):1190–1196. https://doi.org/10.15585/mmwr.mm7244a3
3. Pingali C, Yankey D, Elam-Evans LD, et al. Vaccination coverage among adolescents aged 13–17 Years—National Immunization Survey–Teen, United States, 2022. *MMWR Morb Mortal Wkly Rep*. 2023;72(34): 912–919. https://doi.org/10.15585/mmwr.mm7234a3
4. Lu PJ, Hung MC, Srivastav A, et al. Surveillance of vaccination coverage among adult populations—United States, 2018. *MMWR Surveill Summ*. 2021; 70(3):1–26. https://doi.org/10.15585/mmwr.ss7003a1
5. Omer SB, Enger KS, Moulton LH, Halsey NA, Stokley S, Salmon DA. Geographic clustering of nonmedical exemptions to school immunization requirements and associations with geographic clustering of pertussis. *Am J Epidemiol*. 2008; 168(12):1389–1396. https://doi.org/10.1093/aje/kwn263
6. Centers for Disease Control and Prevention. Supplementary Table 1. Vaccination coverage among adolescents aged 13–17 years—National Immunization Survey–Teen, United States, 2022. 2023. Available at: https://stacks.cdc.gov/view/cdc/132006#tabs-2. Accessed January 4, 2024.
7. Centers for Disease Control and Prevention. Vaccination coverage among adolescents (13–17 years). 2023. Available at: https://data.cdc.gov/Teen-Vaccinations/Vaccination-Coverage-among-Adolescents-13-17-Years/ee48-w5t6/about_data. Accessed January 4, 2024.
8. Centers for Disease Control and Prevention. Survey of state immunization information system legislation. 2018. Available at: https://www2a.cdc.gov/vaccines/iis/iissurvey/legislation-survey.asp. Accessed January 4, 2024.
9. Centers for Disease Control and Prevention. IISAR data participation rates and maps. 2022. Available at: https://www.cdc.gov/vaccines/programs/iis/annual-report-iisar/rates-maps-table.html. Accessed January 4, 2024.

# State Mandates for Hearing Aid Coverage: An Opportunity for Improving Access to Hearing Health

*Emmanuel E. Garcia Morales, PhD, and Nicholas S. Reed, AuD, PhD*

**ABOUT THE AUTHORS**

*Both authors are with the Cochlear Center for Hearing and Public Health, Department of Epidemiology, Johns Hopkins Bloomberg School of Public Health, Baltimore, MD.*

**See also Arnold et al., p. 407.**

Often overlooked, hearing loss is a common chronic condition and an important factor in overall health. Twenty-three percent of Americans 12 years and older have at least mild hearing loss.[1] However, the prevalence increases with age from less than 1.0% of those younger than 20 years[1] to 65% of those 71 years and older and 96% of those 90 years and older.[2] Hearing loss ranges in severity from mild (~66% of cases), to moderate (~28%), to severe or profound (~6%).

Early public health research on hearing loss focused on the association between unaddressed hearing loss among children and outcomes such as lower educational achievement and poorer speech and language development. Subsequent studies have shown the protective effects and importance of early intervention and language access (e.g., language services such as teaching American Sign Language, amplification, cochlear implantation, or some combination of these) and have led to widespread programs such as the universal newborn hearing–screening program tied to federal funding in the 1990s.

More recently, a shift in focus suggests that hearing loss among older adults is associated with lower health-related quality of life,[3] incident dementia,[4] depression,[5] and increased health care expenditures.[6] Importantly, most observational studies find that hearing aid use provides a protective effect against negative outcomes. A landmark randomized controlled trial assessing the effectiveness of hearing intervention in reducing cognitive decline over three years among older adults, the ACHIEVE (Aging and Cognitive Health Evaluation in Elders) trial, reported a null overall effect; however, a prespecified subanalysis found that hearing intervention reduced cognitive change among older adults at increased risk for cognitive decline (e.g., those with poorer overall health, lower socioeconomic status).[7]

Hearing aids, a noninvasive, minimal-risk intervention, are the most common and versatile (e.g., indicated for most degrees of hearing loss) treatment of hearing loss but are underutilized. Estimates suggest that only between 16% and 30% of American adults who might benefit from a hearing aid own and use one.[2] The barriers to hearing care are multifactorial, but often noted key barriers are accessibility and affordability.[8] The estimated cost at $4700 for a typical pair of hearing aids and accompanying professional services is prohibitive for many Americans, especially given hearing services minimal insurance coverage.[8]

Hearing aids and related services are a statutory exclusion under Medicare, the primary health insurance provider for older Americans. Although many Medicare Advantage programs include hearing aid coverage, evidence on the details and effectiveness of these benefits on hearing aid adoption is limited. As of 2016, only 28 states had some level of Medicaid hearing aid coverage for adults, with benefits varying significantly from state to state.[9]

Recent policies have attempted to improve the accessibility and affordability of hearing care. The Over-the-Counter Hearing Aid Act of 2017 (passed as a rider on the US Food and Drug Administration [FDA] Reauthorization Act of 2017) required the FDA to develop criteria and to implement a new category for a regulated class of over-the-counter hearing aids. These devices would be available to the public without the need to see a licensed professional as a means to decrease access barriers to hearing care. The new FDA regulations became official in November 2022, and any realized increase in hearing aid uptake is still uncertain. The Build Back Better Act of 2021 included provisions that removed the statutory exclusion and expanded hearing care under Medicare; the act passed the US House of Representative but ultimately failed by a single vote in the US Senate.

AJPH April 2024, Vol. 114, No. 4

In recognition of hearing aids' importance for people with hearing loss, some states and US territories have enacted mandates requiring private health insurance to cover the cost of hearing aids. In an exemplary exercise of policy surveillance, in this issue of the *AJPH*, Arnold et al. (p. 407) found that as of 2023, there are 28 state mandates in place (27 by the end of 2022 and an additional one in Vermont starting in 2023) requiring private health insurance to cover hearing aids. Unsurprisingly, the authors found vast heterogeneity across state mandates, with variability in exemptions and exceptions of included populations, coverage limits, and intervals for how often benefits could be claimed—a key consideration given the limited lifespan of a hearing aid (~3–7 years).[8] The detailed report puts the generosity of these mandates into perspective, as some benefit limits would not cover the average cost of a pair of hearing aids and would leave Americans on the hook for a substantial remaining bill.

Perhaps consistent with the history of the research described, Arnold et al. found that hearing aid policies and state mandates favored US children and adolescents. Because of multiple state mandates, the overall proportion of US individuals whose private health insurance covers at least some costs related to a hearing aid has increased over the past 15 years (2008–present); however, deeper surveillance revealed differences by age group. The proportion of children and adolescents with hearing aid coverage increased from 3.4% to 18.7%, whereas adults aged 19 to 64 years were left behind with only a 0.3% to 4.6% increase. A combination of established research translating to policy, a smaller target population that requires fewer resources to guarantee coverage, and ageism (e.g., overlooked concern for older adults) likely plays a role in the disparities in coverage. However, given the recent work and trial findings, improving hearing care access for older Americans could have an important impact on the overall well-being of society—perhaps even being cost-effective because health care expenditures would be reduced.

In their article, Arnold et al. suggest that higher coverage could be achieved with the implementation of a federal-level mandate or with the relaxation of state mandate exceptions, particularly those pertaining to age limits. However, as the authors mention, the reach of these state mandates is limited, as they do not apply to private employer self-insured group health plans, which cover most privately insured workers.

Moving forward, an important consideration is the need for a deeper understanding of how increased coverage and which aspects of coverage (e.g., plan generosity) translate into realized increases in hearing aid uptake and sustained hearing aid use. Importantly, the authors have provided a valuable contribution to science and have laid the foundation for developing causal inference and econometric models to assess the effectiveness of mandates by publicly disseminating the output of this surveillance research, which compiles and categorizes details of the various state mandates with information on when they go into effect. These data could be a catalyst for new, innovative research and offer a unique opportunity to spur new interest in hearing care research from public health researchers not previously engaged in this area.

Policy surveillance examines the link between law and public health, and it contributes to the development of effective and equitable policies. At the same time, it allows the monitoring of such policies to ensure that these remain relevant to the needs of the population they intend to serve. Policy surveillance analysis pertaining to hearing health care was overlooked until now. The work of Arnold et al. will ease the monitoring and evaluation of these hearing aid mandates for the benefit of the US population while providing new information to consider in the larger framework of hearing care policy research moving forward as their work isolates the effect of new initiatives (e.g., over-the-counter hearing aids) and proposes comprehensive approaches (e.g., combining mandates with Medicare expansion) for improving hearing care uptake in the United States. AJPH

## CORRESPONDENCE

Correspondence should be sent to Emmanuel E. Garcia Morales, PhD, Johns Hopkins Bloomberg School of Public Health, 2024 E. Monument St, Suite 2-700, Baltimore, MD 21205 (e-mail: egarci18@jhu.edu). Reprints can be ordered at http://www.ajph.org by clicking the "Reprints" link.

## PUBLICATION INFORMATION

Full Citation: Garcia Morales EE, Reed NS. State mandates for hearing aid coverage: an opportunity for improving access to hearing health. *Am J Public Health*. 2024;114(4):361–363.

Acceptance Date: January 27, 2024.

DOI: https://doi.org/10.2105/AJPH.2024.307620

## CONTRIBUTORS

Both authors conceptualized, drafted, and revised the editorial.

## CONFLICTS OF INTEREST

E. E. Garcia Morales has no conflicts of interest to report. N. S. Reed sits on the advisory board of Neosensory.

## REFERENCES

1. Goman AM, Lin FR. Prevalence of hearing loss by severity in the United States. *Am J Public Health*. 2016;106(10):1820–1822. https://doi.org/10.2105/AJPH.2016.303299
2. Reed NS, Garcia-Morales EE, Myers C, et al. Prevalence of hearing loss and hearing aid use among US Medicare beneficiaries aged 71 years and older. *JAMA Netw Open*. 2023;6(7):e2326320.

https://doi.org/10.1001/jamanetworkopen.2023.26320

3. Chia EM, Wang JJ, Rochtchina E, Cumming RR, Newall P, Mitchell P. Hearing impairment and health-related quality of life: the Blue Mountains Hearing Study. *Ear Hear*. 2007;28(2):187–195. https://doi.org/10.1097/AUD.0b013e31803126b6
4. Deal JA, Betz J, Yaffe K, et al. Hearing impairment and incident dementia and cognitive decline in older adults: the Health ABC Study. *J Gerontol A Biol Sci Med Sci*. 2017;72(5):703–709. https://doi.org/10.1093/gerona/glw069
5. Lawrence BJ, Jayakody DMP, Bennett RJ, Eikelboom RH, Gasson N, Friedland PL. Hearing loss and depression in older adults: a systematic review and meta-analysis. *Gerontologist*. 2020;60(3):e137–e154. https://doi.org/10.1093/geront/gnz009
6. Foley DM, Frick KD, Lin FR. Association between hearing loss and healthcare expenditures in older adults. *J Am Geriatr Soc*. 2014;62(6):1188–1189. https://doi.org/10.1111/jgs.12864
7. Lin FR, Pike JR, Albert MS, et al. Hearing intervention versus health education control to reduce cognitive decline in older adults with hearing loss in the USA (ACHIEVE): a multicentre, randomised controlled trial. *Lancet*. 2023;402(10404):786–797. https://doi.org/10.1016/S0140-6736(23)01406-X
8. Blazer DG, Domnitz S, and Liverman CT, eds. *Hearing Health Care for Adults: Priorities for Improving Access and Affordability*. Washington, DC: National Academies Press; 2016.
9. Arnold ML, Hyer K, Chisolm T. Medicaid hearing aid coverage for older adult beneficiaries: a state-by-state comparison. *Health Aff (Millwood)*. 2017;36(8):1476–1484. https://doi.org/10.1377/hlthaff.2016.1610

# Social Justice and Public Health: A Public Health of Consequence, April 2024

*Farzana Kapadia, PhD, MPH*

**ABOUT THE AUTHOR**

*Farzana Kapadia is* AJPH *deputy editor, and professor of epidemiology, School of Global Public Health, New York University, New York.*

"Of all the forms of inequality, injustice in health care is the most shocking and inhumane."

—*Martin Luther King Jr.*

Martin Luther King Jr. delivered this well-known quotation March 25, 1966, at the second convention of the Medical Committee for Human Rights. This quotation resonates as strongly today as it did almost 60 years ago—not only because of steadfast recognition of the multiple systems of oppression that create and sustain social inequality and social injustice but also because of how these coalesce to perpetuate health inequities. In emphasizing health and health care, King recognized that high-quality health care—especially for those most marginalized in our society—was a right that had to be protected and valued as a public good.

This Public Health of Consequence looks at *AJPH* publications that extend and build on King's words and his work as it evolved and connects the complex, complicated, and insidious ways systematic inequality and oppression undermine health equity and social justice. I use examples from this issue of *AJPH* to highlight social determinants of health and how high-quality health care needs to be accessible to all to achieve population health.

## SOCIAL DISADVANTAGE AND ADVERSE HEALTH

First, Koester et al. (p. 366) address the intertwined issues of food insecurity among low-income families and children and how childcare centers can help reduce this insecurity by participating in the Child and Adult Care Feeding Program (CACFP). Unlike the Supplemental Nutrition Assistance Program and the Special Supplemental Nutrition Program for Women, Infants, and Children, the CACFP is a less well-known program that subsidizes healthy meals for children by reimbursing licensed childcare centers and daycare homes for those meals—sites that are more likely to serve children of low-income parents.[1,2] Koester et al. note that concerted efforts to make childcare providers aware of the CACFP and provide guidance on how to overcome administrative hurdles to enrollment are necessary, highlighting how difficult it can be to access federal food assistance programs.

Next, Ward et al. (p. 387) provide the first, to their knowledge, multiyear and nationwide analysis of fatal and nonfatal police shootings, providing evidence of racial disparities in total injury burden that are more severe than shown in previous studies that examined fatal shootings alone. These findings, as summarized by Zare (p. 384) and Nix (p. 382), are evidence of the lack of accountability at local, state, and federal levels for police officers' use of deadly force—reflecting the structural racism that is deeply rooted in efforts to control and subjugate people of color and people from low-income communities.

Finally, two research articles that merit recognition deal with issues that affect historically marginalized people. Tran et al. (p. 424) report findings showing that transgender and nonbinary people, particularly those from minoritized racial and ethnic backgrounds, experience greater exposure to conversion practices that begin at younger ages. These findings are especially troubling in the current US sociopolitical landscape, where more and more states are passing legislation that is hostile to transgender and nonbinary individuals as well as the broader sexual and gender minority community. Facente et al. (p. 435) show that funding for syringe exchange programs, one of the most cost-effective HIV prevention interventions, does not meet the level necessary and recommended by the Centers for Disease Control and Prevention to offer comprehensive programming to reduce HIV and other physical and mental health burdens among injection drug users.

In addition, an editorial by Wagner and Michaels (p. 372) highlights the importance of occupational safety as fundamental to public health. Although the COVID-19 pandemic prompted attention to the health and safety—both physical and mental—of frontline essential and health care workers, who are overwhelmingly of low income and people of color, the integration of occupational safety and public health beyond emergency situations is necessary. And as occupation and occupational hazards are social determinants of health, government agencies that provide oversight and protect against occupational hazards require greater funding and resources to protect and promote the health of workers, their families, and their communities.

## SOCIAL DISADVANTAGE TO SOCIAL JUSTICE

The articles in this issue add to the growing body of literature on the social, political, and economic policies and practices that continue to contribute to and exacerbate health and health care inequities. They further highlight how the patterns of social disadvantage are sharper and more damaging to health among minoritized racial and ethnic groups, sexual and gender minorities, and people who use drugs.

For public health professionals, a social justice approach to promoting health and well-being requires that we continue tackling structural racism and discrimination in all its forms, income and educational inequality, housing and food insecurity, and occupational and environmental hazards—the fundamental drivers of health inequalities in our population. Continuing to do so is our shared responsibility if we seek to uphold King's legacy of fighting for health as a public good for all people. AJPH

### CORRESPONDENCE

Correspondence should be sent to Farzana Kapadia, PhD, MPH, New York University, School of Global Public Health, 708 Broadway, Room 729, New York, NY 10003 (e-mail: farzana.kapadia@nyu.edu). Reprints can be ordered at http://www.ajph.org by clicking the "Reprints" link.

### PUBLICATION INFORMATION

Full Citation: Kapadia F. Social justice and public health: a Public Health of Consequence, April 2024. *Am J Public Health*. 2024;114(4):364–365.

Acceptance Date: January 23, 2024.

DOI: https://doi.org/10.2105/AJPH.2024.307610

### CONFLICTS OF INTEREST

The author has no conflicts of interest to disclose.

### REFERENCES

1. Nestle M. Equitable access to the USDA's food assistance programs: policies needed to reduce barriers and increase accessibility. *Am J Public Health*. 2023;113(suppl 3):S167–S170. https://doi.org/10.2105/AJPH.2023.307480
2. Asada Y, Schermbeck R, Thiede K, Chriqui JF. Opportunities to improve access to and retention in the Child and Adult Care Food Program: key recommendations from early childcare providers in Illinois, December 2020–July 2021. *Am J Public Health*. 2023;113(suppl 3):S231–S239. https://doi.org/10.2105/AJPH.2023.307433

# Family Child Care Providers' Experience With the Child and Adult Care Food Program During the COVID-19 Pandemic

*Brenda Davis Koester, MS, Stephanie Sloane, PhD, Katherine E. Speirs, PhD, Elizabeth T. Powers, PhD, and Rachel A. Gordon, PhD*

**ABOUT THE AUTHORS**

*Brenda Davis Koester is with the Center for Social and Behavioral Science, Stephanie Sloane is with the Family Resiliency Center, and Elizabeth T. Powers is with the Department of Economics, University of Illinois Urbana-Champaign. Katherine E. Speirs is with the Norton School of Family & Consumer Economics, University of Arizona, Tucson. Rachel A. Gordon is with the College of Health and Human Services, Northern Illinois University, DeKalb.*

AJPH April 2024, Vol. 114, No. 4

Addressing children's nutritional health in child care settings is important, because 60% of all children under age 5 years spend a significant portion of their waking hours in nonparental care.[1] Meals and snacks eaten in these settings often provide most of a young child's daily food and nutrient intake.[2] The nutritional quality of these meals is important, as adequate nutrition is critical to healthy development in early childhood.[3] There is abundant evidence that low-income children are at a greater risk for poor nutrition.[4]

The Child and Adult Care Food Program (CACFP), a federally funded program designed to support young children's equitable access to nutrition and healthy development,[5] subsidizes nutritious meals and snacks for low-income children in center- and family-based child care. The program is administered by state agencies through sponsoring organizations (henceforth, sponsors).[6] Early child care programs participating in CACFP have been shown to serve healthier food than nonparticipating child care centers and homes,[7] and emerging evidence indicates that children who receive CACFP-funded meals are less likely to experience food insecurity.[8]

Family child care providers are an important access point for CACFP.[3,9] Millions of children in the United States receive care in family child care settings,[10] which are estimated to represent more than 70% of all child care providers.[11] Children from low-income, racial and ethnic minority households are more likely to be enrolled in family child care than higher-income and majority race/ethnicity children,[12] and many family child care providers are low-income themselves, with higher documented rates of food insecurity than in the general public.[13]

There is evidence that the COVID-19 pandemic exacerbated inequities in food access,[14] particularly for low-income families and families of color.[15,16] The pandemic also affected child care in unprecedented ways. One of the most significant impacts was widespread child care closures, which prevented children from accessing nutritious CACFP-funded food through their child care provider.[17] Nationwide, the number of CACFP meals claimed by child care providers dropped dramatically in the first three months of the pandemic.[18]

The federal government took several steps to mitigate the impact of the pandemic on child care and children's feeding programs.[19] In response to unprecedented pandemic-related program operation challenges, the Food and Nutrition Service of the US Department of Agriculture (USDA) authorized temporary waivers to core policy elements of CACFP as authorized by the Families First Coronavirus Response Act.[20] One waiver allowed providers to serve meals outside of standard mealtimes, another allowed parents to take food home even when the children were not present, and another permitted flexibility regarding the specific foods that providers served to children to meet CACFP meal pattern requirements.[21] Providers were eligible to use any or all of the waivers. Implementation of waivers varied among states, and little is known about how the waivers were operationalized in the field, particularly in the child care setting.[22]

Here, we summarize insights on child care providers' experiences participating in CACFP during the COVID-19 pandemic, obtained through surveys with a convenience sample of family child care providers conducted in early fall 2021 (method described in the Appendix, available as a supplement to the online version of this article at http://www.ajph.org). Providers gave voice to the problems they experienced utilizing the temporary programmatic waivers, difficulties they had providing nutritious food to children, and obstacles they faced in operating their family child care. Rural–urban differences were also of interest. Access to CACFP is more limited in rural areas because of the ways the geographic concentration of poverty affects CACFP benefit levels[23] and the documented barriers for rural areas in accessing healthy food.[24]

## KNOWLEDGE OF AND EXPERIENCE WITH WAIVERS

Prior evidence has shown that COVID-19 relief funds were effective in providing critical short-term support for child care programs.[25] However, there is uneven evidence of the contribution of CACFP programmatic waivers for child care providers, particularly family-based child care.[26] Previously identified barriers to using programmatic waivers included limited program capacity due to issues such as staffing, storage, and transportation.[26] Importantly, we found that many of the licensed family child care providers that we surveyed had little knowledge of CACFP program waivers. For instance, 40.6% of providers reported they had not heard of the waivers at all, and 44.1% had no knowledge of at least one of the waivers. Those who had heard about the waivers most commonly learned about them from their CACFP sponsor or monitor (32.9%), their child care resources and referral agency (10.5%), or the statewide network of such agencies (9.8%).

The overwhelming majority of our sample (85.9%) reported that they never used a waiver. One provider even noted, "Wish I would've known about the waivers because it would have helped my families." Several providers who were aware of the waivers, but did not use them, indicated they did not understand the waivers. Among providers who used one or more of the waivers, few reported problems associated with their use. One provider mentioned that the mealtime flexibility waiver helped with school-age students' online learning schedules, and others talked about the waivers helping support the families of the children in their care whom they perceived needing food support: "The children were able to still get nutritious meals when program attendance wasn't allowed. Many families needed those meals." Providers indicated reasons they had stopped using the waivers, which included that their child care program had reopened and they were serving meals in person; that there was no longer interest from the families in taking meals home; and that grocery availability had improved.

Providers' lack of awareness is surprising, given that CACFP connects every family child care provider to a sponsor who should have provided them with information about the waivers. A prior study found that child care providers who participated in CACFP were more likely to connect families in their care with food resources than non-CACFP-participating providers.[17] Communication challenges (e.g., confusing program guidance) have been identified as barriers to CACFP participation[27] and to the implementation of healthy eating standards.[28] A study of state CACFP administrators found that they experienced difficulty receiving timely and clear communication from the USDA, which translated into downstream communication challenges for program participants.[26] CACFP sponsoring organizations and participating child care centers also reported confusion that was due to changing and inconsistent rules and guidance for COVID-19.[29,30] These communication-related challenges resulted in diminished access to nutritious meals for children and families who were already likely to face nutrition inequities.[16]

Family child care providers who participate in CACFP are an important focus of policy efforts to support children's nutritional health and equitable access to nutritional meals. Few providers used or were aware of CACFP programmatic waivers during the COVID-19 pandemic, which was a missed opportunity for children's nutrition, particularly as providers that used waivers found them beneficial. Identifying effective ways to directly communicate to providers in a timely and clear manner is critical for current programmatic needs as well as for future public health crises.

## CHALLENGES DURING THE PANDEMIC

During the pandemic, family child care providers struggled to purchase food for their business. Almost all of the providers (95.8%) we surveyed said they noticed higher food prices since March 2020, with a majority reporting difficulty at times purchasing the food they needed for their child care. The most frequent reasons that providers gave were that food prices had increased during COVID-19, that grocery stores had trouble keeping the items they wanted or needed in stock, and that they didn't have enough money to buy the food they needed for their day care. We also sought to understand if providers in rural areas had more food-related challenges than those in urban areas. In our sample, providers in rural areas did not report more difficulty purchasing food than providers in urban areas.

Our survey results indicated that providers were currently experiencing more difficulty, both in making meals and snacks that children wanted to eat and in purchasing food that complied with CACFP menu requirements, than they were before March 2020. Providers mentioned that grocery shortages required additional travel and time to find certain foods and that they sometimes had to make trips to multiple stores. Difficulty finding items created additional complications, such as needing to rearrange CACFP menus (for themes and illustrative quotes from open-ended questions, see Table A, available as a supplement to the online version of this article at http://www.ajph.org). Other providers mentioned the poor quality and short shelf life of available foods, particularly fruits and vegetables. Others pointed out that certain items required by meal patterns were hard to find (e.g., whole grain items). One provider mentioned that reduced enrollment had affected their economy of scale. Many providers also mentioned that children's picky eating was challenging. Some suggested that these behaviors had gotten worse since COVID-19, whereas others saw them as ongoing. However, despite these challenges, many said they felt that their participation in CACFP supported the healthy eating habits of children in their care.

Our study also found that providers reported higher food costs, significantly more difficulty finding the food they needed, and more difficulty making CACFP-compliant meals and snacks in fall 2021 than before the pandemic. Because CACFP reimbursement does not cover the full cost of meals, providers must pay the difference out of pocket. Our findings reinforce other studies that have also identified the ways that meeting CACFP meal patterns is challenged by limited food availability and high food costs.[31] Contrary to our expectations, there were few rural–urban differences.

An important priority should be helping providers address financial hardships such as rising food prices. Identifying cross-sector and system-level opportunities to leverage connections, information, and support for providers is critical.[32,33] Sponsors could help connect providers with food assistance programs (e.g., the Supplemental Nutrition Assistance Program, or SNAP) and charitable food assistance (e.g., food pantries), and provide information about budgeting and stretching resources.

## ADDITIONAL COVID-19–RELATED CONCERNS

Overall, providers were worried about their personal financial situation, the sustainability and future of their child care business, and purchasing food compliant with CACFP menu requirements (Table 1). Many providers reported difficulty finding protective equipment and cleaning supplies and an increase in the cost of supplies. A few mentioned that COVID-19–related cleaning was burdensome and took time away from interacting with children. The toll of added worry and stress that the pandemic created on the physical and mental health of the providers themselves was mentioned frequently. Providers voiced concern about the impact on their immediate family, and some commented that they felt the children in their care experienced greater stress and anxiety than before the pandemic. A majority reported they were somewhat or very worried about the future health and safety of children after the pandemic.

## IMPACT OF COVID-19 ON CHILD CARE OPERATION

Providers' concern about their financial situation was not surprising, given that over 75% of providers reported financial loss due to COVID-19, with another 7.7% reporting they had not yet experienced a financial loss but expected to in the future. One contributing factor was that many providers were still operating under capacity. One quarter of providers reported that they were operating at under 50% of their capacity, 23.8% at between 51% and 75% of their capacity, and 50.3% at 76% or more of their capacity. Comparable pre-COVID-19 capacity information is not available. These results are critical, as fewer children enrolled in care means that fewer children can access the benefits of healthy food through the CACFP program. Responses about additional COVID-19 impacts illuminated some reasons that providers were operating under capacity. These included parents working from home, parents wanting different schedules, families losing employment, and exposure-related closings. Providers also mentioned not being able to find reliable assistants and the inability to employ assistants due to reduced capacity. We also sought to understand if providers in rural areas faced more financial hardships than those in urban areas. Our results indicated that although providers in rural areas

**TABLE 1— Illinois Family Child Care Providers' Concerns About Child Care Program During and After COVID-19 Pandemic**

| When It Comes to the Current and Future Sustainability of Your Child Care Program, How Much Do You Worry About— | Very Much, % | Somewhat, % | Undecided, Not Much, or Not at All, % |
|---|---|---|---|
| Paying myself | 50.0 | 28.9 | 21.1 |
| Making rent or mortgage payments | 37.3 | 34.5 | 28.2 |
| Making utility payments | 38.0 | 35.9 | 26.1 |
| Paying for health insurance and other benefits | 41.8 | 26.2 | 32.0 |
| Finding and paying for protective equipment and cleaning supplies | 27.5 | 39.4 | 42.5 |
| Whether families will come back after the pandemic is over | 31.9 | 25.5 | 42.6 |
| Purchasing food that meets the CACFP menu requirements | 24.6 | 38.7 | 36.7 |
| Health and safety of children after the pandemic is over | 48.3 | 29.4 | 22.3 |

*Note.* CACFP = Child and Adult Care Food Program. The response options "undecided," "not much," and "not at all" were collapsed. Sample size was n = 143.

did not report more financial loss than providers in urban areas, they were more likely to report operating under capacity.

Many providers in our study reported that they experienced a financial loss, had reduced enrollment, were operating under capacity, and had difficulty finding and paying assistants. These challenges have been documented for family child care providers statewide, with 48.2% of all Illinois child care providers reporting they considered quitting because of economic stress from COVID-19.[34] Even before the pandemic, numbers of family child care providers were declining.[35] Such declines reduce children's access to nutritional supports through CACFP, particularly among lower-income and non-White families, who are more likely to use family child care.[36] Our finding that rural providers were more likely to report operating under capacity is of note. Future research should seek to understand the drivers of this relationship and whether it has continued after the pandemic.

Providers' significant worries about the financial sustainability of their child care operation are not surprising, given that child care providers overall are low-income earners.[12] Thirty-eight percent of our sample fell below the federal poverty level (according to the US Department of Health and Human Services; https://bit.ly/3SQxX6q). Food insecurity among child care providers is higher than in the general public,[37] and providers' food security status influences their feeding practices with children.[12] Providers' physical and mental health are also predictors of quality in family child care.[38] Providing nutritional support to providers, who play a critical role in the child-serving ecosystem, can further support the health and well-being of children.[32]

COVID-19 disrupted the food safety net, and the government responded with speed and great flexibility. However, we have presented evidence that communication to providers was poor, and lack of knowledge overwhelmingly prevented the providers in our sample from taking advantage of COVID-19 waivers that would have helped children. These are issues that were also evident in the CACFP program before the pandemic. An important question dramatically highlighted by COVID-19 is how to improve communication of CACFP policies to families, providers, and state agencies. Given the recent USDA focus on advancing nutrition security and equity,[39] family child care providers and their participation in CACFP are essential to consider if we are to meet the goal of connecting all Americans with healthy, safe, affordable foods and to ensure equitable access to nutrition for all children. AJPH

## CORRESPONDENCE

Correspondence should be sent to Brenda Davis Koester, 105 Observatory, 1901 South Mathews Ave, Urbana, IL 61801 (e-mail: bkoester@illinois.edu). Reprints can be ordered at http://www.ajph.org by clicking the "Reprints" link.

## PUBLICATION INFORMATION

Full Citation: Koester BD, Sloane S, Speirs KE, Powers ET, Gordon RA. Family child care providers' experience with the Child and Adult Care Food Program during the COVID-19 pandemic. *Am J Public Health*. 2024;114(4):366–371.

Acceptance Date: November 26, 2023

DOI: https://doi.org/10.2105/AJPH.2023.307557

## CONTRIBUTORS

B. D. Koester led the design of the study, the drafting, review, and revision of the article, and the data management, analysis, and interpretation. All authors contributed to the conceptualization and design of the study, assisted with interpretation of the data, reviewed the article for intellectual content, and approved the final version of the article as submitted.

## ACKNOWLEDGMENTS

Support for this research was provided in part by a grant from the Robert Wood Johnson Foundation. Support was also provided by the Christopher Family Food and Family Program at the Family Resiliency Center at the University of Illinois Urbana-Champaign.

We thank the family child care providers for their participation in this study.

**Note.** The views given here do not necessarily reflect the views of the Robert Wood Johnson Foundation.

## CONFLICTS OF INTEREST

The authors have no conflicts of interest to declare.


## REFERENCES


1. National Center for Education Statistics. Early Childhood Program Participation. 2019. Available at: https://nces.ed.gov/pubs2017/2017101REV.pdf. Accessed February 19, 2023.
2. Institute of Medicine. *Early Childhood Obesity Prevention Policies: Goals, Recommendations, and Potential Actions.* Washington, DC: National Academies Press; 2011. https://doi.org/10.17226/13124.
3. Benjamin-Neelon SE. Position of the Academy of Nutrition and Dietetics: benchmarks for nutrition in child care. *J Acad Nutr Diet.* 2018;118(7):1291–1300. https://doi.org/10.1016/j.jand.2018.05.001
4. Larson N, Story M. Barriers to equity in nutritional health for US children and adolescents: a review of the literature. *Curr Nutr Rep.* 2015;4(1):102–110. https://doi.org/10.1007/s13668-014-0116-0
5. Gordon RA, Kaestner R, Korenman S, Abner K. The Child and Adult Care Food Program: who is served and why? *Soc Serv Rev.* 2011;85(3): 359–400. https://doi.org/10.1086/662607
6. Adams G, Hernandez F. The Child and Adult Care Food Program and home-based child care providers: expanding participation. Urban Institute. 2021. Available at: https://www.urban.org/research/publication/child-and-adult-care-food-program-and-home-based-child-care-providers. Accessed February 16, 2024.
7. Zaltz DA, Hecht AA, Neff RA, et al. Healthy eating policy improves children's diet quality in early care and education in South Carolina. *Nutrients.* 2020;12(6):1753. https://doi.org/10.3390/nu12061753
8. Heflin C, Arteaga I, Gable S. The Child and Adult Care Food Program and food insecurity. *Soc Serv Rev.* 2015;89(1):77–98. https://doi.org/10.1086/679760
9. Cohen JFW, Stowers KC, Odoms-Young A, Franckle RL. A call for theory to guide equity-focused federal child nutrition program policy responses and recovery efforts in times of public health crisis. *J Acad Nutr Diet.* 2023;123(1):15–28. https://doi.org/10.1016/j.jand.2022.07.016
10. National Survey of Early Care and Education Project Team. *Number and Characteristics of Early Care Education (ECE) Teachers and Caregivers: Initial Findings From the National Survey of Early Care and Education (NSECE).* Washington, DC: Office of Planning, Research and Evaluation Administration for Children and Families, US Dept of Health and Human Services; 2013.
11. Porter T, Paulsell D, Del Grosso P, Avellar S, Hass R, Vuong L. A review of the literature on home-based child care: implications for future directions. 2010. Available at: https://www.acf.hhs.gov/sites/default/files/documents/opre/lit_review.pdf. Accessed November 14, 2023.
12. Laughlin L. Who's minding the kids? Child care arrangements: spring 2011. Current Population Reports. US Census Bureau. 2013. Available at: https://www.census.gov/library/publications/2013/demo/p70-135.html. Accessed February 16, 2024.
13. Swindle T, Phelps J, Schrick B, Johnson SL. Hungry is not safe: a mixed methods study to explore food insecurity in early care and education. *Appetite.* 2021;167:105626. https://doi.org/10.1016/j.appet.2021.105626
14. Kar A, Motoyama Y, Carrel AL, Miller HJ, Le HTK. COVID-19 exacerbates unequal food access. *Appl Geogr.* 2021;134(June):102517. https://doi.org/10.1016/j.apgeog.2021.102517
15. Bonney J, Campbell E, Chang DI, et al. Children's access to healthy food suffers when child care programs close their doors. *NAM Perspectives.* 2021. https://doi.org/10.31478/202104f
16. Kuhns C, Adams G. Child care and feeding young children during the pandemic: exploring the role of the Child and Adult Care Feeding Program. Urban Institute. 2020. Available at: https://www.urban.org/sites/default/files/publication/102619/child-care-and-feeding-young-children-during-the-pandemic_0.pdf. Accessed September 4, 2020.
17. Stephens L, Rains C, Benjamin-Neelon SE. Connecting families to food resources amid the covid-19 pandemic: a cross-sectional survey of early care and education providers in two US states. *Nutrients.* 2021;13(9):3137. https://doi.org/10.3390/nu13093137
18. Bauer KW, Chriqui JF, Andreyeva T, et al. A safety net unraveling: feeding young children during COVID-19. *Am J Public Health.* 2021;111(1): 116–120. https://doi.org/10.2105/AJPH.2020.305980
19. Dunn CG, Kenney E, Fleischhacker SE, Bleich SN. Feeding low-income children during the COVID-19 pandemic. *N Engl J Med.* 2020;382(18):e40. https://doi.org/10.1056/NEJMp2005638
20. US Dept of Agriculture Food and Nutrition Service. Child nutrition COVID-19 waivers. 2022. Available at: https://www.fns.usda.gov/fns-disaster-assistance/fns-responds-covid-19/child-nutrition-covid-19-waivers. Accessed July 24, 2022.
21. Food Research & Action Center. Child and Adult Care Food Program: USDA waivers. Available at: https://frac.org/wp-content/uploads/CACFP-New-USDA-Waivers-for-COVID-19.pdf. Accessed July 24, 2022.
22. Dev DA, Garcia AS, Dzewaltowski DA, et al. Provider reported implementation of nutrition-related practices in childcare centers and family childcare homes in rural and urban Nebraska. *Prev Med Rep.* 2020;17:101021. https://doi.org/10.1016/j.pmedr.2019.101021
23. Speirs KE, Gordon RA, Powers ET, Koester BD, Fiese BH. Licensed family child care providers' participation in the Child and Adult Care Food Program (CACFP): greater benefits and fewer burdens in highly urban areas? *Early Educ Dev.* 2020;31(2):153–176. https://doi.org/10.1080/10409289.2019.1648087
24. Losada-Rojas LL, Ke Y, Pyrialakou VD, Gkritza K. Access to healthy food in urban and rural areas: an empirical analysis. *J Transp Health.* 2021;23: 101245. https://doi.org/10.1016/j.jth.2021.101245
25. Smith L, Bagley A, Reef G, Sarkar M. COVID-19 relief bolstered child care programs in crisis. Bipartisan Policy Center. 2022. Available at: https://bipartisanpolicy.org/explainer/child-care-programs-crisis. Accessed October 17, 2022.
26. Dev DA, Hillburn C, Luxa J, et al. Implementation of federal waivers for feeding children in early care and education during the COVID-19 pandemic. *J Nutr Educ Behav.* 2022;54(10):925–938. https://doi.org/10.1016/j.jneb.2022.07.005
27. Lee DL, Vitale EH, Marshall SK-D, Hecht C, Beck LT, Ritchie LD. Child and Adult Care Food Program participation benefits, barriers and facilitators for independent child care centers in California. *Nutrients.* 2022;14(21):4449. https://doi.org/10.3390/nu14214449
28. Lessard L. Implementation of revised nutrition standards in US Department of Agriculture's Child and Adult Care Food Program. *J Nutr Educ Behav.* 2020;52(5):535–538. https://doi.org/10.1016/j.jneb.2019.10.011
29. Loefstedt K, Erinosho T, Jana B, Vu M, Ward D. COVID-19 pandemic on efforts to promote nutrition and quality care at early care and education programs. *Curr Dev Nutr.* 2022;6(suppl 1):139. https://doi.org/10.1093/cdn/nzac051.055
30. Erinosho T, Jana B, Loefstedt K, Vu M, Ward D. Experiences pertaining to child nutrition and care provision among early care and education stakeholders, sponsors, and center directors during the COVID-19 pandemic: a multi-method study. *Front Public Health.* 2022;10:999272. https://doi.org/10.3389/fpubh.2022.999272
31. Thompson H, Askelson NM, Evans S, Kersten S, Starin K, Brady P. Serving children healthy food during the COVID-19 pandemic: qualitative interviews with Child and Adult Care Food Program–participating child care providers. Report to Iowa Department of Education. 2021. Available at: https://ppc.uiowa.edu/sites/default/files/2022-01/Serving%20Healthy%20Food%20-%20Final%20Remediated.pdf. Accessed March 14, 2021.
32. Miller AL, Stein SF, Sokol R, et al. From zero to thrive: a model of cross-system and cross-sector relational health to promote early childhood. *Infant Ment Health J.* 2022;43(4):624–637. https://doi.org/10.1002/imhj.21996
33. Dooyema CA, Hall K, Tovar A, Bauer KW, Lowry-Warnock A, Blanck HM. Leveraging federal, state, and facility-level early care and education systems and providers toward optimal child nutrition in the first 1000 days. *Am J Public Health.* 2022;12(suppl 8):S779–S785. https://doi.org/10.2105/AJPH.2022.307082
34. Norton J, Salrin R, Lee C, Whitehead J, Illinois Network of Child Care Resource and Referral Agencies. Illinois Salary and Staffing Survey of Licensed Child Care Facilities: FY 2021. 2021. Available at: https://www.dhs.state.il.us/page.aspx?item=143721#a_toc61. Accessed January 5, 2023.
35. Herman ER, Breedlove ML, Lang SN. Family child care support and implementation: current challenges and strategies from the perspectives of providers. *Child Youth Care Forum.* 2021;50(6): 1037–1062. https://doi.org/10.1007/s10566-021-09613-5

36. Lee EK, Parolin Z. The care burden during COVID-19: a national database of child care closures in the United States. *Socius.* 2021;7:1–10. https://doi.org/10.1177/23780231211032028
37. Dynia JM, Koury AJ, Bates RA, McGinnis CP. Food insecurity in a nationally representative sample of child care workers [white paper]. 2019. Available at: https://sproutfive.org/food-insecurity-in-a-nationally-representative-sample-of-child-care-workers. Accessed January 25, 2023.
38. Bromer J, Korfmacher J. Providing high-quality support services to home-based child care: a conceptual model and literature review. *Early Educ Dev.* 2017;28(6):745–772. https://doi.org/10.1080/10409289.2016.1256720
39. Bleich SN, Dean S. The USDA's actions to promote and elevate nutrition security during the first 1000 days. *Am J Public Health.* 2022;112(suppl 8):773–775. https://doi.org/10.2105/AJPH.2022.307078

# Work Matters: Mainstreaming Worker Health and Safety Is Not Limited to Pandemic Response

*Gregory R. Wagner, MD, and David Michaels, PhD, MPH*

**ABOUT THE AUTHORS**

*Gregory R. Wagner is with the Harvard T. H. Chan School of Public Health, Boston, MA. David Michaels is with the George Washington University Milken Institute School of Public Health, Washington, DC.*

AJPH April 2024, Vol. 114, No. 4

During the depths of the COVID-19 pandemic, with stay-at-home orders, quiet urban streets punctuated by ambulance sirens, the frequent sound of helicopters transferring critically ill patients, widespread fear and anxiety, hospital understaffing, and protective equipment shortages, the continued work and enormous commitment of essential public-facing workers highlighted the importance of work as a determinant of the health status of workers, their families, communities, and the country. People who worked outside their homes—in hospitals, chronic care facilities, public safety, transportation, commercial delivery, and food production and sale—were celebrated as "heroes." Daily press stories made it clear: work matters for worker and community health and well-being.

But the spotlight shifted as vaccines became widely available, fear abated, the risk of infection from going to and being at work was less pronounced, and many workers began suffering from burnout and other mental health challenges. Workers willing to take care of the sick and elderly, people delivering packages that we were no longer sanitizing, and teachers who were trying to protect their own health in poorly ventilated classrooms, were no longer national heroes, and their ongoing importance faded from the media.

The experience of the recent pandemic underscores the need, advocated by Alfredo Morabia, the editor-in-chief of *AJPH*, to maintain a focus on the centrality of work or its absence in the lives of virtually everyone by bringing worker health and safety into the mainstream of public health.[1]

The importance of "mainstreaming" worker health and safety is not limited to pandemic response. Work policies, practices, and exposures influence the health of workers and their families outside of work in obvious and subtle ways. Work is central to the lives of people who work, providing financial and social support and purpose; thus, work is a major driver of overall well-being. Poor and hazardous working conditions can cause or contribute to injury, disease, premature death, burnout, and addiction.[2] For many, work is a source of health insurance, an important factor in access to some degree of sickness care for many workers and their families. And the absence of work drives poverty, inequality, and despair. The consequences of the quality of work are felt by workers, their families, and the communities in which they live.

Nevertheless, although the World Health Organization has for decades noted that health is more than the absence of disease and has recognized that employment and working conditions have powerful effects on health and health equity,[3] work and the potential to improve working conditions are too often overlooked as an opportunity for public health engagement.

## OLD HAZARDS WITH GROWING CONSEQUENCES

There have been many missed opportunities for collaborative approaches, combining general public health and occupational health expertise and authorities, that aim to prevent or mitigate disease. A few recent examples of the inadequacy of the public health system's response to well-known work hazards that are emerging in new and dangerous forms illustrate many of the weaknesses of these systems.

### Airborne Pathogens

In the face of the pandemic, it is difficult to recall that coronaviruses have long been recognized as one of the pathogens causing mild to moderate respiratory illness, often called the "common cold." Workers are regularly infected by airborne pathogens that include coronavirus and influenza, pass infections on to fellow workers, and bring infections home. In addition to those employed in health care settings, teachers, retail workers, and others in public-facing jobs have higher risk of respiratory infections.[4] For many jobs, particularly office-based work, respiratory infections are a major cause of work absence.[5] Unlike in other high-income countries, paid sick leave that would enable workers to stay home when they might infect others is far from universal in the United States.

The novel SARS-CoV-2 virus (the causative agent of COVID-19) is a ramped-up version of the pathogen causing colds. Workplace transmission of airborne pathogens like coronavirus has been tolerated without regulation or interventions for years. Early evidence and common sense identified the risk of infection transmission in nursing homes, hospitals, and meat-processing plants, but the risk to other workers was generally ignored, delaying public health efforts to protect workers with heightened risk.

As a rule, the responsibility and authority for public health action resides in local, county, and state health departments. Public health authorities, strapped for resources, do not have the expertise, and do not consider it within their domain to enter workplaces and use their powers to reduce risk to workers. That is seen as the responsibility of a federal agency, the Occupational Safety and Health Administration (OSHA). But OSHA did not have adequate tools in place to require employers to take steps necessary to protect their employees from SARS-CoV-2, even those in health care facilities.[6]

## Climate Change–Related Hazards

The climate crisis is increasing the risk to workers from exposure to wildfire smoke, extreme heat, vector-borne illnesses, and other hazards.[7]

Wildfires are increasing, creating smoke that travels great distances, elevating toxic exposures associated with respiratory and cardiovascular disease. Everyone in New York City and Washington, DC, including outdoor workers, experienced the highly polluted air from Canadian wildfires for days in 2023.

A recent National Academies report found that the nation is unprepared to provide respiratory protection for most workers exposed to airborne viruses or wildfire smoke.[8] The response to the report was almost complete silence from Congress or the federal agencies whose job it is to protect the public's health.

Extreme heat exposure, in both outdoor and indoor workplaces, is also becoming more common and more deadly. Heat not only kills directly but also increases the risk of renal failure, cardiovascular disease, ischemic stroke, and workplace injuries.[9,10] Federal OSHA's standard setting process is extremely slow and resource intensive. Although a few state OSHA plans have standards requiring rest breaks, shade, and rehydration, regulations that cover much of the country are unlikely to be issued in the next several years.

## Respirable Crystalline Silica

Silica dust is another well-known deadly resurging hazard. Although both federal and California OSHA plans have standards requiring employers to limit exposure, the fabrication of countertops made from "engineered" stone has resulted in dozens of California workers developing silicosis. In severe cases, some workers have died, and others have needed lung transplants.[11]

## COORDINATION FAILURES HAVE CONSEQUENCES

In addressing each of these hazards, collaboration and communication between the occupational safety and health (OSH) regulatory system and the mainstream public health system have been inadequate or absent. Although for decades work has been acknowledged as a "social determinant of health" nationally and internationally,[2,3] the separation of OSH from mainstream public health has, if anything, grown.

Before the passage of the Occupational Safety and Health Act in 1970, many state and local governments had workplace inspection units. Some of those state offices transitioned to become state OSHA plans, but others atrophied or disappeared. During the COVID-19 pandemic, few state and local government agencies other than a limited number of state OSHA programs routinely responded to workplace outbreaks in which many workers were sickened.

OSH is too often viewed as a field apart, with distinct knowledge, attitudes, and beliefs. It is pigeonholed as "industrial health," concerned with conditions of the past that will gradually fade away in the United States through a combination of regulation and deindustrialization. It may be misunderstood as focused exclusively on injuries from work and their compensation.

Research investigations published in this and other scientific journals repeatedly confirmed the association of COVID-19 risk with workplace exposures, and that work outside the home contributed to disparities in illness and death.[12,13] Early in the pandemic, workplaces—including nursing homes, hospitals, meatpacking facilities, prisons, and retail establishments—played an important role in spreading the virus throughout much of the country, especially rural areas.[14–16] Yet there was little coordination between the state and local public health agencies that played a lead role in the nation's pandemic response and the federal and state OSHA programs with authority over workplaces.

In addition, much of the public health messaging from the Centers for Disease Control and Prevention stressed the importance of actions individuals could take, emphasizing handwashing, maintaining six feet of social distance, and mask wearing.

In contrast, occupational health experts recommended the application of the fundamental principles of worker protection: the hierarchy of controls.[17] These experts recognized that to control the workplace spread of SARS-CoV-2, it would be more effective to make the environment safer for all rather than by exclusively relying on individuals to change their behaviors.

Applying the hierarchy to COVID-19 risk reduction, the first steps are to eliminate the exposure through keeping sick and potentially infectious workers out of the workplace and by utilizing engineering controls that provide virus-free air. Although useful in conjunction with other controls, personal protective equipment like respirators is not as effective as environmental interventions. We believe that wider implementation of the hierarchy of controls would have helped slow the workplace spread of the virus, saving many lives.

The chasm between OSH and mainstream public health is mirrored in mainstream medicine, where medical treatment of illness and injuries from work is often separated from the rest of the health care system. Workers' compensation insurance systems vary by state, with differences in standards of diagnosis and proof for compensation of injuries and diseases from work. Many people with injuries or illnesses caused or made worse by workplace exposures elect to avoid entering the workers' compensation system, shifting the costs of work-related conditions from the employer (where, by law, they belong) to the worker and their families, their coworkers, and taxpayers. Other barriers to obtaining compensation, including shrinking pools of key medical personnel able and willing to diagnose conditions as occupational when reaching that conclusion, result in both time-consuming engagement with an often-unfamiliar administrative process and substandard levels of payment for providing treatment.[18,19]

## CLOSING THE GAP

Public health policy and funding priorities are often set by measuring or enumerating conditions of concern. When only compensated injuries and diseases are counted as work-related, there is substantial undercounting of the extent of problems and, consequently, the importance of working conditions to health, safety, and well-being.[20,21]

Efforts to integrate OSH with mainstream public health and health care run into strong headwinds. Data tying health and illness to work are limited and often lack the granularity to be useful.[22,23] Both health and exposure surveillance are critical to the recognition of problems, the design and evaluation of interventions, and the recognition of disparities. The adoption of electronic medical records offered hope that individuals' work could be tied to health outcomes and that information about their industries and occupations could result in a better understanding of their work exposures. But even if information about work and work exposures is included in the electronic medical record, most clinicians are inadequately trained and are generally too stressed by their own workplace demands to link diagnosis and treatment to the work of their working patients.

The failure to integrate OSH and mainstream public health has resulted in disparate levels of protection. There is limited recognition that workers are often exposed "first and worst" to toxic chemicals, and that the same exposures can escape the workplace perimeter and adversely affect local communities and beyond. This is a particular environmental justice concern for communities with little political power, including low-income ones, where workplaces with significant chemical hazards are often situated.[24]

Although, overall, workers generally start out healthier than many nonworking community members, the levels of protection afforded them at work through governmental regulation and enforcement are limited and reflect an implicit social belief that workers are getting paid for their health risk at work and if they don't like it, they can leave. But too many leave work because of adverse health effects from work.

People who work full-time spend almost a third of their waking lives at or getting to or from work. Work and work-related activities are a potential source of both adverse and beneficial exposures that may determine worker health, safety, and well-being as well as the health of their communities. However, research into the contributions of work to chronic disease risk is limited. Most occupational diseases are indistinguishable from diseases of "everyday life" such as chronic obstructive pulmonary disease, cardiovascular disease, cancer, and asthma. To understand the risk conferred by workplace toxic exposures and stressors, investigators need to take into consideration work exposures, including the policies governing work. Too often, when chronic disease prevention scientists and practitioners turn their attention to the workplace, their focus is on motivating modification of individual choices and habits, using the workplace as a convenient venue to access individuals for health promotion interventions. A more useful approach was taken by Berkman et al., who demonstrated that an intervention designed specifically to increase employees' control over work time and supervisors' awareness and support of work–family balance resulted in improved worker health.[25]

Given the central role work plays in determining the health of workers, their families, and communities, the separation of worker protection and mainstream public health has worked to the detriment of everyone. To actually address work as a social determinant of health, now is the time to begin reintegrating these fields.

Public health is a sprawling, diverse, and multilayered system intended to protect the health, safety, and well-being of all people and their communities. Public health success is so "normal" that, absent emergencies, funding support for public health agencies dwindles. Agencies with different roles in protecting public health and well-being are often given limited power and inadequate funding, compete with one another for limited resources, and fail to collaborate or even communicate with one another. This results, unfortunately, in the "suboptimization" of overall public protection. The examples presented earlier as well as our decades of experience in public health, occupational health and safety, and sickness care, in roles including practice, research, teaching, advocacy, and organizational leadership in and out of the government, have led us to believe that these complex problems will benefit from the mainstream public health and OSH communities working closely and continually together for improved prevention and protection for all. This can be achieved when those involved with "traditional public health" and those engaged in OSH commit to understanding, embracing, and acting on the concept that work is a key determinant of personal, family, and community health and that the conditions of work, and both the public and enterprise-specific policies that influence them, are broadly important. In this way, not only will future pandemic response be more effective and outbreaks of work-related disease, injury, and death be better investigated, mitigated, and prevented, but quotidian public health problems and opportunities will be addressed more effectively as well. AJPH

## CORRESPONDENCE

Correspondence should be sent to Gregory R. Wagner, MD, 655 Huntington Ave, 1-1405, Boston, MA 02445 (e-mail: gwagner@hsph.harvard.edu). Reprints can be ordered at http://www.ajph.org by clicking the "Reprints" link.

## PUBLICATION INFORMATION

Full Citation: Wagner GR, Michaels D. Work matters: mainstreaming worker health and safety is not limited to pandemic response. *Am J Public Health*. 2024;114(4):372–376.

Acceptance Date: December 16, 2023.

DOI: https://doi.org/10.2105/AJPH.2023.307565

## CONTRIBUTORS

Both authors contributed equally to the conceptualization, writing, and revision of this work.

## ACKNOWLEDGMENTS

We acknowledge financial support from the McElhattan Foundation. D. Michaels also receives financial support from the Health Action Alliance.

## CONFLICTS OF INTEREST

The authors have no conflicts of interest to disclose.

## REFERENCES

1. Morabia A. Bringing workers safety, health, and well-being front and center in public health. *Am J Public Health*. 2023;113(6):597. https://doi.org/10.2105/AJPH.2023.307304
2. Frank J, Mustard C, Smith P, et al. Work as a social determinant of health in high-income countries: past, present, and future. *Lancet*. 2023;402(10410):1357–1367. https://doi.org/10.1016/S0140-6736(23)00871-1
3. Marmot M, Friel S, Bell R, Houweling TA, Taylor S; Commission on Social Determinants of Health. Closing the gap in a generation: health equity through action on the social determinants of health. *Lancet*. 2008;372(9650):1661–1669. https://doi.org/10.1016/S0140-6736(08)61690-6
4. Anderson NJ, Bonauto DK, Fan ZJ, Spector JT. Distribution of influenza-like illness (ILI) by occupation in Washington State, September 2009–August 2010. *PLoS One*. 2012;7(11):e48806. https://doi.org/10.1371/journal.pone.0048806
5. Blanchet Zumofen MH, Frimpter J, Hansen SA. Impact of influenza and influenza-like illness on work productivity outcomes: a systematic literature review. *Pharmacoeconomics*. 2023;41(3):253–273. https://doi.org/10.1007/s40273-022-01224-9
6. Michaels D, Wagner GR, Ryan L. Lessons from COVID-19 for protecting workers in the next pandemic. *JAMA*. 2023;330(1):23–24. https://doi.org/10.1001/jama.2023.8229
7. Schulte PA, Jacklitsch BL, Bhattacharya A, et al. Updated assessment of occupational safety and health hazards of climate change. *J Occup Environ Hyg*. 2023;20(5-6):183–206. https://doi.org/10.1080/15459624.2023.2205468
8. Samet JM, Holm SM, Jayaraman S. Respiratory protection for the nation: a report from the National Academies of Sciences, Engineering, and Medicine. *JAMA*. 2022;327(11):1023–1024. https://doi.org/10.1001/jama.2022.1318
9. Wang JC, Chien WC, Chu P, Chung CH, Lin CY, Tsai SH. The association between heat stroke and subsequent cardiovascular diseases. *PLoS One*. 2019;14(2):e0211386. https://doi.org/10.1371/journal.pone.0211386
10. Park J, Pankratz NMC, Behrer A. Temperature, workplace safety, and labor market inequality. IZA Discussion Paper No. 14560. Available at: https://doi.org/10.2139/ssrn.3892588. Accessed January 22, 2024.
11. Fazio JC, Gandhi SA, Flattery J, et al. Silicosis among immigrant engineered stone (quartz) countertop fabrication workers in California. *JAMA Intern Med*. 2023;183(9):991–998. https://doi.org/10.1001/jamainternmed.2023.3295
12. Gebreegziabher E, Bui D, Cummings KJ, et al. Temporal assessment of disparities in California COVID-19 mortality by industry: a population-based

retrospective cohort study. *Ann Epidemiol.* 2023;87:51–52e.2. https://doi.org/10.1016/j.annepidem.2023.09.003

13. Cummings KJ, Beckman J, Frederick M, et al. Disparities in COVID-19 fatalities among working Californians. *PLoS One.* 2022;17(3):e0266058. https://doi.org/10.1371/journal.pone.0266058
14. Chen YH, Glymour M, Riley A, et al. Excess mortality associated with the COVID-19 pandemic among Californians 18–65 years of age, by occupational sector and occupation: March through November 2020. *PLoS One.* 2021;16(6):e0252454. https://doi.org/10.1371/journal.pone.0252454
15. Taylor CA, Boulos C, Almond D. Livestock plants and COVID-19 transmission. *Proc Natl Acad Sci USA.* 2020;117(50):31706–31715. https://doi.org/10.1073/pnas.2010115117
16. Sims KM, Foltz J, Skidmore ME. Prisons and COVID-19 spread in the United States. *Am J Public Health.* 2021;111(8):1534–1541. https://doi.org/10.2105/AJPH.2021.306352
17. Sehgal NJ, Milton DK. Applying the hierarchy of controls: what occupational safety can teach us about safely navigating the next phase of the global COVID-19 pandemic. *Front Public Health.* 2021;9:747894. https://doi.org/10.3389/fpubh.2021.747894
18. Spieler EA. (Re)assessing the grand bargain: compensation for work injuries in the United States, 1900–2017. *Rutgers U Law Rev.* 2017;69(3):891–1013. Available at: https://www.rutgerslawreview.com/wp-content/uploads/2018/03/2-EmilyASpielerAssessing the.pdf. Accessed February 2, 2024.
19. Michaels D. Adding inequality to injury: the costs of failing to protect workers on the job. US Occupational Safety and Health Administration. 2015. Available at: https://www.osha.gov/sites/default/files/inequality_michaels_june2015.pdf. Accessed January 22, 2024.
20. Gunter MM. An update on SOII undercount research activities. *Monthly Labor Review. U.S. Bureau of Labor Statistics.* 2016; (September). https://doi.org/10.21916/mlr.2016.41
21. Spieler EA, Wagner GR. Counting matters: implications of undercounting in the BLS survey of occupational injuries and illnesses. *Am J Ind Med.* 2014;57(10):1077–1084. https://doi.org/10.1002/ajim.22382
22. Armenti K, Sweeney MH, Lingwall C, Yang L. Work: A social determinant of health worth capturing. *Int J Environ Res Public Health.* 2023;20(2):1199. https://doi.org/10.3390/ijerph20021199
23. Steege AL, Silver S, Mobley A, Sweeney MH. Work as a key social determinant of health: the case for including work in all health data collections. NIOSH Science Blog. February 16, 2023. Available at: https://blogs.cdc.gov/niosh-science-blog/2023/02/16/sdoh. Accessed January 22, 2024.
24. Michaels D, Bullard R. Environmental justice is essential in the workplace and at home: no worker should be forced to choose between an unsafe job and unemployment. *The Nation.* Oct. 22, 2021. Available at: https://www.thenation.com/article/economy/workplace-environmental-justice. Accessed January 22, 2024.
25. Berkman LF, Kelly EL, Hammer LB, et al. Employee cardiometabolic risk following a cluster-randomized workplace intervention from the Work, Family and Health Network, 2009–2013. *Am J Public Health.* 2023;113(12):1322–1331. https://doi.org/10.2105/AJPH.2023.307413

# Inequities in Academic Publishing: Where Is the Evidence and What Can Be Done?

*Meredith Loui, BA, and Steven C. Fiala, MPH*

**ABOUT THE AUTHORS**

*Meredith Loui is with the Department of Prevention and Community Health, the George Washington University, Washington, DC. Steven C. Fiala is with the Oregon Health Authority Public Health Division, and the Oregon Health and Science University-Portland State University School of Public Health, Portland. Steven C. Fiala is also a deputy editor for* AJPH.

In the June 2021 *New York Times* article "Medical Journals Blind to Racism as Health Crisis, Critics Say," *AJPH* was highlighted as publishing more articles mentioning "racism" than four peer journals.[1] Although the comparison of a public health journal to medical journals like *JAMA* and the *Lancet* may be questionable, the article prompted *AJPH* to reflect on why it may be leading in this area without explicit initiatives to do so and to seek to more systematically understand diversity, equity, and inclusion (DEI) in academic publishing broadly.[2]

Attempting to understand the landscape of DEI in academic publishing has been an exciting journey thus far but has generated many uncertainties for further exploration. It is a challenging topic to investigate not only because of the sensitivity and reflexivity required for studying (and ultimately confronting) the structural oppression underlying DEI inequities but also because of the ambiguity of the shorthand term "DEI." Although "diversity," "equity," and "inclusion" can be individually defined, together the words form a cryptic abbreviation that seems ever present on organizational Web site home pages but often lacks definition or meaning. Unsurprisingly, this ambiguity bleeds over into the field of academic publishing, similarly rendering DEI a challenging topic on which to report.

Our first step in understanding the landscape of DEI in academic publishing was to identify what has been reported to date through a rudimentary literature search. This preliminary exploration proved more challenging than expected. Although our search was neither exhaustive nor systematic, we were surprised by the dearth of peer-reviewed literature readily available on the topic, as well as the variety of facets that the topic could encompass from gender to impact of author or reviewer homogeneity.[3,4] Simple literature review findings largely focused on race/ethnicity and gender inequities in academic publishing, which can be studied with demographic survey data or specific algorithms.[5] The concentrated nature of the literature had us questioning whether we were missing a large part of the available evidence. The "diversity" of published research may also engage with other author characteristics, such as disability status, seniority status, and country from which an article originates, given the impact that an author's identity can have on the publication journey. However, in our simple literature review we found that few author characteristics besides race, ethnicity, and gender are explored in peer-reviewed articles other than commentaries.[6]

We describe the current state of our knowledge on the prevalence of exclusion in academic publishing, the mechanisms by which exclusion is perpetuated and reinforced, and journal-specific initiatives to create a more diverse, equitable, and inclusive field.

## THE PREVALENCE OF EXCLUSION

Although direct evidence of exclusion based on race, ethnicity, age, ability, and other factors is limited, exclusion likely exists in academic publishing as in other disciplines. Limited evidence should not bar action, and there is a dire need to establish shared goals for DEI in academic publishing and baseline measures to track progress on related interventions and their effectiveness. This requires a shared understanding of what it means to create an equitable system for publishing scientific information and a common approach to measuring the prevalence of exclusion despite the sensitive nature of collecting demographic information from authors for reasons ranging from innocuous (e.g., forgetting to complete author profiles) to traumatic (e.g., past negative experiences with disclosing aspects of one's identity).

## JOURNAL MECHANISMS OF EXCLUSION

Although individuals from majority cultures are often permitted to perform research and publish on minoritized people's lived experiences (referred to as "health equity tourism"),[7] minoritized people are often excluded from writing on topics outside their lived experience and relegated to areas that align with their cultural identities that journals may perceive as less rigorous (e.g., population- or community-level qualitative research). Journals may require reflexivity statements from authors to investigate potential bias and appropriateness of authorship depending on the topic, as well as statements attesting to the inclusion of people with lived experience in authorship when research is conducted with minoritized communities. Interventions have been designed to address similar colonizing issues such as "helicopter research" and "ethics dumping" by asking authors who conduct research in another country or with indigenous populations to complete a survey focused on the ethical, cultural, and scientific considerations specific to inclusivity in global research.[8–12] Submitting authors can be asked to reflect on why local research contributors were or were not included as authors and to provide an optional disclosure statement on inclusion practices to be shared with peer reviewers and readers.

Journals can also take a more proactive approach to diversifying submissions, including outreach to organizations often excluded from publishing such as historically Black colleges and universities, centers for hearing or sight-impaired persons, and community-based or grassroots organizations engaged in public health. Journals can solicit the perspectives of historically excluded communities in calls for articles or through invited editorials, as well as by incentivizing academics to coproduce submissions with community organizations. Efforts to diversify submissions will also benefit from complementary journal supports that facilitate equitable access to submission. These supports could include promoting AuthorAid and other free publishing resources, providing editorial assistance to authors with English as a second language, waiving open access or article processing fees for researchers in low- or middle-income countries, and providing educational webinars that demystify journal processes. Journals can also institutionalize accessibility as a value through formal positions or advisory bodies.

Diversifying the peer reviewers who inform journal decisions may increase DEI. Interventions could include inviting peer reviewers with lived experience who may fall outside typical professional and practice networks and ensuring that research on certain populations or in specific locations is reviewed by those with similar lived experiences. Looking beyond individuals in academia and practice to open peer review opportunities to community members with relevant experience could significantly expand the expertise in a field beyond theoretical and conceptual knowledge and into a more practical realm. However, journals and authors should be prepared for the peer review process to take longer if inviting and training community peer reviewers and would need to provide financial incentives to honor community members' time and expertise.

Complementary interventions to diversify journal editors and editorial boards may also be needed, which could include open calls for new editors rather than tapping people in known networks, establishing DEI-specific editor positions, and preserving editorial board positions for those with certain lived experiences. For example, *JAMA* has committed to appointing a full-time, senior-level director of equity to promote equity at *JAMA* and guide the equity efforts of other JAMA Network journal editors.[13]

Funding priorities may also be a mechanism of exclusion in academic publishing.[14] Public and private funders' priorities tend to be biased toward quantitative over interdisciplinary research, which privileges disciplines more often populated by non-Latino White researchers.[15,16] Expanding the types of articles eligible for publication may diversify the voices reflected in scientific publications, including more conversational, plain language articles written by researchers. For example, the *Health Affairs* "Narrative Matters" article type allows personal stories about experiences with the health care system to highlight important public policy issues, and *AJPH*'s "Notes From the Field" and "Qualitative Notes From the Field" formats introduced in 2021 and 2023, respectively, feature local public health practice experiences that may inform best practices.[17,18] Creating more space for qualitative and mixed-methods research in journals with historically quantitative leanings may feed back into funder considerations of methodological flexibility.

## PROFESSIONAL MECHANISMS OF EXCLUSION

Minoritized individuals in academic public health may lack opportunities to be mentored by faculty with whom they identify and feel comfortable, which leaves those interested in publishing with few opportunities to participate in the peer review process and article development. Faculty with minoritized identities are often left with little time for mentorship, given pressure to commit their time to committees and boards, especially those focused on DEI, and requests to review articles focused on minoritized populations. Compensation for positions in academic publishing also act as a driver for exclusion. Journal editors often receive little to no compensation for their work, so these roles likely attract individuals who are financially stable and can afford a position that largely functions as a "résumé builder." Similarly, internships in academic publishing are often unpaid, requiring individuals who hold these positions to receive financial support through other means. Historically, minoritized populations come from backgrounds that are more financially unstable, rendering unpaid or low-paying positions in publishing unfeasible.

Although diversifying the professional pipeline is critical to increasing DEI in scientific publishing, not all interventions are under a journal's control. Publisher-led interventions could focus on opportunities for students and early career professionals, including student editor and editorial board positions, paid internships, and health equity fellowships targeted to minoritized populations. Student and early career mentorships in peer review could be especially beneficial given that peer review is often considered part of the "hidden curriculum" in academia, with little to no formal training offered on the process. Several journals are implementing programs to address the myriad ways that individuals from historically oppressed and underrepresented groups are barred from scholarly publishing. *Health Affairs* collaborated with the Robert Wood Johnson Foundation to create a fellowship program for early career health equity researchers to increase the quantity and quality of articles published by individuals from historically underrepresented backgrounds.[19] *The Lancet* developed the Elsevier Rising TIDE (tomorrow, inclusion, diversity, equity) paid internship program to increase access for students and early career professionals from racially and socioeconomically diverse backgrounds to networking, mentorship, and leadership development opportunities in a funded capacity.[20] Lastly, JAMA Network journals developed or expanded editorial fellowships that allow early career faculty across many disciplines to engage deeply in the editorial process, with the goals of advancing scholarship that addresses the needs of diverse communities and of increasing representation among researchers writing and reviewing scientific articles.[21–24]

## MOVING FORWARD TOGETHER

Academic publishing's commitment to DEI is evidenced by the numerous initiatives across public health, social science, clinical medicine, and biomedical journals. For example, the Lancet Group now includes a diversity pledge in all commissioning letters, reviewer invitation letters, media and press release protocols, marketing and conference support, and brand and partner guidelines.[25] *JAMA*'s recent editorial "Equity and the JAMA Network" outlines the editorial priorities and approaches that *JAMA* is advancing to promote DEI.[13] Although journal-specific DEI commitments and interventions should be lauded, ongoing opportunities for shared learning and growth as a field may be needed to challenge current norms. A formal community of practice to share lessons learned and promising practices may catalyze the change needed to alter publishing from a club to a community and expand the current modest landscape of formal research on exclusion in scholarly publishing in the process.

The state of the literature on DEI in scholarly publishing is limited and fragmented. A preliminary exploration of the literature reveals an overall paucity of published research on the prevalence of, mechanisms of, and interventions for exclusion in academic publishing as well as a lack of quantitative evidence in the articles identified and reviewed. Given the absence of a cohesive evidence base and lack of formal research, *AJPH* is performing a scoping review of the literature on DEI in academic public health, biomedical, clinical medicine, and social science publishing to more robustly identify and synthesize knowledge on this relatively nascent topic. Results from a scoping review could identify both promising practices for wider dissemination and ongoing gaps in DEI practices requiring focused attention and resources.

*AJPH* is also recording journals' active data collection on their own publishing practices. Preliminary results indicate that some journals are embracing the challenge and collecting data on gender, geographical location, career stage, institution, race, ethnic origin, and other demographics.[26,27] These measures will aid journals in understanding which subgroups more frequently submit articles or assume roles in the publishing process (i.e., as reviewers or editors), and they can shed light on which subgroups may be systematically excluded or underrepresented as authors, reviewers, or editors. Finally, *AJPH* is conducting a randomized controlled trial that compares the standard double masked peer review process to a triple masked process to determine whether masking the identities of all involved parties (authors, reviewers, editors) influences editorial decision-making and acceptance rates compared with the standard double masked process.[27] The goal of these initiatives is to grant journals insight into the trends of who and what they are publishing to address biases that may arise. AJPH

## CORRESPONDENCE

Correspondence should be sent to Meredith Loui, 1918 F St, NW, Washington, DC 20052 (e-mail: meredithloui@gwmail.gwu.edu). Reprints can be ordered at http://www.ajph.org by clicking the "Reprints" link.

## PUBLICATION INFORMATION

Full Citation: Loui M, Fiala SC. Inequities in academic publishing: where is the evidence and what can be done? *Am J Public Health*. 2024;114(4): 377–381.

Acceptance Date: January 7, 2024.

DOI: https://doi.org/10.2105/AJPH.2024.307587

## CONTRIBUTORS

M. Loui conceptualized the article, wrote the first draft, and oversaw the review and editing process. S. C. Fiala contributed to writing, critically reviewed the article, and provided overarching suggestions and revisions. Both authors approved the final version to be published.

## ACKNOWLEDGMENTS

This work was funded by the Robert Wood Johnson Foundation (RWJF; grant 79725).

To ask about and expand on simple literature review findings, we convened a workshop on DEI in academic publishing in April 2023 with editors from *AJPH* and other leading public health, biomedical, and social science journals, including *Nature Medicine*, *JAMA*, *Social Science and Medicine*, *Health Affairs*, *PLOS*, *Preventive Medicine*, and the *Lancet*. Workshop participants reflected on summary statements developed from simple literature review findings (Table A, available as a supplement to the online version of this article at http://www.ajph.org)[28–38] and offered practitioner perspectives on current challenges to diversity, equity, and inclusion in academic publishing and potential interventions. Although workshop participants anecdotally supported several statements, there was general consensus on the dearth of literature.

We are thankful to all journal representatives participating in this community of practice, all of whom contributed to this work. Our continued efforts would not be possible without them: Luisa Borrell (*Preventive Medicine*), Ross Brownson (*Annual Review of Public Health*), Vanessa Carels (*PLOS One*), Susan Elliott (*Social Science and Medicine*), Preeti Malani (*JAMA*), Raymond McGhee (RWJF), João Monteiro (*Nature Medicine*), Miriam Sabin (the *Lancet*), Rodrigo Reis (the Brown School of Public Health), and Vabren Watts (*Health Affairs*).

## CONFLICTS OF INTEREST

The authors have no conflicts of interest to disclose.

## REFERENCES

1. Mandavilli A. Medical journals blind to racism as health crisis, critics say. *New York Times*. 2021. https://www.nytimes.com/2021/06/02/health/jama-racism-bauchner.html. Accessed February 8, 2024.
2. Morabia A. Why is *AJPH* publishing more than other major journals about race and racism? *Am J Public Health*. 2021;111(9):1557. https://doi.org/10.2105/AJPH.2021.306461
3. Chatterjee P, Werner RM. Gender disparity in citations in high-impact journal articles. *JAMA Netw Open*. 2021;4(7):e2114509. https://doi.org/10.1001/jamanetworkopen.2021.14509
4. Murray D, Siler K, Lariviere V, et al. Author–reviewer homophily in peer review. *BioRxiv*. 2018;400515. https://doi.org/10.1101/400515
5. Bell ML, Fong KC. Gender differences in first and corresponding authorship in public health research submissions during the COVID-19 pandemic. *Am J Public Health*. 2021;111(1):159–163. https://doi.org/10.2105/AJPH.2020.305975
6. Brown N, Leigh J. Ableism in academia: where are the disabled and ill academics? *Disabil Soc*. 2018;33(6):985–989. https://doi.org/10.1080/09687599.2018.1455627
7. Lett E, Adekunle D, McMurray P, et al. Health equity tourism: ravaging the justice landscape. *J Med Syst*. 2022;46(3):17. https://doi.org/10.1007/s10916-022-01803-5
8. Nature addresses helicopter research and ethics dumping. *Nature Medicine*. June 2, 2022. Available at: https://www.nature.com/articles/d41586-022-01423-6. Accessed September 20, 2023.
9. Announcing a new PLOS policy on inclusion in global research. *PLOS*. September 27, 2021. Available at: https://theplosblog.plos.org/2021/09/announcing-a-new-plos-policy-on-inclusion-in-global-research. Accessed September 19, 2023.
10. Best practice in research reporting. *PLOS ONE*. Available at: https://journals.plos.org/plosone/s/best-practices-in-research-reporting. Accessed September 20, 2023.
11. Raising the bar on sex and gender reporting in research. *Nat Med*. 2022;28(6):1099. https://doi.org/10.1038/s41591-022-01860-w
12. Research ethics. *Nature Medicine*. Available at: https://www.nature.com/nm/editorial-policies/ethics-and-biosecurity#sex-gender-sexual-orientation. Accessed September 20, 2023.
13. Fontanarosa PB, Flanagin A, Ayanian JZ, et al. Equity and the JAMA Network. *JAMA*. 2021;326(7): 618–620. https://doi.org/10.1001/jama.2021.9377
14. Hoppe TA, Litovitz A, Willis KA, et al. Topic choice contributes to the lower rate of NIH awards to African-American/Black scientists. *Sci Adv*. 2019; 5(10):eaaw7238. https://doi.org/10.1126/sciadv.aaw7238
15. Stickley T, O'Caithain A, Homer C. The value of qualitative methods to public health research, policy and practice. *Perspect Public Health*. 2022; 142(4):237–240. https://doi.org/10.1177/17579139221083814
16. Kozlowski D, Larivière V, Sugimoto CR, Monroe-White T. Intersectional inequalities in science. *Proc Natl Acad Sci U S A*. 2022;119(2):e2113067119. https://doi.org/10.1073/pnas.2113067119
17. *Health Affairs*. Narrative matters. Available at: https://www.healthaffairs.org/topic/narrativematters. Accessed February 8, 2024.
18. Morabia A. Notes From the Field: a repository of best practices. *Am J Public Health*. 2022;112(8): 1079. https://doi.org/10.2105/AJPH.2022.306957
19. *Health Affairs*. Health affairs fellowships. Available at: https://www.healthaffairs.org/health-affairs-fellowships. Accessed September 20, 2023.
20. Lee MY. Elsevier inclusion & diversity data snapshot 2023. March 8, 2023. Available at: https://beta.elsevier.com/connect/elsevier-inclusion-and-diversity-data-snapshot-2023?trial=true. Accessed September 21, 2023.
21. Ongur D. *JAMA Psychiatry* Editorial fellow. *JAMA Psychiatry*. 2022;79(3):e214077. https://doi.org/10.1001/jamapsychiatry.2021.4077
22. Christakis DA, Duncan AF. Introducing the *JAMA Pediatrics* editorial fellowship. *JAMA Pediatr*. 2023;177(8):755. https://doi.org/10.1001/jamapediatrics.2023.1721
23. Josephson SA. *JAMA Neurology* editorial fellow. *JAMA Neurol*. 2023;80(11):1135. https://doi.org/10.1001/jamaneurol.2023.3552
24. Roberson ML, Shinkai K. Introducing the *JAMA Dermatology* editorial fellowship. *JAMA Dermatol*. 2023;159(5):e230471. https://doi.org/10.1001/jamadermatol.2023.0471
25. Advancing equity, diversity, and inclusion: commitments. *Lancet*. Available at: https://www.thelancet.com/equity-diversity-inclusion/commitments?section=statement. Accessed September 20, 2023.
26. Farley S. Following through on our commitment to diversity, equity, and inclusion. *PLOS Blog*. 2021. Available at: https://theplosblog.plos.org/2021/10/following-through-on-our-commitment-to-diversity-equity-and-inclusion. Accessed December 13, 2023.
27. Triple-masking v double-masking: a trial of scientific publication in public health (TripleMasking). NCT06067633. October 5, 2023. Available at: https://clinicaltrials.gov/study/NCT06067633?term=DEI&id=NCT06067633&rank=1. Accessed December 12, 2023.
28. Dawson J, Coggins NL, Dolechek M, Fosado G. Toolkits for equity: an antiracist framework for scholarly publishing. *Serials Review*. 2020;46(3): 170–174.
29. Deahl R. Why publishing is so White. *Publishers Weekly*. May 11, 2016. Available at: http://quote.ucsd.edu/jskrentny/files/2015/09/Why-Publishing-Is-So-White.pdf. Accessed February 8, 2024.
30. Erosheva EA, Grant S, Chen MC, Lindner MD, Nakamura RK, Lee CJ. NIH peer review: criterion

scores completely account for racial disparities in overall impact scores. *Sci Adv.* 2020;6(23): eaaz4868. https://doi.org/10.1126/sciadv.aaz4868

31. King EB, Avery DR, Hebl MR, Cortina JM. Systematic subjectivity: how subtle biases infect the scholarship review process. *J Manag.* 2018;44(3): 843–853. https://doi.org/10.1177/0149206317743553
32. O'Connor EE, Cousar M, Lentini JA, Castillo M, Halm K, Zeffiro TA. Efficacy of double-blind peer review in an imaging subspecialty journal. *AJNR Am J Neuroradiol.* 2017;38(2):230–235. https://doi.org/10.3174/ajnr.A5017
33. Salazar JW, Claytor JD, Habib AR, Guduguntla V, Redberg RF. Gender, race, ethnicity, and sexual orientation of editors at leading medical and scientific journals: a cross-sectional survey. *JAMA Intern Med.* 2021;181(9):1248–1251. https://doi.org/10.1001/jamainternmed.2021.2363
34. Taylor S, Spilka S, Monahan K, Mulhern I, Wachter J. Evaluating equity in scholarly publishing. *Learned Publishing.* 2020;33(4):353–367. https://doi.org/10.1002/leap.1301
35. Roberts SO, Mortenson E. Challenging the White = neutral framework in psychology. *Perspect Psychol Sci.* 2023;18(3):597–606. https://doi.org/10.1177/17456916221077117
36. Cheon BK, Melani I, Hong YY. How USA-centric is psychology? An archival study of implicit assumptions of generalizability of findings to human nature based on origins of study samples. *Soc Psychol Pers Sci.* 2020;11(7):928–937. https://doi.org/10.1177/1948550620927269
37. Forscher PS, Cox WTL, Brauer M, Devine PG. Little race or gender bias in an experiment of initial review of NIH R01 grant proposals. *Nat Hum Behav.* 2019;3(3):257–264. https://doi.org/10.1038/s41562-018-0517-y
38. Huang J, Gates AJ, Sinatra R, Barabási AL. Historical comparison of gender inequality in scientific careers across countries and disciplines. *Proc Natl Acad Sci U S A.* 2020;117(9):4609–4616. https://doi.org/10.1073/pnas.1914221117

# Unveiling the Unseen: Documenting and Analyzing Nonfatal Shootings by Police

*Justin Nix, PhD*

**ABOUT THE AUTHOR**

*Justin Nix is a distinguished associate professor in the School of Criminology and Criminal Justice at the University of Nebraska Omaha, where he co-directs the Violence Intervention and Policing Research Lab and coordinates the Master of Arts program. His research centers on policing, with emphasis on legitimacy and police use of force.*

**See also Zare, p. 384 and Ward et al., p. 387.**

AJPH April 2024, Vol. 114, No. 4

The 2014 fatal shooting of Michael Brown by Officer Darren Wilson in Ferguson, Missouri, prompted what criminologist Lawrence Sherman called the Second Great Awakening of "both public and scholarly sentiment against avoidable police shootings."[1(p424)] (The First Great Awakening occurred in the 1970s and 1980s, when 50 large cities prohibited officers from shooting nonviolent, fleeing suspects.) Since then, an interdisciplinary array of scholars have drawn on newly available, more comprehensive databases tracking deadly police–citizen interactions (e.g., Fatal Encounters, Mapping Police Violence, and *The Washington Post*'s Fatal Force database) to test hypotheses about the causes[2,3] and public health consequences[4] of these interactions, as well as disparities therein.[5,6] This body of research has revealed an annual average of approximately 1000 fatalities attributable to police gunfire in the United States. However, the scope of these studies has been limited by the paucity of data on nonfatal police shootings.[7] Though nonfatal police shootings, by definition, do not involve fatalities, they nevertheless constitute uses of deadly force (i.e., force likely to cause death) by police officers.

## A WELCOME ADDITION TO THE LITERATURE

Ward et al. (p. 387) have addressed this limitation by meticulously abstracting and manually verifying data from the Gun Violence Archive (GVA) to compile the first multiyear, nationwide analysis of injurious shootings by US police officers. Several key findings emerged. First, their work reveals that from 2015 to 2020, 4741 people were nonfatally injured by police gunfire—an average of 790 per year. Second, the authors document clear incident- and person-level differences in police shooting outcomes. For example, compared with police shootings involving unarmed persons, those involving persons armed with a knife or other cutting instrument were nearly twice as likely to be fatal (odds ratio = 1.92, see Table 4). Meanwhile, police shootings involving non-Hispanic Black victims were less likely than those involving non-Hispanic White victims to be fatal (though readers should bear in mind that race/ethnicity was unknown for 29% of victims).[7] Finally, the authors point out that some groups are overrepresented in injurious police shootings given their representation in the US population. As but one example, "[u]nhoused victims comprise nearly 3% of injured people, despite representing just 0.2% of the US population" (p. 394). Without knowing how often police interactions with unhoused persons do not result in the use of deadly force, it is difficult to make sense of this disparity. But, to be sure, this is an understudied population in the police-use-of-force literature, so simply calculating this disparity is an important contribution.

The next step for researchers is to focus on discerning the causal mechanisms at work here. Are officers firing more rounds, on average, when they confront people armed with knives?[8] Does proximity to trauma care[9] or agency policies regarding when officers can render aid[10] account for some of the observed victim-level differences in shooting outcomes? Are officers more likely to use deadly force when interacting with unhoused persons? Hopefully this study by Ward et al. will inspire researchers to do the additional work necessary to unpack some of their findings and answer these questions.

## INTRODUCING SPOTLITE

It bears mentioning that Ward et al. restricted their focus to injurious shootings by police officers, leaving it unclear how often noninjurious police shootings occur. It seems unlikely that these incidents are as reliably reported by local media and subsequently included in the Gun Violence Archive. However, since Ward et al. completed their study, a new data set has been made available by the Cline Center for Advanced Research at the University of Illinois Urbana-Champaign. Their Systematic Policing Oversight Through Lethal-force Incident Tracking Environment (SPOTLITE) data primarily originate from Gun Violence Archive and Fatal Encounters and include "any discharge of a firearm by law enforcement personnel as well as any other use of force by law enforcement personnel that produces a lethal outcome."[11]

Unfortunately, at this time, the SPOTLITE data are incident-level, and users cannot easily determine which incidents resulted in fatalities, nonfatal injuries, or no injuries (the Cline Center is still working on an individual-level data set, which they will release later). However, users can merge SPOTLITE with GVA using the gva_id variable. Doing so reveals that SPOTLITE extracted 14 320 deadly force incidents from GVA between 2015 and 2020—an average of 2387 per year (data downloaded January 4, 2024). Ward et al. extracted 10 308 injurious shootings over the same period, or 1718 each year on average (reported in Table 1). If we assume the difference in each research team's total is noninjurious shootings (i.e., incidents wherein officers shot and missed), it would mean there were 4012 such shootings from 2015 to 2020, or 669 each year on average.

Relying on the figures Ward et al. reported in Table 1, this would mean that from 2015 to 2020, approximately 31% of all known police shootings resulted in at least one fatality, 41% resulted in nonfatal injuries, and 28% resulted in no injuries. It would also mean that all the research published in the last 10 years drawing on data from *The Washington Post*, Fatal Encounters, and Mapping Police Violence was relying on a nonrandom sample of only about one third of all incidents involving police use of deadly force. Depending on the research question, complete omission of two thirds of the phenomenon we seek to understand may produce statistically biased estimates of the causes and consequences of said phenomenon, or a misunderstanding of the causal mechanisms altogether. Thus, many of these studies will likely need to be replicated with GVA or SPOTLITE data.

## CONCLUSION

Including nonfatal shootings in research on the causes and consequences of police use of deadly force is critical, because, as Ward et al. correctly note, "[U]nderestimating the true scale of injury impact is a further injustice and may obstruct progress toward preventive action and reforms" (p. 394). And, to be clear, we should be trying to prevent unnecessary and avoidable uses of deadly force (i.e., force likely to cause death)—not merely those that do, in fact, result in death. Going forward, I encourage scholars working in this space to take advantage of the data being compiled by GVA and SPOTLITE, which are more comprehensive than any of the other data sets available at this time. AJPH

### CORRESPONDENCE

Correspondence should be sent to Justin Nix, 6001 Dodge St, 218 CPACS, Omaha, NE 68182 (e-mail: jnix@unomaha.edu). Reprints can be ordered at https://ajph.org by clicking the "Reprints" link.

### PUBLICATION INFORMATION

Full Citation: Nix J. Unveiling the unseen: documenting and analyzing nonfatal shootings by police. *Am J Public Health*. 2024;114(4):382–383.

Acceptance Date: January 18, 2024.

DOI: https://doi.org/10.2105/AJPH.2024.307609

### ACKNOWLEDGMENTS

I extend my thanks to Ian Adams, Geoff Alpert, Ajay Singh, and Jay Jennings for their helpful feedback on an earlier draft.

### CONFLICTS OF INTEREST

The author has no conflicts of interest to report.

### REFERENCES

1. Sherman LW. Reducing fatal police shootings as system crashes: research, theory, and practice. *Annu Rev Criminol*. 2018;1(1):421–449. https://doi.org/10.1146/annurev-criminol-032317-092409
2. Kivisto AJ, Ray B, Phalen PL. Firearm legislation and fatal police shootings in the United States. *Am J Public Health*. 2017;107(7):1068–1075. https://doi.org/10.2105/AJPH.2017.303770
3. Nagin DS. Firearm availability and fatal police shootings. *Ann Am Acad Pol Soc Sci*. 2020;687(1):49–57. https://doi.org/10.1177/0002716219896259
4. Bor J, Venkataramani AS, Williams DR, Tsai AC. Police killings and their spillover effects on the mental health of Black Americans: a population-based, quasi-experimental study. *Lancet*. 2018;392(10144):302–310. https://doi.org/10.1016/S0140-6736(18)31130-9
5. Edwards F, Esposito MH, Lee H. Risk of police-involved death by race/ethnicity and place, United States, 2012–2018. *Am J Public Health*. 2018;108(9):1241–1248. https://doi.org/10.2105/AJPH.2018.304559
6. Schwartz GL, Jahn JL. Mapping fatal police violence across us metropolitan areas: overall rates and racial/ethnic inequities, 2013–2017. *PLoS One*. 2020;15(6):e0229686. https://doi.org/10.1371/journal.pone.0229686
7. Nix J, Shjarback JA. Factors associated with police shooting mortality: a focus on race and a plea for more comprehensive data. *PLoS One*. 2021;16(11):e0259024. https://doi.org/10.1371/journal.pone.0259024
8. Zimring FE. *When Police Kill*. Cambridge, MA: Harvard University Press; 2017.
9. Carr BG, Bowman AJ, Wolff CS, et al. Disparities in access to trauma care in the United States: a population-based analysis. *Injury*. 2017;48(2):332–338. https://doi.org/10.1016/j.injury.2017.01.008
10. Band RA, Salhi RA, Holena DN, Powell E, Branas CC, Carr BG. Severity-adjusted mortality in trauma patients transported by police. *Ann Emerg Med*. 2014;63(5):608–614e3. https://doi.org/10.1016/j.annemergmed.2013.11.008
11. Jennings J, Singh A, Althaus S, Martin M, Bajjalieh J, Robbennolt J. Cline Center SPOTLITE United States Dataset. University of Illinois at Urbana-Champaign; 2023.

# Disparities in Policing From Theory to Practice

*Hossein Zare, PhD, MS*

**ABOUT THE AUTHOR**

*Hossein Zare is with the Department of Health Policy and Management, Johns Hopkins Bloomberg School of Public Health, Baltimore, MD, and the University of Maryland Global Campus, Adelphi.*

**See also Nix, p. 382 and Ward et al., p. 387.**

In recent years, high-profile police use-of-force encounters with individuals of color (e.g., George Floyd in Minneapolis, Minnesota; Breonna Taylor in Louisville, Kentucky; Jacob Blake in Kenosha, Wisconsin) have increased the long-standing scrutiny of law enforcement actions and deepened the mistrust between communities and police when police behave inappropriately.

Disparities in policing are indeed multifaceted issues that cannot be adequately understood solely by examining individual instances of violence. Analyzing how these events reflect broader systemic oppression is essential to gaining a comprehensive understanding. It requires exploring historical and ongoing patterns of discrimination, socioeconomic inequalities, neighborhood disadvantage, and the influence of power dynamics on policing practices. By recognizing and addressing these systemic factors, we are in a better position to address disparities in policing and reduce incidents of police violence.

Theoretically, disparities in policing can be explained by three theories: majority-minority communities, conflict theory of law, and minority threat hypothesis–group threat theory. In majority-minority communities, the high level of violent crime leads to more police encounters and a greater need for police presence, which increases the risk of fatal outcomes.[1] According to majority-minority communities, individuals living in lower-income, distressed communities of color, characterized by higher poverty rates, greater residential segregation, and elevated levels of violent crime, are more likely to experience social control measures, including heightened policing. Multiple studies have consistently shown that racial/ethnic minorities, particularly Black people and Hispanic people, are more likely to be subjected to more intense law enforcement practices than White people.[2]

The conflict theory of law suggests that policing enforces social control that benefits those in power, resulting in intensified policing and potential use of force.[3] This argument means that areas with a higher population of non-Whites, particularly Black people, could have larger police forces mainly because of Whites' fear and perceived economic threat.[4] Finally, the minority threat hypothesis and group threat theory propose that minority-serving areas and socially marginalized populations experience more aggressive policing and lethal outcomes because these groups are seen as threatening the established order and power structure.[5] On the community side, it might also lead to an increase in hate crimes targeting these minority groups.[6] Without taking these theories into consideration, there is a possibility of misinterpreting or misreading research findings.

The study conducted by Ward et al. (p. 387) addressed a gap in the existing research on police violence by explicitly focusing on nonfatal shooting incidents. This study utilized a comprehensive data set, thereby offering valuable insights into the disparities in policing. Additionally, it highlights some essential findings that merit further explanation and analysis. In addressing various aspects related to this study and similar research, I highlight in the following sections several significant factors that directly or indirectly influence the subject matter.

## SIZE AND COMPOSITION OF THE POPULATION

It is crucial to consider the size of the population when analyzing data on fatal and nonfatal police shootings. Although the frequency of such incidents can be higher among the White population, this interpretation can be misleading without considering population size. Many studies have reported that Black and Hispanic people have higher rates of fatal police shootings than White people,[2] that they are 50% more likely to experience some form of force in interactions with police.[7] The demographic composition plays a role in the occurrence of police shootings—for example, when the Black and Hispanic populations at the county level increased by one unit, the rate of police shootings increased by 1.5 and 1.6, respectively.[8]

## NEIGHBORHOOD AND GEOGRAPHICAL DISPARITIES

Neighborhood context can influence interactions and police decision-making.

Police are more likely to use fatal force in areas with economic disadvantage, racial conflict, high crime rates, and a high proportion of vulnerable and low-income populations—more specifically, communities of color.[9] These disparities were most pervasive in suburbs, where Black people were arrested 4.5 times more often than White people for quality-of-life (disorderly behaviors in public) offenses.[10] The characteristics of these neighborhoods influence police decisions to increase social control through more arrests, upgraded crime classifications, and the use of more coercive actions in interactions with citizens. Studies on police violence should consider geographical disparities; failure to do so can lead to misleading findings that unintentionally favor a lower rate of police disparities for non-White populations.

To delve deeper into this subject, I conducted a county-level analysis using Mapping Police Violence data and *Washington Post* fatal force data from 2015 to 2020, aligning with the timeframe used in Ward et al.'s study. The analysis specifically examined the influence of race and location on incidents of fatal shootings. The findings revealed a higher prevalence of police fatal shootings in areas characterized by high social vulnerability, particularly affecting individuals from diverse racial backgrounds. When I compared low- and high-social vulnerability areas, the rate of fatal shootings for White people increased by 2.25 times, whereas Black people experienced a 7.5 times increase. Alarmingly, Hispanic people faced a 12-fold increase in fatal shooting deaths in high-social vulnerability areas.[9] Examining neighborhood-level disparities in police violence requires an examination of the problem from the structural level.

## CHARACTERISTICS OF POLICE OFFICERS

As mentioned by Ward et al., injuries resulting from shootings by sheriff's departments and state police have been shown to have a higher likelihood of being lethal compared with injuries from shootings by local police departments. The study by Ward et al. pointed out the significance of giving more attention to local police departments in addressing violent crime. Local police departments have an advantage in combating violent crime through their involvement with communities and familiarity with the local environment. Increasing accountability both at the system level and individual level is crucial for preventing firearm injuries. Law enforcement policymakers may reduce disparities in policing by increasing "front-end restrictions on officer discretion or increased back-end accountability"[11]; paying more attention to work-related factors, victims, and police gender and race/ethnicity; and ensuring the protection of police officers while carrying out their duties by implementing a system of double-distributed accountability.

## LACK OF GOOD DATA

Existing data sets—such as the *Washington Post*'s Police Shootings, Mapping Police Violence, and Gun Violence Archive—have deficiencies in capturing individual factors. One major issue is the missing observation of race and ethnicity in these data sets. Ward et al. found that approximately 29% of the data they analyzed were missing race or ethnicity information, with a higher occurrence among non-White populations (determined by the study team's assigned race). The issue of missing data goes beyond just race and ethnicity; important individual factors such as age, location, officers involved, names of victims, and officer race/ethnicity are often missing or not consistently reported in available data sets. Many studies have emphasized the lack of reliable and comprehensive data on addressing disparities in policing; this highlights the essential need for policymakers and relevant organizations to take action to address this issue effectively.

Deep concerns remain about the historical and structural racism and discrimination that have resulted in stringent social control of communities of color and low-income people. There is growing recognition that current federal and state police accountability policies are largely inadequate,[12] and that more must be done to address the systematic causes of disparities in policing. *AJPH*

### CORRESPONDENCE

Correspondence should be sent to Hossein Zare, Room 337, 624 N Broadway, Baltimore, MD 21205 (e-mail: hzare1@jhu.edu). Reprints can be ordered at http://www.ajph.org by clicking the "Reprints" link.

### PUBLICATION INFORMATION

Full Citation: Zare H. Disparities in policing from theory to practice. *Am J Public Health*. 2024;114(4): 384–386.

Acceptance Date: January 8, 2024

DOI: https://doi.org/10.2105/AJPH.2024.307588

### ACKNOWLEDGMENTS

This study is funded by the Bloomberg American Health Initiative (Johns Hopkins Bloomberg School of Public Health, 1600108087).

**Note.** The contents are solely the author's responsibility and do not necessarily represent the official views of the funding agencies.

### CONFLICTS OF INTEREST

The author has no known competing financial interests or personal relationships that could have appeared to influence the work reported in this article.

## REFERENCES


1. Holmes MD, Painter MA, Smith BW. Race, place, and police-caused homicide in US municipalities. *Justice Q.* 2019;36(5):751–786. https://doi.org/10.1080/07418825.2018.1427782
2. Zare H, Meyerson NS, Delgado P, Spencer M, Gaskin DJ, Thorpe RJ Jr. Association between neighborhood and racial composition of victims on fatal police shooting and police violence: an integrated review (2000–2022). *Soc Sci.* 2022; 11(4):153. https://doi.org/10.3390/socsci11040153
3. Turk AT. Conflict and criminality. *Am Sociol Rev.* 1966;31(3):338–352. https://doi.org/10.2307/2090822
4. Stults BJ, Baumer EP. Racial context and police force size: evaluating the empirical validity of the minority threat perspective. *Am J Sociol.* 2007; 113(2):507–546. https://doi.org/10.1086/518906
5. Blalock HM. *Toward a Theory of Minority-Group Relations.* New York, NY: Wiley; 1967.
6. Cikara M, Fouka V, Tabellini M. Hate crime increases with minoritized group rank. Harvard Business School Working Paper No. 21-075 (last revised 2022). Available at: https://papers.ssrn.com/sol3/papers.cfm?abstract_id=3863364. Accessed February 16, 2024.
7. Fryer RG. An empirical analysis of racial differences in police use of force. *J Polit Econ.* 2019; 127(3):1210–1261. https://doi.org/10.1086/701423
8. Helms, R, Costanza, SE. Contextualizing race: a conceptual and empirical study of fatal interactions with police across US counties. *J Ethn Crim Justice.* 2020; 18(1):43–71. https://doi.org/10.1080/15377938.2019.1692748
9. Zare H, Meyerson NS, Delgado P, et al. How place and race drive the numbers of fatal police shootings in the US: 2015–2020. *Prev Med.* 2022;161:107132. https://doi.org/10.1016/j.ypmed.2022.107132
10. Beck B. Broken windows in the cul-de-sac? Race/ethnicity and quality-of-life policing in the changing suburbs. *Crime Delinq.* 2019;65(2): 270–292. https://doi.org/10.1177/0011128717739568
11. Goff PA, Rau H. Predicting bad policing: theorizing burdensome and racially disparate policing through the lenses of social psychology and routine activities. *Ann Am Acad Pol Soc Sci.* 2020; 687(1):67–88. https://doi.org/10.1177/0002716220901349
12. Legal Defense Fund (LDF). LDF issues statement on the failure to advance the George Floyd Justice in Policing Act of 2021 (September 22, 2021). Available at: https://www.naacpldf.org/press-release/ldf-issues-statement-on-the-failure-to-advance-the-george-floyd-justice-in-policing-act-of-2021/?gclid=CjwKCAiAxP2eBhBiEiwA5puhNY3G5_X12OZ0jldW1it0MsnWOQoTDmmMe2UBjjHDw4ekYu_hWs54xRoCDgEQAvD_BwE. Accessed February 16, 2024.

# National Burden of Injury and Deaths From Shootings by Police in the United States, 2015–2020

*Julie A. Ward, RN, PhD, MN, Javier Cepeda, PhD, MPH, Dylan B. Jackson, PhD, MS, Odis Johnson Jr, PhD, Daniel W. Webster, ScD, MPH, and Cassandra K. Crifasi, PhD, MPH*

**See also Nix, p. 382 and Zare, p. 384.**

**Objectives.** To describe all-outcome injurious shootings by police and compare characteristics of fatal versus nonfatal injurious shootings nationally.

**Methods.** From July 2021 to April 2023, we manually reviewed publicly available records on all 2015–2020 injurious shootings by US police, identified from Gun Violence Archive. We estimated injury frequency, case fatality rates, and relative odds of death by incident and victim characteristics.

**Results.** A total of 1769 people were injured annually in shootings by police, 55% fatally. When a shooting injury occurred, odds of fatality were 46% higher following dispatched responses than police-initiated responses. Injuries associated with physically threatening or threat-making behaviors, behavioral health needs, and well-being checks were most frequently fatal. Relative to White victims, Black victims were overrepresented but had 35% lower odds of fatal injury when shot.

**Conclusions.** This first multiyear, nationwide analysis of injurious shootings by US police suggests that injury disparities are underestimated by fatal shootings alone. Nonpolicing responses to social needs may prevent future injuries.

**Public Health Implications.** We call for enhanced reporting systems, comprehensive evaluation of emerging reforms, and targeted investment in social services for equitable injury prevention. (*Am J Public Health*. 2024;114(4):387–397. https://doi.org/10.2105/AJPH.2023.307560)

AJPH April 2024, Vol. 114, No. 4

Firearm injuries are a public health crisis, annually costing 45 000 lives and more than 1 million disability-adjusted life years in the United States alone.[1,2] Harms associated with use of firearms are compounded and reinforced by underreporting, inadequate funding for prevention, and other structural inequities.[2] Among the most underreported but societally impactful forms of firearm injury are shootings by police, which result in 1000 US fatalities annually[1] and likely contribute to worsening public perceptions of policing. According to a Pew Research Center survey, in 2020, just 35% of US adults agreed that police use the right amount of force in all situations, and 34% believed that police treat racial and ethnic groups equally.[3] These views have fueled national policy debates about public safety reforms[4] and calls for public health action against violence by police,[5] but data needed for empirical decision-making are lacking because of persistent gaps in national use-of-force injury surveillance.

Owing to their relative comprehensiveness, inclusion of contextual data, and minimal reporting lag, news media repositories (e.g., Fatal Encounters, Mapping Police Violence, *The Guardian*'s The Counted, *The Washington Post*'s Fatal Force, and Gun Violence Archive [GVA]) are currently the best available sources for a national accounting of injuries by police use of deadly force. Alternative data sources include accountability systems of the US Federal Bureau of Investigation (including the recently phased-out Supplemental Homicide Reports, replaced by National Use-of-Force Data Collection), the Centers for Disease Control and Prevention's (CDC's) National Vital Statistics

System, and CDC's National Violent Death Reporting System. These 3 federal systems underestimate fatal injuries by police shootings through insufficient agency participation, inconsistencies in cause-of-death designation, and inconsistent state participation, respectively.[6–9] Some states and localities maintain accessible databases, but these sources are not nationally representative.[10,11] Of all national data sources, only National Use-of-Force Data Collection and GVA document fatal and nonfatal shootings by police.

The various media repositories produce comparable national estimates of fatal injuries from police use of force.[7,12] These sources have been used to describe disparities in fatal injuries by age,[13,14] race,[11,13,15] gender,[13] armed status,[15,16] mental health status,[15] and other characteristics, including US region.[13,15,17] In an illustrative analysis by Nix et al. of 2015 shooting fatalities (n = 990), 50% of people killed in police shootings were White, 26% were Black, and 96% were men. The average age of victims was 37 years. Most victims were armed (82% with a deadly weapon or replica gun, 5.5% with a vehicle), and 9% were unarmed. Twenty-five percent involved signs of mental distress or history of mental illness according to reports by journalists and police at the time.[18] Although collectively illuminating, by failing to account for nonfatal injuries, fatality studies still likely underestimate the national burden of injury from shootings by on-duty police.

Few studies have examined nonfatal injuries, leaving the frequency and characteristics of these shootings uncertain. In 1 analysis of 11 urban police and sheriffs' departments with publicly available injury data, fatalities comprised 53% of injurious shootings by police.[19] Another analysis of 4 state-mandated databases estimated 56% of people injured in police shootings died.[10] A broadly inclusive study describing 2015 GVA-listed "officer involved incidents" (n = 1907) reported 49% of incidents were fatal.[20] In these studies, fatal injuries were associated with older victim age,[10,20] White versus Black racial identity,[10,19] multiple police shooters,[19] and nonofficer weapon possession.[10,20] Odds of fatality were higher from injuries to victims armed with knives or blunt-force objects, compared with firearms, and lower among vehicularly armed victims (knife: odds ratio [OR] = 2.20; blunt object: OR = 2.33; vehicle: OR = 0.26).[20] Unarmed victims had higher odds of survival than armed victims.[10] When nonfatal injuries were included, injury disparities most affecting people who are Black were projected to be more severe than when estimated from fatalities alone.[10]

In sum, open-source data repositories of police use of force are reliable and informative resources that have produced broad understanding of fatal shootings by police nationally. However, fatal shootings may represent little more than half of all injurious shootings by police. To date, no published studies have examined the full and current burden of physical injury from shootings by on-duty US law enforcement officers. The objectives of this exploratory study were to (1) describe total people injured or killed in shootings by police in the United States using an up-to-date, multiyear nationwide data set and (2) compare characteristics of fatal versus nonfatal injurious shootings nationally.

## METHODS

We extracted and compiled data representing incidents and victim characteristics from GVA's linked articles and other publicly available sources. GVA is a database of fatal and nonfatal US gun violence events, identified from approximately 7500 media, law enforcement, government, and commercial sources daily since 2013.[21] Incidents are cataloged by date, location, and gun violence type. Data abstraction occurred from July 2021 to April 2023 for shootings by police occurring January 1, 2015, through December 31, 2020. The abstraction team consisted of 15 students from the Johns Hopkins Bloomberg School of Public Health. All 14 155 incidents designated as "officer involved incidents" were manually reviewed for eligibility and identification of case characteristics at least once. Abstractors received standardized training and a randomly assigned subset of incidents. In addition, a blinded 10% of incidents were repetitively assigned for quality assurance. Median total case assignment was 1100 (range = 460–5525).

Cases were restricted to include only incidents of shots fired by 1 or more law enforcement officers, resulting in injuries to people who were not responding officers. Accidental discharges, policing occupational injuries, injuries by bullet alternatives exclusively (e.g., rubber bullets, taser), shootings without injury, and self-inflicted injuries were excluded. GVA-designated "suicide by cop" shootings (i.e., shootings presumed to have been intentionally provoked) were retained.

### Measures

Abstracted variables included situational characteristics (e.g., response type, incident type, shooting location, weapon involvement), victim demographics (e.g., gender, age, race, ethnicity), victim

AJPH April 2024, Vol. 114, No. 4

characteristics (e.g., housed or unhoused, armed status and weapon type, injury outcome), and a limited set of shooting-officer characteristics (e.g., on- or off-duty status, alone or accompanied, agency affiliation). Abstractors additionally identified and described incidents in which mental or behavioral health conditions were explicitly named in association with the shooting or its initiating incident. These cases were rereviewed and confirmed. Definitions of all abstracted variables are provided in Appendix A (available as a supplement to the online version of this article at https://ajph.org).

Abstractors categorically coded all descriptors using a combination of deductive and inductive techniques, aiming for objective reflection of best-available reporting. Abstractors cross-referenced fatal incidents with Fatal Encounters. Race and ethnicity designations were made when specified by sources or following 2-person concordant review of a published photo, an approximation of socially assigned identities.[22] If ambiguous or unreported, abstractors selected "unknown." All other coding uncertainties were discussed in weekly meetings. Post hoc review of repetitively assigned incidents revealed strong coding consistency; rare discrepancies were resolved through additional source review by the first author.

## Analyses

We calculated counts and proportions for total incidents and injuries, entirely nonfatal incidents versus incidents with at least 1 fatality, and nonfatal injuries versus fatal injuries. We calculated case fatality rates for incident and person characteristics. For each characteristic, we estimated odds of fatal injury outcome from a random-intercept model, in which victims were nested within incidents. We defined reference categories to support intuitive comparisons, based on majority representation (e.g., local police agencies, non-Hispanic White ethno-racial designation, masculine gender), or simplicity of the comparator (e.g., unarmed victim, shooting-related initiating incident). For age, regression models first included only age-specified victims (i.e., excluding "juvenile," "adult," or decade-approximated descriptive ages), then categorically examined all victims as "juvenile" (ages 0–17 years) or "adult" (ages ≥ 18 years). In adjusted models, we estimated the effect of each characteristic after accounting for incident-level clustering and holding all other incident and person variables constant. Confidence intervals were calculated based on an $\alpha$ of .05.

Estimates reflect injurious shootings by officers ostensibly acting "in the line of duty," including shootings by on-duty officers, on- and off-duty officers in a multiple-officer response, off-duty officers acting in an on-duty capacity (e.g., performing investigative activities, identifying oneself as police), and incidents without explicitly reported duty status. In sensitivity analyses, we compared estimates under more restrictive duty-status criteria (i.e., only explicitly on duty or both on and off-duty) and maximally inclusive duty-status criteria (i.e., also off-duty officers working security positions and off-duty officers not acting in a law-enforcement capacity). We performed analyses with Stata version 16.1 (StataCorp LP, College Station, TX) and the melogit command with clustering by incident.

# RESULTS

From 2015 to 2020, there were 10 308 incidents of US law enforcement officers shooting their firearms and injuring 1 or more people (Table 1). These incidents resulted in 5874 fatalities and 4741 individuals with nonfatal gunshot injuries, a 55.3% case fatality rate (Table 2). On average, 1769 people were injured annually (979 fatally; 790 nonfatally; Table 3). Examined monthly, injury frequency appeared cyclical but otherwise stable over the 6-year period (Appendix B, available as a supplement to the online version of this article at https://ajph.org).

## Incident Characteristics

In more than half of injurious shooting incidents, a nonofficer was armed with a firearm (56%; n = 5738); 4% involved nonofficer possession of a BB gun or replica gun (n = 403). Combined, 58% of these incidents involved a fatality. Knives were involved in 15% of incidents (n = 1543; 68% fatal), and a vehicle was reportedly weaponized against an officer in 8% of incidents (n = 806; 36% fatal). In another 8%, no weapon was involved (n = 785; 54% fatal). In 1.5% of incidents, a nonofficer reportedly gained control of a service weapon (n = 98) or nearly did so (n = 46; Appendix C, available as a supplement to the online version of this article at https://ajph.org).

Injurious shootings typically involved multiple police responders (81%; Appendix C), most frequently from a local police department (local police: 62%; sheriff's office: 23%; Table 1). Fourteen percent of incidents with at least 1 fatality occurred during a single-officer response, compared to 18% of nonfatal-injury incidents (Appendix C). Dispatch by emergency services preceded 62% of injurious incidents; officer-initiated encounters preceded 36% of incidents. The most common reasons for police involvement before

**TABLE 1— Fatal and Nonfatal Injurious Shooting Incidents, by Event Characteristic: United States, 2015–2020**

| Incident Characteristic | Nonfatal Injurious Incident, No. | Fatal Incident, No. | % Fatal | Total Injurious Shooting Incidents, No. (%) |
|---|---|---|---|---|
| Total | 4467 | 5841 | 56.7 | 10 308 (100) |
| Agency type | | | | |
| Local police | 2867 | 3481 | 54.8 | 6348 (61.6) |
| Sheriff's office | 982 | 1412 | 59.0 | 2394 (23.2) |
| State police | 227 | 341 | 60.0 | 568 (5.5) |
| National agency | 73 | 103 | 58.5 | 176 (1.7) |
| Special jurisdiction | 50 | 28 | 35.9 | 78 (0.8) |
| Constable or marshal | 5 | 5 | 50.0 | 10 (0.1) |
| Multiple shooting agencies | 209 | 441 | 67.8 | 650 (6.3) |
| Unknown | 54 | 30 | 35.7 | 84 (0.8) |
| Response type | | | | |
| On view | 1752 | 1952 | 52.7 | 3704 (35.9) |
| Dispatched to 911 call | 2588 | 3783 | 59.4 | 6371 (61.8) |
| By subject | 53 | 56 | 51.4 | 109 (1.1) |
| Unknown | 74 | 50 | 40.3 | 124 (1.2) |
| Incident type | | | | |
| Shooting | 438 | 525 | 54.5 | 963 (9.3) |
| Assault | 155 | 249 | 61.6 | 404 (3.9) |
| Disorderly conduct or dispute or disturbance | 162 | 236 | 59.3 | 398 (3.9) |
| Domestic incident (disturbance, dispute, or violence) | 566 | 1048 | 64.9 | 1614 (15.7) |
| Investigative | 243 | 294 | 54.7 | 537 (5.2) |
| Robbery or carjacking | 408 | 398 | 49.4 | 806 (7.8) |
| Burglary | 122 | 101 | 45.3 | 223 (2.2) |
| Stolen vehicle | 79 | 57 | 41.9 | 136 (1.3) |
| Suicidal or behavioral health crisis | 238 | 392 | 62.2 | 630 (6.1) |
| Suspicious person or vehicle | 263 | 286 | 52.1 | 549 (5.3) |
| Threats | 71 | 144 | 67.0 | 215 (2.1) |
| Traffic stop | 789 | 811 | 50.7 | 1600 (15.5) |
| Trespassing | 73 | 101 | 58.0 | 174 (1.7) |
| Warrant or arrest | 376 | 592 | 61.2 | 968 (9.4) |
| Weapon complaint | 203 | 245 | 54.7 | 448 (4.3) |
| Well-being check | 54 | 101 | 65.2 | 155 (1.5) |
| Other[a] | 150 | 203 | 57.5 | 353 (3.4) |
| Unknown | 77 | 58 | 43.0 | 135 (1.3) |

*Note.* Includes on duty, both on and off duty, off duty but acting as on duty, and unknown duty status.
[a]Included within "other" incidents are vehicle collision, fire, hostage, involuntary commitment, pedestrian stop, vandalism, vehicle collision, escaped prisoner responses, immigration-related incidents, disaster responses, evictions, parole checks, dog complaints, fraud, and fare evasion.

injurious shootings were traffic stops (16% of incidents, 51% fatal), domestic incidents (16% of incidents, 65% fatal), shots fired (9% of incidents, 55% fatal), and warrants (9% of incidents, 61% fatal). Suicidal crises represented 6% of injurious incidents (62% fatal). Rarer but more frequently fatal injurious shootings included well-being checks (2% of incidents, 65% fatal) and threats (e.g., an armed person verbalizing intent to harm; 2% of incidents, 67% fatal; Table 1).

**TABLE 2— Fatally and Nonfatally Injured Persons, by Event or Person Characteristic: United States, 2015–2020**

| Incident or Person Characteristic | Nonfatally Injured, No. | Fatally Injured, No. | % Fatal | Total Injured Persons, No. (%) |
|---|---|---|---|---|
| Total | 4741 | 5874 | 55.3 | 10 615 (100) |
| Person weapon | | | | |
| Unarmed | 478 | 477 | 49.9 | 955 (9.0) |
| Firearm | 2418 | 3356 | 58.1 | 5774 (54.4) |
| BB or replica gun | 154 | 210 | 57.7 | 364 (3.4) |
| Total gun[a] | 2572 | 3566 | 58.1 | 6138 (57.8) |
| Knife or cutting/stabbing instrument | 491 | 1040 | 67.9 | 1531 (14.4) |
| Vehicle | 495 | 279 | 36.0 | 774 (7.3) |
| Blunt object | 76 | 123 | 61.8 | 199 (1.9) |
| Other | 118 | 121 | 50.6 | 239 (2.3) |
| Unknown | 511 | 268 | 34.4 | 779 (7.3) |
| Age[b] | | | | |
| Range, y | < 1–93 | 6–91 | | |
| Mean of known ages, y (n = 9467; 59.8% fatal) | 33 | 37 | ... | 35.4 |
| Median of known ages, y (n = 9467; 59.8% fatal) | 30 | 35 | ... | 33 |
| Total juvenile count (< 18 y) | 212 | 105 | 33.1 | 317 (3.0) |
| Total adult count (≥ 18 y) | 4315 | 5733 | 57.1 | 10 048 (94.7) |
| Unknown | 214 | 36 | 14.4 | 250 (2.4) |
| Gender | | | | |
| Cisgender man | 4369 | 5613 | 56.2 | 9982 (94.0) |
| Cisgender woman | 287 | 248 | 46.4 | 535 (5.0) |
| Transgender | 1 | 10 | 90.9 | 11 (0.1) |
| Unknown | 84 | 3 | 3.4 | 87 (0.8) |
| Race/ethnicity | | | | |
| Non-Hispanic White | 1106 | 2500 | 69.3 | 3606 (34.0) |
| Non-Hispanic Black | 863 | 1363 | 61.2 | 2226 (21.0) |
| Hispanic, any race | 424 | 1004 | 70.3 | 1428 (13.5) |
| American Indian or Alaska Native | 23 | 105 | 82.0 | 128 (1.2) |
| Asian or Pacific Islander | 25 | 106 | 80.9 | 131 (1.2) |
| Other[c] or multiple | 20 | 20 | 50.0 | 40 (0.4) |
| Unknown | 2280 | 776 | 25.4 | 3056 (28.8) |
| Unhoused person | 94 | 184 | 66.2 | 278 (2.6) |
| Behavioral health involvement, incident[d] | 793 | 1611 | 67.0 | 2404 (22.6) |

*Note.* Includes on duty, both on and off duty, off duty but acting as on duty, and unknown duty status.
[a]Includes "firearm," "multiple with firearm," and "BB or replica gun." Does not include "service weapon concern," which was only assessed at the incident level.
[b]Age was entered as specified, where applicable. Otherwise, age was categorized as juvenile (ages 0–17 years), adult (ages ≥ 18 years), or unknown.
[c]Includes Middle Eastern-North African.
[d]Behavioral health incidents include suicidal or self-harming behaviors, substance use, diagnosis of serious mental illness relevant to the incident, disability that may have been misinterpreted as a mental or behavioral health issue, and transportation or response to inpatient behavioral health facility.

## Injured Person Characteristics

In victim-level analysis, weapon status, shooting-agency type, response type, and incident type were proportionately similar to incident-level descriptions (Appendix C). Victims' ages ranged from younger than 1 to 93 years; 95% were adults. Nonfatally injured people tended to be younger than fatally injured (nonfatal median age: 30 years; interquartile range [IQR] = 24–40 years; fatal median

**TABLE 3— People Injured in Fatal and Nonfatal Shootings by Police, by Year: United States**

| Year | Nonfatally Injured, No. | Fatally Injured, No. | % Fatal | Total People Injured, No. |
|---|---|---|---|---|
| 2015 | 777 | 916 | 54.1 | 1693 |
| 2016 | 761 | 940 | 55.3 | 1701 |
| 2017 | 810 | 970 | 54.5 | 1780 |
| 2018 | 821 | 1026 | 55.5 | 1847 |
| 2019 | 765 | 990 | 56.4 | 1755 |
| 2020 | 807 | 1032 | 56.1 | 1839 |
| Mean | 790 | 979 | 55.4 | 1769 |
| Total | 4741 | 5874 | 55.3 | 10 615 |

age: 35 years; IQR = 27–45 years). Sixty-seven percent of juveniles who were shot were not killed. Men and boys comprised 94% of victims. Race or ethnicity was identified for 71% of victims (n = 7559). When specified, 48% of people were described as non-Hispanic White (n = 3606; 69% fatal), 29% non-Hispanic Black (n = 2226; 61% fatal), and 19% Hispanic of any race (n = 1428; 70% fatal). Seventy-five percent of victims with unknown ethno-racial identities were nonfatally injured (Table 2). Among unarmed victims with assigned race-ethnicity, 40% were non-Hispanic White (n = 282), 35% were non-Hispanic Black (n = 245), and 21% were Hispanic (n = 144; fatal and nonfatal injuries included, data not shown). Nearly 3% of victims (n = 278) were unhoused, of whom 66% were fatally shot. Across incident types, 23% of injured people were shot in incidents involving mental or behavioral health issues (n = 2404; 67% fatal; Table 2). Forty-three percent of unhoused victims were injured in a such incidents (n = 120; data not shown).

Unadjusted logistic regression models suggest that compared with unarmed injured people (n = 955; 9%), odds of a fatal injury were significantly higher for injured people who were armed with a firearm (OR = 1.47; 95% confidence interval [CI] = 1.24, 1.74), BB or replica gun (OR = 1.43; 95% CI = 1.07, 1.91), knife (OR = 2.38; 95% CI = 1.91, 2.97), or blunt-force object (OR = 1.74; 95% CI = 1.20, 2.53). Odds of fatality were lower for injured people armed with a vehicle (OR = 0.52; 95% CI = 0.41, 0.66). Compared with shooting injuries during an officer-initiated interaction, odds of fatality were higher from injuries following dispatched interactions (OR = 1.46; 95% CI = 1.32, 1.63). Compared with injuries from police shootings following an on-view or dispatched "shots-fired" incident, odds of fatality were higher following incidents involving verbal threats (OR = 1.92; 95% CI = 1.32, 2.79), well-being checks (OR = 1.74; 95% CI = 1.14, 2.65), domestic incidents (OR = 1.72; 95% CI = 1.41, 2.11), suicidal or behavioral health crises (OR = 1.52; 95% CI = 1.19, 1.95), assaults (OR = 1.44; 95% CI = 1.08, 1.90), and warrant or arrest attempts (OR = 1.37; 95% CI = 1.11, 1.70). Odds of fatality were lower during traffic stops and other potentially vehicle-involved incidents (e.g., burglaries, robberies, or carjackings, and stolen vehicles). Incidents involving behavioral health concerns had 2.1-times-higher odds of fatal injury than injuries in incidents without such concerns (95% CI = 1.83, 2.45). Injuries from shootings by sheriff's departments and state police were more likely to be lethal than injuries from shootings by local police departments (Table 4).

Demographically, odds of fatality increased by 3% with each year of victim age (95% CI = 1.03, 1.04) and were lower for injured women compared with men (OR = 0.61; 95% CI = 0.48, 0.76). Among people with identified race/ethnicity, odds of fatality were lower among non-Hispanic Black victims (OR = 0.65; 95% CI = 0.56, 0.76) compared with non-Hispanic White victims, and higher among American Indian or Alaska Native victims (OR = 2.29; 95% CI = 1.33, 3.95) and Asian or Pacific Islander victims (OR = 2.12; 95% CI = 1.25, 3.58). In the adjusted model, Hispanic victims were also estimated to have higher odds of fatality (OR = 1.22; 95% CI = 1.04, 1.44), and fewer incident types were statistically significantly associated with fatal injury. All other inferences were unchanged (Table 4).

## Sensitivity Analysis

Estimates calculated from alternative duty-status inclusion criteria varied rarely and minimally from the main analysis. Results based on more restrictive or maximally inclusive on-duty status criteria are provided in Appendix D (available as a supplement to the online version of this article at https://ajph.org).

## DISCUSSION

In this study of 1769 annual injuries from shootings by police over a 6-year period, 45% of injured persons were

**TABLE 4— Logistic Regression Models Predicting Odds of Fatal vs Nonfatal Injury: United States, 2015–2020**

| Incident or Person Characteristic | OR (95% CI) | AOR (95% CI) |
|---|---|---|
| Officer duty status | | |
| On duty (Ref) | 1 | 1 |
| On and off duty | 1.43 (0.30, 6.71) | 1.22 (0.28, 5.40) |
| Off duty acting as on duty | 0.43 (0.27, 0.70) | 0.82 (0.50, 1.35) |
| Unknown | 0.34 (0.21, 0.55) | 1.16 (0.67, 2.02) |
| Person weapon | | |
| Unarmed (Ref) | 1 | 1 |
| Firearm | 1.47 (1.24, 1.74) | 1.37 (1.14, 1.65) |
| BB or replica gun | 1.43 (1.07, 1.91) | 1.23 (0.90, 1.67) |
| Knife or cutting/stabbing instrument | 2.38 (1.91, 2.97) | 1.92 (1.52, 2.44) |
| Vehicle | 0.52 (0.41, 0.66) | 0.55 (0.42, 0.71) |
| Blunt object | 1.74 (1.20, 2.53) | 1.43 (0.96, 2.13) |
| Other | 1.03 (0.74, 1.43) | 0.82 (0.58, 1.16) |
| Unknown | 0.47 (0.37, 0.60) | 0.72 (0.56, 0.93) |
| Agency type | | |
| Local police (Ref) | 1 | 1 |
| Sheriff's office | 1.24 (1.10, 1.40) | 1.26 (1.11, 1.42) |
| State police | 1.32 (1.07, 1.64) | 1.45 (1.16, 1.82) |
| National agency | 1.18 (0.82, 1.71) | 1.15 (0.79, 1.69) |
| Special jurisdiction | 0.38 (0.21, 0.68) | 0.67 (0.38, 1.19) |
| Constable or marshal | 0.66 (0.15, 2.90) | 0.80 (0.16, 3.94) |
| Multiple shooting agencies | 1.79 (1.45, 2.22) | 1.57 (1.26, 1.96) |
| Unknown | 0.38 (0.22, 0.67) | 1.12 (0.63, 2.01) |
| Single officer response | | |
| No (Ref) | 1 | 1 |
| Yes | 0.69 (0.60, 0.79) | 0.79 (0.68, 0.91) |
| Unknown | 0.38 (0.27, 0.52) | 0.75 (0.53, 1.07) |
| Age | | |
| Where specified (n = 9467)[a] | 1.03 (1.03, 1.04) | *Not included in model* |
| Adult (≥ 18 y; Ref) | 1 | 1 |
| Juvenile (< 18 y) | 0.32 (0.24, 0.44) | 0.63 (0.46, 0.86) |
| Unknown | 0.09 (0.06, 0.15) | 0.52 (0.34, 0.81) |
| Gender | | |
| Cisgender man (Ref) | 1 | 1 |
| Cisgender woman | 0.61 (0.48, 0.76) | 0.73 (0.58, 0.92) |
| Transgender | 11.11 (1.12, 110.18) | 9.05 (0.89, 91.79) |
| Unknown | 0.02 (< 0.01, 0.06) | 0.14 (0.04, 0.49) |
| Race/ethnicity | | |
| Non-Hispanic White (Ref) | 1 | 1 |
| Non-Hispanic Black | 0.65 (0.56, 0.76) | 0.85 (0.74, 0.98) |
| Hispanic, any race | 1.07 (0.91, 1.25) | 1.22 (1.04, 1.44) |
| American Indian or Alaska Native | 2.29 (1.33, 3.95) | 2.55 (1.48, 4.37) |
| Asian or Pacific Islander | 2.12 (1.25, 3.58) | 2.20 (1.32, 3.68) |

*Continued*

nonfatally injured, consistent with previous estimates from 4 states' mandated reporting.[10] Compared with estimates drawn from fatal shootings only, victim and incident characteristics were proportionately similar in categorical age, gender, involvement of unarmed victims, and other characteristics.[18] However, when nonfatally injured people were included, proportionately more victims were identified as non-Hispanic Black. Case fatality rates varied by incident characteristics. Few would disagree that a fatality is the most severe and irreversible potential outcome of a shooting, but nonfatal injuries are also physically and psychologically impactful. Situations with low case fatality rates are among the most underexamined incidents in previous research on fatal shootings by police.

Incidents with high case fatality rates generally involved complaints of physically threatening or threat-making behaviors (e.g., assaults, verbalized threats, domestic incidents, suicidal and self-harming incidents). Threat perception among police may be amplified by a prominent, and often racialized, emphasis on threat anticipation and officer self-protection in US policing culture and training.[23] Absent explicit threats, officers may anticipate increased threat during incidents such as traffic stops or domestic violence episodes, which are more frequently associated with police occupational homicides.[24] One potential exception to this pattern in threat-related, more frequently fatal injuries was well-being checks. Well-being checks were 74% more likely to be associated with fatal injury, despite not explicitly or necessarily involving pre-encounter threats of harm. In these cases, the probable involvement of callers and dispatchers

## TABLE 4— Continued

| Incident or Person Characteristic | OR (95% CI) | AOR (95% CI) |
|---|---|---|
| Other[b] or multiple | 0.38 (0.17, 0.83) | 0.46 (0.22, 0.97) |
| Unknown | 0.10 (0.07, 0.15) | 0.14 (0.10, 0.20) |
| Unhoused | | |
| No or unknown (Ref) | 1 | 1 |
| Yes | 0.99 (0.99, 1.00) | 1.00 (1.00, 1.00) |
| Response type | | |
| On view (Ref) | 1 | 1 |
| Dispatched to 911 call | 1.46 (1.32, 1.63) | 1.32 (1.11, 1.56) |
| By subject | 1.00 (0.63, 1.59) | 0.76 (0.46, 1.25) |
| Unknown | 0.58 (0.37, 0.91) | 1.11 (0.62, 1.98) |
| Incident type | | |
| Shooting (Ref) | 1 | 1 |
| Assault | 1.44 (1.08, 1.90) | 1.18 (0.87, 1.61) |
| Disorderly conduct or dispute or disturbance | 1.25 (0.94, 1.65) | 1.24 (0.92, 1.68) |
| Domestic incident (disturbance, dispute, or violence) | 1.72 (1.41, 2.11) | 1.43 (1.15, 1.77) |
| Investigative | 0.93 (0.73, 1.19) | 1.18 (0.88, 1.58) |
| Robbery or carjacking | 0.75 (0.60, 0.94) | 0.92 (0.73, 1.16) |
| Burglary | 0.66 (0.46, 0.93) | 0.66 (0.46, 0.95) |
| Stolen vehicle | 0.51 (0.33, 0.79) | 0.95 (0.60, 1.50) |
| Suicidal or behavioral health crisis | 1.52 (1.19, 1.95) | 1.09 (0.83, 1.43) |
| Suspicious person or vehicle | 0.89 (0.70, 1.14) | 1.11 (0.85, 1.46) |
| Threats | 1.92 (1.32, 2.79) | 1.89 (1.26, 2.82) |
| Traffic stop | 0.81 (0.67, 0.98) | 1.21 (0.95, 1.54) |
| Trespassing | 1.13 (0.77, 1.65) | 1.29 (0.86, 1.95) |
| Warrant or arrest | 1.37 (1.11, 1.70) | 1.66 (1.26, 2.18) |
| Weapon complaint | 1.03 (0.79, 1.34) | 0.91 (0.69, 1.21) |
| Well-being check | 1.74 (1.14, 2.65) | 1.32 (0.85, 2.05) |
| Other[c] | 1.16 (0.87, 1.55) | 1.26 (0.92, 1.72) |
| Unknown | 0.60 (0.39, 0.93) | 1.49 (0.86, 2.60) |
| Behavioral health–related incident[d] | | |
| None (Ref) | 1 | 1 |
| Any | 2.12 (1.83, 2.45) | 1.41 (1.22, 1.63) |

*Note.* AOR = adjusted odds ratio; CI = confidence interval; OR = odds ratio. Odds predicted with 2-level mixed-effects logistic regression models. Includes on duty, both on and off duty, off duty but acting as on duty, and unknown duty status.
[a]OR represents change in odds of fatality for each additional year of victim age.
[b]Includes Middle Eastern-North African.
[c]Included within "other" incidents are fire, hostage, vandalism, vehicle collision, pedestrian stop, involuntary commitment, subject-initiated, escaped prisoner responses, immigration-related incidents, disaster responses, evictions, parole checks, dog complaints, fraud, and fare evasion.
[d]Behavioral health incidents include suicidal or self-harming behaviors, substance use, diagnosis of serious mental illness relevant to the incident, disability that may have been misinterpreted as a mental or behavioral health issue, and transportation or response to inpatient behavioral health facility.

may be a source of relayed alarm, prompting readiness for threat perception.[25,26] Of all injuries, 61% followed dispatched incidents; these injuries were 1.46-times more likely to be fatal than injuries following on-view responses.

Among injured people, victims identified as non-Hispanic Black comprised 29% of race-identified injured people in this study. This compares to 26% of victims in a single-year sample of fatal shootings and 13% of the total US population.[18,27] Injured non-Hispanic Black people had 35% higher odds of surviving than non-Hispanic White injured people. Police may be more apt to fire shots that nonfatally injure people whom they perceive as Black because of biased assumptions of criminality that, in combination with amplified threat perception, may lead to more impulsive, emotional, longer-distance, or otherwise less-accurate shots. Racial disparities in most policing judgments and interactions are well-known.[6,28,29] Still, for incidents that may be dismissed as rare, such as shootings by police, underestimating the true scale of injury impact is a further injustice and may obstruct progress toward preventive action and reforms.

Also relatively underexamined in previous research are injuries among people who were unhoused or experiencing symptoms of behavioral health conditions. Unhoused victims comprised nearly 3% of injured people, despite representing just 0.2% of the US population.[30] Behavioral health needs were associated with 23% of injured persons; they were twice as likely to die from their injuries as other victims. These represent instances in which not only are "the marginalized . . . further criminalized" but they are also victimized by a system that is inadequately designed to meaningfully address social needs.[26(p771)]

Mechanisms for less potentially injurious triaging of social services exist. In 2022, the National Suicide Prevention Lifeline 988 was introduced, yet complementary local systems for improved access to social services without entrenched criminal legal system involvement (e.g., nonpolice mobile units) remain uncommon[31] despite strong public health alignment.[32] Public support is high for alternative approaches (e.g., diversion to mental health services, police and mental health co-responder models),[4] but cost remains a barrier to more widespread implementation.[31] Future analysis of incidents at the intersection of dispatched responses and social or behavioral health needs may inform feasibility, design, outreach, and equity-oriented impact analyses of new crisis-support systems.

## Strengths and Limitations

This study affirmed and expanded upon previous understandings of shootings by police in the United States, providing the first estimate of total injured persons nationally over multiple years. With this larger data set, previously excluded states and relatively rarer incident types could be examined. Still, some limitations exist. First, police perspectives (themselves often reconstructed "observations of observations,"[33(p146)] which may be subject to recall and social desirability bias) are known to be overrepresented in media accounts of shootings by police.[34] To diversify considered narratives, abstractors reviewed multiple sources, including bystander accounts, surveillance videos, legal documents, and articles not linked to the original GVA record. In addition, the study's inclusion period was defined to allow case details to develop and be represented. Still, some reporting bias is likely. More subjective variables, such as those involving interpretation of intent (e.g., declaring a vehicle weaponized or a service weapon nearly acquired), may be especially subject to dominant narratives and should be interpreted accordingly.

Second, the use of media sources inherently relies on assumptions of newsworthiness, adequate reporting capacity, and resulting news coverage, which may vary by time and place. Consistency with previous studies' fatal injury estimates is assuring of source validity. Still, nonfatal injuries may be less consistently or less thoroughly reported, leading to nonrandom missingness. Counts of "unspecified" or "unknown" characteristics are signals of underreporting, highlighting continued need for mandatory surveillance of all-outcome shootings by police. The relatively more developed repertoire of open-source repositories for fatalities adds to known information asymmetry. This limitation restricted our ability to precisely calculate national injury disparities. Still, our estimates of fatal and nonfatal injuries, though conservative, are substantial improvements over previous projections of total and subgroup injury burden.

Finally, we only examined injurious shootings in this study; other mechanisms of deadly force exist, and nonfatal shootings without injury were not included. Future research should analyze determinants of survival. This analysis did not account for differences in frequency of policing activities or the unequal distribution of risk in the prerequisite condition of encountering police. Disparities were interpreted on a per-capita basis, but results may not reflect individual risk for injury.

## Public Health Implications

In 2002, American criminologist James Fyfe observed, "ours is a democracy that does not tell us how often we are forcibly injured or killed by the people we pay to protect us."[35(p88)] Twenty years later, despite ongoing criticism and controversy surrounding use of deadly force by police, US accountability systems remain persistently inadequate. Nonfatal injurious shootings by police are governed by the same use-of-force policies as fatal shootings and appear similar in frequency and circumstance. However, the historical exclusion of nonfatal injuries from surveillance and research has led to underestimated injury disparities and underexamined shooting incidents, particularly at the margins of policing. Of all injurious shootings by police, incidents involving well-being checks, behavioral health concerns, suicidal crises, and unhoused persons were among the most frequently fatal. Inadequate services for people who are unhoused, insufficient supports for managing mental illness and substance use, and inequitable social and economic protections for minoritized populations are potential areas for priority response.[11,36] Evaluations of emerging public safety reforms should monitor fatal and nonfatal shootings by police to assess impact overall and among disproportionately affected groups.

Additional research is needed regarding the role of societal firearm prevalence in shootings by police, characteristics of shootings in rural and other historically underexamined regions, the role of decision-making in single- and multiple-officer responses, and frequency of non-injurious shootings. Researchers and justice advocates would also benefit from analyses of how and for whom publicly known contextual details of police shootings evolve. Finally, improved and sustained investments in reliable data and accountability systems remain essential to the prevention of firearm injuries from armed policing responses. AJPH

## ABOUT THE AUTHORS

Julie A. Ward is with the Department of Medicine, Health, and Society, the Program in Public Policy Studies, and the Center for Research on Inequality and Health at Vanderbilt University, Nashville, TN. Javier Cepeda is with the Department of Epidemiology at the Johns Hopkins Bloomberg School of Public Health, Baltimore, MD. Dylan B. Jackson is with the Department of Population, Family, and Reproductive Health at the Johns Hopkins Bloomberg School of Public Health and the Johns Hopkins Center for Gun Violence Solutions. Odis Johnson Jr is with the Department of Health Policy and Management at the Johns Hopkins Bloomberg School of Public Health, the Johns Hopkins School of Education, and the Johns Hopkins Center for Gun Violence Solutions. Daniel W. Webster and Cassandra K. Crifasi are with the Department of Health Policy and Management at the Johns Hopkins Bloomberg School of Public Health and the Johns Hopkins Center for Gun Violence Solutions.

## CORRESPONDENCE

Correspondence should be sent to Julie A. Ward, PMB 351665, 2301 Vanderbilt Place, Nashville, TN 37235 (e-mail: julie.ward@vanderbilt.edu). Reprints can be ordered at https://ajph.org by clicking the "Reprints" link.

## PUBLICATION INFORMATION

Full Citation: Ward JA, Cepeda J, Jackson DB, Johnson Jr O, Webster DW, Crifasi CK. National burden of injury and deaths from shootings by police in the United States, 2015–2020. *Am J Public Health*. 2024;114(4):387–397.

Acceptance Date: December 8, 2023.

DOI: https://doi.org/10.2105/AJPH.2023.307560

ORCID iD:

Julie A. Ward https://orcid.org/0000-0002-1604-349X

## CONTRIBUTORS

J. A. Ward conceptualized the work, contributed formal analysis, and led the writing of the original draft and revisions. C. K. Crifasi and D. W. Webster provided supervision and secured funding. All authors contributed critical draft revisions, approved the final article as submitted, and agree to be accountable for all aspects of the work.

## ACKNOWLEDGMENTS

Funding to support initial data collection and analysis was provided by New Venture Fund and Joyce Foundation. Additional funding was provided by the Robert Wood Johnson Foundation. J. A. Ward acknowledges support from the National Institute of Child Health and Human Development (T32-HD 094687). J. Cepeda acknowledges support from the National Institute on Drug Abuse (K01DA054521).

This project benefited from the commitment and persistence of a team of data abstractors that included Vaishu Bandaru, Ethan Bartlett, Makenzie Bozer, Annie Brown, Kat Catamura, Brooke Dal Santo, Brandon Hardy, Taylor Johnson, Hami Kang, Nick Meyerson, Isabella Parea, Delilah Ponce, Martina Racioppi, and Alissa Zhu. We thank them for their efforts.

**Note.** Funders had no role in the study design, statistical analyses, interpretation of data or drafting of this article.

## CONFLICTS OF INTEREST

The authors declare no actual or potential conflicts of interest.

## HUMAN PARTICIPANT PROTECTION

This study was reviewed and approved by the Johns Hopkins Bloomberg School of Public Health institutional review board.

## REFERENCES

1. The Johns Hopkins Center for Gun Violence Solutions. A year in review: 2020 gun deaths in the U.S. 2022:40. Available at: https://publichealth.jhu.edu/sites/default/files/2022-05/2020-gun-deaths-in-the-us-4-28-2022-b.pdf. Accessed November 24, 2022.
2. Patel J, Leach-Kemon K, Curry G, Naghavi M, Sridhar D. Firearm injury: a preventable public health issue. *Lancet Public Health*. 2022;7(11):e976–e982. https://doi.org/10.1016/S2468-2667(22)00233-X
3. Pew Research Center. Majority of public favors giving civilians the power to sue police officers for misconduct. Pew Research Center. July 9, 2020. Available at: https://www.pewresearch.org/politics/2020/07/09/majority-of-public-favors-giving-civilians-the-power-to-sue-police-officers-for-misconduct. Accessed September 22, 2021.
4. Ward JA, McGinty EE, Hudson T, et al. Reimagining public safety: public opinion on police reform and gun violence prevention by race and gun ownership in the United States. *Prev Med*. 2022;165(pt A):107180. https://doi.org/10.1016/j.ypmed.2022.107180
5. American Public Health Association. Addressing law enforcement violence as a public health issue. 2018. Available at: https://www.apha.org/policies-and-advocacy/public-health-policy-statements/policy-database/2019/01/29/law-enforcement-violence. Accessed June 7, 2023.
6. GBD 2019 Police Violence US Subnational Collaborators. Fatal police violence by race and state in the USA, 1980–2019: a network meta-regression. *Lancet*. 2021;398(10307):1239–1255. https://doi.org/10.1016/S0140-6736(21)01609-3
7. Conner A, Azrael D, Lyons VH, Barber C, Miller M. Validating the National Violent Death Reporting System as a source of data on fatal shootings of civilians by law enforcement officers. *Am J Public Health*. 2019;109(4):578–584. https://doi.org/10.2105/AJPH.2018.304904
8. Feldman JM, Gruskin S, Coull BA, Krieger N. Quantifying underreporting of law-enforcement-related deaths in United States vital statistics and news-media-based data sources: a capture–recapture analysis [erratum in *PLoS Med*. 2017;14(10):e1002449]. *PLoS Med*. 2017;14(10):e1002399. https://doi.org/10.1371/journal.pmed.1002399
9. US Government Accountability Office. Law enforcement: DOJ can improve publication of use of force data and oversight of excessive force allegations. 2021. Available at: https://www.gao.gov/products/gao-22-104456. Accessed November 26, 2022.
10. Nix J, Shjarback JA. Factors associated with police shooting mortality: a focus on race and a plea for more comprehensive data. *PLoS One*. 2021;16(11):e0259024. https://doi.org/10.1371/journal.pone.0259024
11. Zimring FE. *When Police Kill*. Cambridge, MA: Harvard University Press; 2017. https://doi.org/10.4159/9780674978058
12. Comer BP, Ingram JR. Comparing fatal encounters, mapping police violence, and *Washington Post* fatal police shooting data from 2015–2019: a research note. *Crim Justice Rev*. 2023;48(2):249–261. https://doi.org/10.1177/07340168211071014
13. Edwards F, Esposito MH, Lee H. Risk of police-involved death by race/ethnicity and place, United States, 2012–2018. *Am J Public Health*. 2018;108(9):1241–1248. https://doi.org/10.2105/AJPH.2018.304559
14. Bui AL, Coates MM, Matthay EC. Years of life lost due to encounters with law enforcement in the USA, 2015–2016. *J Epidemiol Community Health*. 2018;72(8):715–718. https://doi.org/10.1136/jech-2017-210059
15. Thomas MD, Jewell NP, Allen AM. Black and unarmed: statistical interaction between age, perceived mental illness, and geographic region among males fatally shot by police using case-only design. *Ann Epidemiol*. 2021;53:42–49.e3. https://doi.org/10.1016/j.annepidem.2020.08.014
16. Hemenway D, Azrael D, Conner A, Miller M. Variation in rates of fatal police shootings across US states: the role of firearm availability. *J Urban Health*. 2019;96(1):63–73. https://doi.org/10.1007/s11524-018-0313-z
17. Zare H, Meyerson NS, Delgado P, et al. How place and race drive the numbers of fatal police shootings in the US: 2015–2020. *Prev Med*. 2022;161:107132. https://doi.org/10.1016/j.ypmed.2022.107132
18. Nix J, Campbell BA, Byers EH, Alpert GP. A bird's eye view of civilians killed by police in 2015: further evidence of implicit bias. *Criminol Public Policy*. 2017;16(1):309–340. https://doi.org/10.1111/1745-9133.12269
19. Hanink PA, Renner M, Bates CJ. Lethality of police shootings and proximity to trauma centers.

*Homicide Stud*. 2022;27(1):120–141. https://doi.org/10.1177/10887679221116546

20. Hou Y. *Fatal and Non-Fatal Police Shootings in the United States, 2015: An Examination of Open-Source Data*. PhD dissertation. City University of New York. 2022. Available at: https://academicworks.cuny.edu/gc_etds/4682. Accessed September 1, 2022.
21. Gun Violence Archive. General methodology. Available at: https://www.gunviolencearchive.org/methodology. Accessed October 4, 2021.
22. White K, Lawrence JA, Tchangalova N, Huang SJ, Cummings JL. Socially-assigned race and health: a scoping review with global implications for population health equity. *Int J Equity Health*. 2020;19(1):25. https://doi.org/10.1186/s12939-020-1137-5
23. Sierra-Arévalo M. American policing and the danger imperative. *Law Soc Rev*. 2021;55(1):70–103. https://doi.org/10.1111/lasr.12526
24. Blair JM, Fowler KA, Betz CJ, Baumgardner JL. Occupational homicides of law enforcement officers, 2003–2013: data from the National Violent Death Reporting System. *Am J Prev Med*. 2016;51(5, suppl 3):S188–S196. https://doi.org/10.1016/j.amepre.2016.08.019
25. Gillooly JW. "Lights and sirens": variation in 911 call-taker risk appraisal and its effects on police officer perceptions at the scene. *J Policy Anal Manage*. 2021;41(3):762–786. https://doi.org/10.1002/pam.22369
26. Herring C. Complaint-oriented policing: regulating homelessness in public space. *Am Sociol Rev*. 2019;84(5):769–800. https://doi.org/10.1177/0003122419872671
27. Centers for Disease Control and Prevention, National Center for Health Statistics. National Vital Statistics System, Mortality 1999–2020 on CDC WONDER Online Database, released in 2021. Multiple Cause of Death Files, 1999–2020, as compiled from data provided by the 57 vital statistics jurisdictions through the Vital Statistics Cooperative Program. November 20, 2022. Available at: https://wonder.cdc.gov/ucd-icd10.html. Accessed November 26, 2022.
28. Epp CR, Maynard-Moody S, Haider-Markel D. Beyond profiling: the institutional sources of racial disparities in policing. *Public Adm Rev*. 2017;77(2):168–178. https://doi.org/10.1111/puar.12702
29. Thompson HA. The racial history of criminal justice in America. *Du Bois Rev*. 2019;16(1):221–241. https://doi.org/10.1017/S1742058X19000183
30. Henry M, de Sousa T, Roddey C, Gayen S, Bednar TJ. Abt Associates. *The 2020 Annual Homeless Assessment Report (AHAR) to Congress*. The US Department of Housing and Urban Development, Office of Community Planning and Development; 2021:102. Available at: https://www.huduser.gov/portal/sites/default/files/pdf/2020-ahar-part-1.pdf. Accessed September 7, 2022.
31. Fix RL, Bandara S, Fallin MD, Barry CL. Creating comprehensive crisis response systems: an opportunity to build on the promise of 988. *Community Ment Health J*. 2022;59(2):205–208. https://doi.org/10.1007/s10597-022-01017-6
32. Spolum MM, Lopez WD, Watkins DC, Fleming PJ. Police violence: reducing the harms of policing through public health–informed alternative response programs. *Am J Public Health*. 2023;113(suppl 1):S37–S42. https://doi.org/10.2105/AJPH.2022.307107
33. Van Maanen J. Beyond account: the personal impact of police shootings. *Ann Am Acad Pol Soc Sci*. 1980;452:145–156.
34. Walker D. "There's a camera everywhere": how citizen journalists, cellphones, and technology shape coverage of police shootings. *Journalism Pract*. 2021;16(10):2022–2039. https://doi.org/10.1080/17512786.2021.1884990
35. Fyfe JJ. Too many missing cases: holes in our knowledge about police use of force. *Justice Res Policy*. 2002;4(1-2):87–102. https://doi.org/10.3818/JRP.4.1.2002.87
36. Kaiser Permanente. *Kaiser Permanente Research: Social Needs in America*. 2019:1–7. Available at: https://about.kaiserpermanente.org/content/dam/internet/kp/comms/import/uploads/2019/06/KP-Social-Needs-Survey-Key-Findings.pdf. Accessed September 7, 2022.

# Contribution of Cold Versus Climate Change to Mortality in London, UK, 1976–2019

*Shakoor Hajat, PhD, MSc, David Gampe, PhD, MSc, and Giorgos Petrou, PhD, MRes*

**Objectives.** To quantify past reductions in cold-related mortality attributable to anthropogenic climate change.

**Methods.** We performed a daily time-series regression analysis employing distributed lag nonlinear models of 1 203 981 deaths in Greater London, United Kingdom, in winter months (November–March) during 1976 to 2019. We made attribution assessment by comparing differential cold-related mortality impacts associated with observed temperatures to those using counterfactual temperatures representing no climate change.

**Results.** Over the past decade, the average number of cold days (below 8 °C) per year was 120 in the observed series and 158 in the counterfactual series. Since 1976, we estimate 447 (95% confidence interval = 330, 559) annual cold-related all-cause deaths have been avoided because of milder temperatures associated with climate change. Annually, 241 cardiovascular and 73 respiratory disease deaths have been avoided.

**Conclusions.** Anthropogenic climate change made some contribution to reducing previous cold-related deaths in London; however, cold remains an important public health risk factor.

**Public Health Implications.** Better adaptation to both heat and cold should be promoted in public health measures to protect against climate change. In England, this has been addressed by the development of a new year-round Adverse Weather and Health Plan. (*Am J Public Health*. 2024;114(4): 398–402. https://doi.org/10.2105/AJPH.2023.307552)

AJPH April 2024, Vol. 114, No. 4

Although deaths associated with low ambient temperatures reduced over much of the past century, continued reductions in cold-related vulnerability have generally not been observed in more recent years, meaning that wintertime weather remains an important public health concern for the United Kingdom and elsewhere.[1] As well as improvements in housing, health care and nutrition, historical reductions in cold-related mortality were also likely because of milder winters caused by climate change; however, to our knowledge, this has never been quantified. The fraction of heat-related deaths attributable to climate change has recently been estimated by comparing differential impacts associated with observed temperatures to those using counterfactual temperatures modeled in the absence of anthropogenic climate change.[2] These attribution studies provide the basis for better climate change risk management[3]; however, a similar approach can also be applied to attribute reductions in cold-related deaths to past climate change. Such information can also inform the likelihood of future reductions in cold deaths under climate change scenarios, over which there remains much uncertainty and debate.[4]

The United Kingdom experiences greater cold-related health impacts compared with many of its colder European neighbors, partly from poor insulation of its housing stock,[5] and London is more vulnerable than other UK regions despite milder temperatures.[6] We analyzed extended time-series mortality data sets in relation to observed and counterfactual climate data to quantify past reductions in cold-related deaths in London attributable to anthropogenic climate change.

## METHODS

We obtained daily counts of all-cause, cardiovascular, and respiratory disease deaths in London between 1976 and 2019 from the Office for National Statistics. To characterize exposures, we considered 2 daily mean temperature series. First, we extracted reference data of average temperature from the W5E5 data set representing a bias-corrected reanalysis data set that can be considered quasi-observational for temperature (containing observed trends in global temperatures).[7] Second, we applied a counterfactual version of this data set estimated through the ATTRICI (ATTRIbuting Climate Impacts) approach.[8] This data set approximates a temperature series preserving interannual variability of the quasi-observations but removing long-term global warming trends using a quantile mapping approach, thus representing a non–climate change scenario. Both data sets are available from the Inter-Sectoral Impact Model Intercomparison Project (https://www.isimip.org) on a 0.5° grid. We conducted additional bias correction by using deviations from the observed W5E5 temperature in the quasi-preindustrial period (1901–1920) as reference through quantile mapping to remove local biases remaining in the statistically derived counterfactual data set. (Codes used to bias-correct the counterfactual temperature series are available from the authors upon request.)

We used quasi-Poisson time-series regression to assess short-term associations between daily mean temperature and mortality, adjusting for trend and within-season variability using natural cubic spline (ncs) functions with 4 degrees of freedom (df) per season. We used indicator terms to model day-of-week variations. We then employed distributed lag nonlinear models to flexibly model nonlinear and delayed effects of temperature using cross-basis functions.[9] The model is summarized here:

$$\text{Log}[E(Y_i)] = \alpha + \beta_1 T_{i,j} + \beta_2 \text{ncs}(\text{time}_i, \text{df} = 4/\text{season}) + \beta_3(\text{dow}_i) \quad (1)$$

where $E[Y_i]$ is expected mortality on day $i$; $T_{i,j}$ is the cross-basis matrix of temperature and lag $j$ up to 21 days, using *ncs* functions for both domains with 5df and 4df, respectively; *ncs* = ncs functions of time; and *dow* = day-of-week indicator. We conducted analysis using the observed temperature series, and we then also applied the estimated exposure–response function from this model to the counterfactual temperature series representing no climate change. We then estimated the relative risk (RR) of cold-related death at selected temperatures compared with the minimum mortality temperature (MMT). The MMT is defined as the temperature value at which risk of death is lowest and is determined using statistical model fit (Akaike information criterion [AIC]). We used the most recent decade of data (2010–2019) to derive the risk function because cold risk was relatively stable during this period, thus enabling a direct comparison of differential impacts between the observed and counterfactual temperature series without other secular changes. We derived the percentage of cold-attributable deaths below the MMT by using (RR-1)/RR. Cold effects were restricted to months November through March when evidence for a causal association with mortality is strongest.[10] We conducted analyses with Stata version 17 (StataCorp LP, College Station, TX) and R version 4.3.1 (R Foundation for Statistical Computing, Vienna, Austria).

## RESULTS

Figure 1a shows the annual number of cold days (below 8 °C) in the observed and counterfactual temperature series during the study period. Unsurprisingly, the observed series is associated with milder winters compared with the counterfactual, although a slight reduction in cold days is also evident in the counterfactual series, potentially attributable to the urban heat-island. The negative trend in cold days was statistically significant in the observed series (Mann–Kendall test; $P < .05$) but not in the counterfactual. During 2010 to 2019, the average number of cold days per year was 120 in the observed series and 158 in the counterfactual.

There were 1 203 981 deaths in London during winter months (November–March). Figure A (available as a supplement to the online version of this article at https://ajph.org) shows the seasonally adjusted temperature–mortality relationship in winter during 2010 to 2019. The MMT was estimated at 8 °C, and there was a 27.9% (95% CI = 18.8, 37.7) increased risk of death at −1 °C (approximately the 1st percentile) compared with the MMT. From this model, we estimated the total number of cold-attributable deaths each winter associated with both observed and counterfactual series (Figure 1b). Cold-related deaths have reduced over time, reflecting improved adaptation to wintertime climate, but there was wide year-to-year fluctuation and some degree of

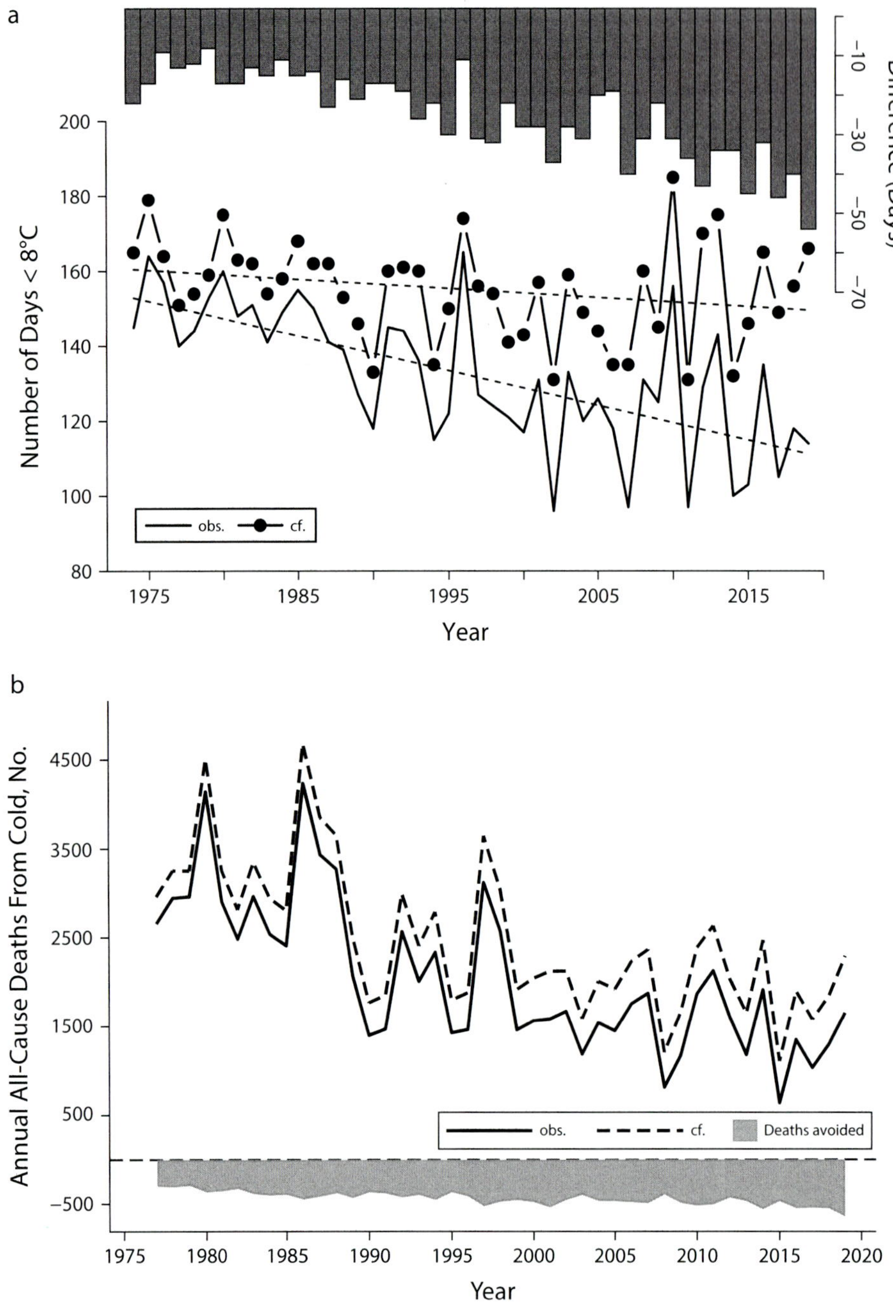


**FIGURE 1— Annual (a) Average Wintertime Temperature and (b) Cold-Related Deaths Associated With the Observed (obs.) and Counterfactual (cf.) Temperature Series: Greater London, UK, November–March 1976–2019**

leveling-off in recent years. Differences in mortality between the 2 temperature series have also widened over time, with the average annual number of cold deaths avoided in the counterfactual series being 447 (95% CI = 330, 559). The annual number of deaths avoided from cardiovascular and respiratory diseases was 241 (95% CI = 190, 289) and 73 (95% CI = 52, 107), respectively.

## DISCUSSION

The damaging effects of anthropogenic climate change on public health are unquestionable, and studies have demonstrated substantial numbers of heat-related deaths already attributable to such changes.[2] Although health impact assessments have previously reported reductions in future cold-related mortality under climate change scenarios,[11] to our knowledge, this is the first study to quantify historic reductions in cold-related mortality attributable to the degree of anthropogenic climate change that has already occurred.

In the most recent winter in our data set (winter 2018–2019), we estimate 639 fewer cold-related deaths in London associated with counterfactual temperature, amounting to 70.1 wintertime deaths per million people in the population avoided because of climate change. Any continuing gains are, however, likely to be impacted by current trends in other determinants of wintertime health (e.g., the current volatility in global fuel prices). Better housing and other adaptation strategies will almost certainly remain more important in counteracting the negative health impacts of these. For example, Taylor et al. estimated that 168 to 174 annual cold-related deaths per million population in London could be avoided by the 2050s based on current rates of retrofit home energy efficiency measures, and 261 to 269 deaths per million under more ambitious retrofit rates.[12] Improved home energy efficiency also offers other health benefits, including reducing dampness and mold that contribute to asthma, as well decreasing residential space heating demands to help reach Net Zero targets.[13]

## Limitations

Some study limitations are acknowledged. Our assessment only considered 1 pathway by which milder winters affect public health; there are also negative impacts such as enhanced wintertime transmission of zoonotic pathogens.[14] The degree of seasonal control in our statistical models was decided a priori rather than based on AIC; however, model fit was good, and results were robust to greater dfs in ncs and alternative model specifications. Comparison of the observed series with the statistically constructed counterfactual one allows attribution of differential health impacts to climate change in general, but does not provide direct attribution to increased anthropogenic greenhouse gas emissions or changes in aerosol concentrations. Furthermore, the relatively coarse resolution of data, the extraction procedure, and bias-correction of the counterfactual series impose additional sources of uncertainty in the temperature data not characterized in this assessment. Nevertheless, our findings are likely robust to such data considerations.

## Public Health Implications

Although climate change has played a role in reducing wintertime deaths in London, its contribution has been modest, and cold remains an important public health risk factor in the United Kingdom. Better adaptation to both heat and cold should be prioritized in public health plans to protect against climate change. In England, this has been addressed by the development of a new year-round Adverse Weather and Health Plan by the UK Health Security Agency.[15] Wherever cold remains an important determinant of ill health, better longer-term strategies are needed to protect public health and improve resilience to future wintertime weather. AJPH


### ABOUT THE AUTHORS

Shakoor Hajat is with the London School of Hygiene and Tropical Medicine, London, UK. David Gampe is with the Department of Geography, Ludwig-Maximilians-Universität, Munich, Germany. Giorgos Petrou is with the Institute for Environmental Design and Engineering, University College London, London, UK.

### CORRESPONDENCE

Correspondence should be sent to Professor Shakoor Hajat, Centre on Climate Change and Planetary Health and Department of Public Health, Environments and Society, 15-17 Tavistock Place, London WC1H 9SH, UK (e-mail: shakoor.hajat@lshtm.ac.uk). Reprints can be ordered at https://ajph.org by clicking the "Reprints" link.



### PUBLICATION INFORMATION

Full Citation: Hajat S, Gampe D, Petrou G. Contribution of cold versus climate change to mortality in London, UK, 1976–2019. *Am J Public Health*. 2024;114(4):398–402.

Acceptance Date: November 24, 2023.

DOI: https://doi.org/10.2105/AJPH.2023.307552


### CONTRIBUTORS

S. Hajat contributed to conceptualization, study design, analysis, and article writing. D. Gampe contributed to conceptualization, data processing, data visualization, and article revision. G. Petrou contributed to article revision.


### ACKNOWLEDGMENTS

This study was funded by the National Institute for Health and Care Research (NIHR) Health Protection Research Unit in Environmental Change and Health (NIHR200909), a partnership of the London School of Hygiene and Tropical Medicine, the UK Health Security Agency, University College London, and the Met Office.

**Note.** The views expressed are those of the authors and not necessarily those of the NIHR, UK Health Security Agency, or the Department of Health and Social Care.


### CONFLICTS OF INTEREST

The authors have no conflicts of interest.

### HUMAN PARTICIPANT PROTECTION

This study did not involve human participants.

### REFERENCES


1. Arbuthnott K, Hajat S, Heaviside C, Vardoulakis S. Changes in population susceptibility to heat and cold over time: assessing adaptation to climate change. *Environ Health*. 2016;15(suppl 1):33. https://doi.org/10.1186/s12940-016-0102-7
2. Vicedo-Cabrera AM, Scovronick N, Sera F, et al. The burden of heat-related mortality attributable to recent human-induced climate change. *Nat Clim Chang*. 2021;11(6):492–500. https://doi.org/10.1038/s41558-021-01058-x
3. Ebi KL, Ogden NH, Semenza JC, Woodward A. Detecting and attributing health burdens to climate change. *Environ Health Perspect*. 2017;125(8):085004. https://doi.org/10.1289/EHP1509
4. Kinney PL, Schwartz J, Pascal M, et al. Winter season mortality: will climate warming bring benefits? *Environ Res Lett*. 2015;10(6):064016. https://doi.org/10.1088/1748-9326/10/6/064016
5. Association for the Conservation of Energy. The cold man of Europe. 2015. Available at:

https://www.nea.org.uk/wp-content/uploads/2020/11/ACE-and-EBR-briefing-2015-10-Cold-man-of-Europe-update.pdf. Accessed June 26, 2023.

6. Hajat S, Chalabi Z, Wilkinson P, Erens B, Jones L, Mays N. Public health vulnerability to wintertime weather: time-series regression and episode analyses of national mortality and morbidity databases to inform the Cold Weather Plan for England. *Public Health*. 2016;137:26–34. https://doi.org/10.1016/j.puhe.2015.12.015
7. Lange S, Menz C, Gleixner S, et al. WFDE5 over land merged with ERA5 over the ocean (W5E5 v2.0). Potsdam, Germany: ISIMIP Repository; 2021
8. Mengel M, Treu S, Lange S, Frieler K. ATTRICI v1.1—counterfactual climate for impact attribution. *Geosci Model Dev*. 2021;14(8):5269–5284. https://doi.org/10.5194/gmd-14-5269-2021
9. Armstrong B. Models for the relationship between ambient temperature and daily mortality. *Epidemiology*. 2006;17(6):624–631. https://doi.org/10.1097/01.ede.0000239732.50999.8f
10. Arbuthnott K, Hajat S, Heaviside C, Vardoulakis S. What is cold-related mortality? A multi-disciplinary perspective to inform climate change impact assessments. *Environ Int*. 2018;121(pt 1):119–129. https://doi.org/10.1016/j.envint.2018.08.053
11. Martínez-Solanas È, Quijal-Zamorano M, Achebak H, et al. Projections of temperature-attributable mortality in Europe: a time series analysis of 147 contiguous regions in 16 countries. *Lancet Planet Health*. 2021;5(7):e446–e454. https://doi.org/10.1016/S2542-5196(21)00150-9
12. Taylor J, Symonds P, Heaviside C, Chalabi Z, Davies M, Wilkinson P. Projecting the impacts of housing on temperature-related mortality in London during typical future years. *Energy Build*. 2021;249. https://doi.org/10.1016/j.enbuild.2021.111233
13. UK Department of State for Business, Energy and Industrial Strategy. Heat and Buildings Strategy. 2021. Available at: https://www.gov.uk/government/publications/heat-and-buildings-strategy/heat-and-building-strategy-accessible-webpage. Accessed June 26, 2023.
14. Sipari S, Khalil H, Magnusson M, Evander M, Hörnfeldt B, Ecke F. Climate change accelerates winter transmission of a zoonotic pathogen. *Ambio*. 2022;51(3):508–517. https://doi.org/10.1007/s13280-021-01594-y
15. UK Health Security Agency. Adverse Weather and Health Plan. Protecting health from weather related harm, 2023 to 2024. Available at: https://assets.publishing.service.gov.uk/government/uploads/system/uploads/attachment_data/file/1171545/Adverse-weather-health-plan-2023.pdf. Accessed September 8, 2023.

# Comparing Self-Reported and Aggregated Racial Classification for American Indian/Alaska Native Youths in YRBSS: 2021

*Ashton Gatewood, MPH, Amy D. Hendrix-Dicken, MA, and Micah Hartwell, PhD*

**Objectives.** To identify how race and ethnicity were reclassified with survey variables for children self-reporting as American Indian/Alaska Native (AI/AN) using the 2021 Youth Risk Behavior Surveillance System (YRBSS).

**Methods.** We conducted a cross-sectional analysis of the US Centers for Disease Control and Prevention's 2021 YRBSS. YRBSS collects behaviors and demographics of students in grades 9 through 12, including race and ethnicity via self-report, and then reclassifies data into a "raceeth" variable. To examine the classification of AI/AN in YRBSS, we compared AI/AN composition between self-report and raceeth variables.

**Results.** A total of 816 adolescents self-reported as AI/AN alone (145; 17.70%), AI/AN alone with Hispanic/Latino background (246; 30.15%), or AI/AN in combination with 1 or more race (425; 52.08%). Of those, only 145 were classified as being AI/AN in the calculated raceeth variable. With YRBSS survey weighting, the percentage of AI/AN in the raceeth variable was 13.4%.

**Conclusions.** Misclassification, noncollection, or the use of categories such as "other" and "multirace" without allowing disaggregation can misrepresent disease burden, morbidity, and mortality. Consequently, it is critical to disaggregate data to adequately capture race/ethnicity in self-report surveys and data sources. (*Am J Public Health*. 2024;114(4):403–406. https://doi.org/10.2105/AJPH.2023.307561)

AJPH April 2024, Vol. 114, No. 4

Health disparities in the American Indian and Alaska Native (AI/AN) population include lower life expectancy, greater poverty rates, and increased incidence of chronic disease morbidity and mortality as well as diseases of despair, such as suicide-, drug-, and alcohol-related deaths.[1,2] Although members of federally recognized tribes have legal rights to health care to address these inequities, sociopolitical barriers such as blood quantum and tribal enrollment requirements limit access.[2] Furthermore, surveillance systems often result in underreporting of morbidity and mortality, particularly among AI/AN minors.[1,2]

Discrepancies in racial aggregation and reporting are data quality issues that can affect access to critical resources, such as federally funded programs, housing, employment, and health care,[1–3] for more than 8.7 million AI/AN individuals in the United States. Federally funded research built on the biomedical–epidemiologic model requires researchers to use evidence-based assessments of population health status.[2] Yet, inaccuracies or omission of AI/AN data collection and reporting in research, also known as "data genocide," are linked to historical systemic racism and colonization of data methods.[1,2] Given the necessity of reporting accuracy for services and research, our objective was to identify how race and ethnicity were reclassified with survey variables for adolescents self-reporting AI/AN using the

2021 Youth Risk Behavior Surveillance System (YRBSS).

## METHODS

We performed a cross-sectional analysis of the 2021 YRBSS, a biannual survey conducted by the US Centers for Disease Control and Prevention (CDC).[4] A total of 45 states participated in YRBSS 2021 in addition to several US territories and freely associated states.[5] YRBSS collects data regarding health, behaviors, and demographics of students in grades 9 through 12, including race and ethnicity, via self-report.

The survey allowed adolescents to self-report all applicable races. YRBSS reclassifies the adolescents' race and ethnicity into a new variable ("raceeth"), which places individuals in singular race categories when only 1 race is selected, a multiple races category if more than 1 is selected, or the Hispanic grouping regardless of race selection if the response was yes to the prompt, "Are you Hispanic/Latino?" Thus, we included all respondents in the YRBSS data and extracted data from the self-reported race variable, the raceeth variable, and the Hispanic/Latino ethnicity prompt. Our analysis also included those with missing data or reported as "unknown."

To examine the classification of AI/AN in YRBSS, we compared the self-reported variable with the raceeth variable. We calculated and compared the number of adolescents who were categorized as AI/AN in the raceeth variable with their actual self-reported race categories among individuals reporting as AI/AN alone or in combination with racial categories or Hispanic/Latino ethnicity. We first used the unweighted data and then applied the survey design and weighting that YRBSS provided.

## RESULTS

In YRBSS, 816 (4.7%) of 17 232 participants self-reported as AI/AN solely, in conjunction with another race, or in conjunction with Hispanic/Latino ethnicity (Table 1). Among these 816 participants, only 145 adolescents were classified as AI/AN (17.7%), that is, those who reported as AI/AN alone, with no Hispanic/Latino background (the number present in the raceeth variable), which reduces the representation of AI/AN to 0.8% in the YRBSS data overall. Participants self-reporting as AI/AN alone but with Hispanic/Latino ethnicity accounted for 246 of the 816 (30.2%). The remaining participants self-reported AI/AN in combination with 1 or more other races or unknown or missing ethnicity (425; 52.1%). When we applied the survey design and sampling weights from YRBSS, rates of self-report of AI/AN alone or in combination were slightly higher, at 4.9% in the overall data set; however, the AI/AN representation in the raceeth was slightly lower, at 0.7%. Table 1 provides the breakdown of AI/AN race/ethnicity combinations using both unweighted data and when we included the survey design and sampling weights.

## DISCUSSION

Only 17.7% of individuals who self-reported as AI/AN were classified as such in the calculated raceeth variable in YRBSS—limiting the overall representation of AI/AN in YRBSS to approximately 0.8%. The only individuals reported as AI/AN in the computed raceeth variable were those who self-reported as AI/AN only without Hispanic/Latino ethnicity. These findings are consistent with previous work related to the misclassification of AI/AN individuals.[6] Given this methodological approach leading to misclassification, it is likely that other groups are also being classified as multiracial, thus diminishing various facets of identity. Misclassification, noncollection, or the use of categories such as other or multiracial without allowing disaggregation can misrepresent disease burden, morbidity, and mortality.[7]

We applaud YRBSS for providing the self-reported race variable, given its utility beyond the computed raceeth variable; recommend that other national data sets include self-reported race variables; and urge researchers to consider using the self-report variable when assessing ethnoracial disparities when possible. Even categorical self-reporting is not without limitations, which include the lack of standardized definitions, shifts in self-identification throughout the lifespan, and perceived risks or benefits of alignment with certain racial/ethnic groups.

This type of misclassification and lack of data transparency affects policies, programs, and resource allocation, which may ultimately exacerbate health disparities.[1,7] Furthermore, the AI/AN group is the most likely to identify as 2 or more races, which can result in aggregation into multiracial or other categories,[8] likely masking within-group differences and disparities.

### Limitations

Limitations of this study include that YRBSS collects data only from adolescents who attend public or private school, and not all states participate equally in YRBSS.[9] Additionally, the Cherokee Nation and Winnebago Tribe of Nebraska were the only sovereign nations the CDC listed as participating in the high school version of YRBSS in

## TABLE 1— Racial Reporting Among Individuals Reporting as American Indian/Alaska Native (AI/AN) in the 2021 Youth Risk Behavior Surveillance System (YRBSS): United States

| Race Grouping | Unweighted No. (%) | | | | Weighted[a] No. (%) | | | |
|---|---|---|---|---|---|---|---|---|
| | Hispanic/ Latino | Non-Hispanic/ Latino | Unsure and Missing | Total | Hispanic/ Latino | Non-Hispanic/ Latino | Unsure and Missing | Total |
| "raceeth" variable from YRBSS[b] | | | | | | | | |
| AI/AN only | 0 (0) | 145 (100)[c] | 0 (0) | 145 (100) | 0 (0) | 114 (100)[c] | 0 (0) | 114 (100)[c] |
| Self-reported race from YRBSS | | | | | | | | |
| AI/AN only | 246 (30.2) | 145 (17.8)[c] | 12 (1.5) | 403 (49.4) | 317 (37.2) | 114 (13.4) | 15 (1.8) | 447 (52.5) |
| AI/AN, White | 40 (4.9) | 178 (21.8) | 0 (0) | 218 (26.7) | 42 (5) | 143 (16.8) | 0 (0) | 185 (21.8) |
| AI/AN, NH/PI | 4 (0.5) | 0 (0) | 0 (0) | 4 (0.5) | 3 (0.3) | 0 (0) | 0 (0) | 3 (0.3) |
| AI/AN, NH/PI, White | 4 (0.5) | 2 (0.3) | 0 (0) | 6 (0.7) | 9 (1.1) | 0 (0) | 0 (0) | 10 (1.1) |
| AI/AN, Black/African American | 22 (2.7) | 64 (7.8) | 2 (0.3) | 88 (10.8) | 28 (3.3) | 69 (8.1) | 0 (0) | 98 (11.5) |
| AI/AN, Black/African American, White | 5 (0.6) | 32 (3.9) | 0 (0) | 37 (4.5) | 4 (0.4) | 29 (3.4) | 0 (0) | 33 (3.9) |
| AI/AN, Black/African American, NH/PI | 1 (0.1) | 1 (0.1) | 0 (0) | 2 (0.3) | 1 (0.1) | 1 (0.1) | 0 (0) | 2 (0.2) |
| AI/AN, Black/African American, NH/PI, White | 1 (0.1) | 1 (0.1) | 0 (0) | 2 (0.3) | 4 (0.5) | 1 (0.1) | 0 (0) | 5 (0.6) |
| AI/AN, Asian | 6 (0.7) | 4 (0.5) | 0 (0) | 10 (1.2) | 16 (1.8) | 6 (0.8) | 0 (0) | 22 (2.6) |
| AI/AN, Asian, White | 0 (0) | 9 (1.1) | 0 (0) | 9 (1.1) | 0 (0) | 10 (1.2) | 0 (0) | 10 (1.2) |
| AI/AN, Asian, NH/PI | 1 (0.1) | 2 (0.3) | 0 (0) | 3 (0.4) | 0 (0) | 1 (0.2) | 0 (0) | 2 (0.2) |
| AI/AN, Asian, NH/PI, White | 1 (0.1) | 2 (0.3) | 0 (0) | 3 (0.4) | 1 (0.1) | 1 (0.1) | 0 (0) | 2 (0.2) |
| AI/AN, Asian, Black/African American | 2 (0.3) | 1 (0.1) | 0 (0) | 3 (0.4) | 2 (0.2) | 2 (0.3) | 0 (0) | 4 (0.5) |
| AI/AN, Asian, Black/African American, White | 1 (0.1) | 2 (0.3) | 2 (0.3) | 5 (0.6) | 2 (0.2) | 1 (0.1) | 2 (0.2) | 5 (0.6) |
| AI/AN, Asian, Black/African American, NH/PI | 1 (0.1) | 0 (0) | 0 (0) | 1 (0.1) | 2 (0.2) | 0 (0) | 0 (0) | 2 (0.2) |
| AI/AN, Asian, Black/African American, NH/PI, White | 10 (1.2) | 10 (1.2) | 1 (0.1) | 21 (2.6) | 6 (0.7) | 15 (1.8) | 1 (0.1) | 22 (2.6) |
| All race combinations, including other races, not listed | 0 (0) | 1 (0.1) | 0 (0) | 1 (0.1) | 0 (0) | 0 (0) | 0 (0) | 0 (0) |
| Total | 345 (42.3) | 454 (55.6) | 17 (2.1) | 816 (100) | 436 (51.3) | 396 (46.6) | 18 (2.1) | 851 (100) |

*Note.* NH/PI = Native Hawaiian/Pacific Islander. The sample size for the 2021 YRBSS was n = 17 232, from which the computed raceeth variable showed that 0.84% (unweighted sample size: n = 145) of participants were AI/AN, which decreased to 0.66% when YRBSS sampling weights were applied. By self-report, 816 participants identified as AI/AN alone or in combination with other ethnoracial groups, representing 4.73% of the sample and 4.94% (n = 851) when sampling weights were applied.

[a]The Centers for Disease Control and Prevention weights the responses to account for nonresponse at the school and student levels by student demographics. Consequently, the weighted columns are considered representative of the population from which the sample was drawn.

[b]YRBSS reclassifies the adolescents' race and ethnicity into a new variable "raceeth," which places individuals in singular race categories when only 1 race is selected, a multiple races category if more than 1 is selected, or the Hispanic grouping regardless of race selection if the response was yes to the prompt, "Are you Hispanic/Latino?"

[c]Only group included in aggregate "raceeth" variable as AI/AN. YRBSS calculates the raceeth variable and provides it for researchers to use.

2021, although data from both nations were restricted for the purpose of dissemination.[5] These limitations are noteworthy, as Indigenous individuals may be underrepresented in the data, particularly adolescents living on reservations.

## Policy-Level Recommendations

Recommendations for future research include using the lens of critical race theory to understand the historical context of policy,[2] including AI/AN leadership in research processes,[1,3] disaggregating data to adequately capture race/ethnicity in self-report surveys and other data sources,[7] and using data for tangible improvements rather than furthering stigma.[1] Researchers, agencies, and institutions should consider capturing data at the sovereign nation level to more accurately represent the unique experiences, health status, and distribution of various Indigenous people across the United States. To understand and appropriately represent Indigenous experiences, more Indigenous individuals need to be in leadership roles in agencies such as the CDC and research universities to create better methodologies based on lived experience. To that end, the CDC should consult closely with the Tribal Advisory Committee to improve how data from various public health systems are used in research.

## Recommendations for Researchers Using YRBSS

Researchers must remember the importance of how they conceptualize the data they are using and how they explain its methodological limitations. For researchers using YRBSS, it is important to consider the advantages and disadvantages of using the recalculated raceeth variable. Although insufficient sample sizes may prevent the full disaggregation of data, it is the responsibility of researchers to report such limitations clearly. Given the percentage of AI/AN individuals who are multiracial, we recommend that researchers consider creating 2 race categories: 1 for individuals who are AI/AN only, and 1 for individuals who are AI/AN and 1 or more additional races/ethnicities. YRBSS allows this level of flexibility because self-report race data are provided, which is a considerable strength of the data set. AJPH

### ABOUT THE AUTHORS

Ashton Gatewood and Micah Hartwell are with the Office of Medical Student Research, Oklahoma State University College of Osteopathic Medicine at Cherokee Nation, Tahlequah. Amy D. Hendrix-Dicken is with the Department of Pediatrics, University of Oklahoma-Tulsa School of Community Medicine. Micah Hartwell is also with the Department of Psychiatry and Behavioral Sciences, Oklahoma State University Center for Health Sciences, Tulsa. Ashton Gatewood is an enrolled tribal member of Choctaw Nation of Oklahoma and a descendant of Chickasaw Nation. Amy D. Hendrix-Dicken is an enrolled tribal member of Cherokee Nation.

### CORRESPONDENCE

Correspondence should be sent to Ashton Gatewood, 19500 E Ross St, Tahlequah Campus, Tahlequah, OK 74464 (e-mail: ashton.glover-gatewood@okstate.edu). Reprints can be ordered at http://www.ajph.org by clicking the "Reprints" link.

### PUBLICATION INFORMATION

Full Citation: Gatewood A, Hendrix-Dicken AD, Hartwell M. Comparing self-reported and aggregated racial classification for American Indian/Alaska Native youths in YRBSS: 2021. *Am J Public Health*. 2024;114(4):403–406.

Acceptance Date: December 12, 2023.

DOI: https://doi.org/10.2105/AJPH.2023.307561

ORCID iD:

Micah Hartwell https://orcid.org/0000-0001-6810-6571

### CONTRIBUTORS

A. Gatewood and M. Hartwell designed the project. M. Hartwell performed the statistical analyses. All authors interpreted the findings and created the brief.

### CONFLICTS OF INTEREST

The authors have no conflicts of interest declare.

### HUMAN PARTICIPANT PROTECTION

No protocol approval was necessary because data were obtained from secondary sources.

### REFERENCES

1. Friedman J, Hansen H, Gone JP. Deaths of despair and Indigenous data genocide. *Lancet*. 2023;401(10379):874–876. https://doi.org/10.1016/S0140-6736(22)02404-7
2. Haozous EA, Strickland CJ, Palacios JF, Solomon TGA. Blood politics, ethnic identity, and racial misclassification among American Indians and Alaska Natives. *J Environ Public Health*. 2014;2014:321604. https://doi.org/10.1155/2014/321604
3. Kalweit A, Clark M, Ishcomer-Aazami J. Determinants of racial misclassification in COVID-19 mortality data: the role of funeral directors and social context. *Am Indian Cult Res J*. 2021;44(3):15–36. https://doi.org/10.17953/AICRJ.44.3.KALWEIT_ETAL
4. Centers for Disease Control and Prevention. 2021 Youth Risk Behavior Survey data. May 2, 2023. Available at: http://www.cdc.gov/yrbs. Accessed June 20, 2023.
5. Centers for Disease Control and Prevention. YRBS participation history, data quality, and data availability. 2023. Available at: https://www.cdc.gov/healthyyouth/data/yrbs/pdf/2021/2021_hs_participation_history_508.pdf. Accessed January 24, 2024.
6. Conrick KM, Mills B, Schreuder AB, et al. Disparities in misclassification of race and ethnicity in electronic medical records among patients with traumatic injury. *J Racial Ethn Health Disparities*. 2023; Epub ahead of print. https://doi.org/10.1007/s40615-023-01783-3
7. Urban Indian Health Institute. Data genocide of American Indians and Alaska Natives in COVID-19 data. February 19, 2021. Available at: https://www.uihi.org/projects/data-genocide-of-american-indians-and-alaska-natives-in-covid-19-data. Accessed June 21, 2023.
8. Maxim R, Sanchez GR, Huyser KR. Why the federal government needs to change how it collects data on Native Americans. March 30, 2023. Available at: https://www.brookings.edu/articles/why-the-federal-government-needs-to-change-how-it-collects-data-on-native-americans. Accessed November 8, 2023.
9. Centers for Disease Control and Prevention. Overview and methods for the Youth Risk Behavior Surveillance System—United States, 2021. *MMWR Suppl*. 2023;72(1):1–12. https://doi.org/10.15585/mmwr.su7201a1

# Longitudinal Policy Surveillance of Private Insurance Hearing Aid Mandates in the United States: 1997–2022

Michelle L. Arnold, AuD, PhD, Brianna J. Heslin, JD, Madison Dowdy, BS, Stacie P. Kershner, JD, Serena Phillips, DrPH, Brandy Lipton, PhD, and Michael F. Pesko, PhD

See also Garcia Morales and Reed, p. 361.

**Objectives.** To produce a database of private insurance hearing aid mandates in the United States and quantify the share of privately insured individuals covered by a mandate.

**Methods.** We used health-related policy surveillance methods to create a database of private insurance hearing aid mandates through January 2023. We coded salient features of mandates and combined policy data with American Community Survey and Medicare Expenditure Panel Survey–Insurance Component data to estimate the share of privately insured US residents covered by a mandate from 2008 to 2022.

**Results.** A total of 26 states and 1 territory had private insurance hearing aid mandates. We found variability for mandate exceptions, maximum age eligibility, allowable frequency of benefit use, and coverage amounts. Between 2008 and 2022 the proportion of privately insured youths (aged ≤ 18 years) living where there was a private insurance hearing aid mandate increased from 3.4% to 18.7% and the proportion of privately insured adults (19–64 years) increased from 0.3% to 4.6%.

**Conclusions.** Hearing aid mandates cover a small share of US residents. Mandate exceptions in several states limit coverage, particularly for adults.

**Public Health Implications.** A federal mandate would improve hearing aid access. States can also improve access by adopting exception-free mandates with limited utilization management and no age restrictions. (*Am J Public Health*. 2024;114(4):407–414. https://doi.org/10.2105/AJPH.2023.307551)

AJPH April 2024, Vol. 114, No. 4

Hearing loss is the third largest contributor to years lived with disability in global burden of disease[1] and poses a significant public health threat, given its high and growing prevalence and known association with numerous costly outcomes. Hearing loss affects 23% of those aged 12 years and older in the United States and prevalence increases as age increases, so that more than two thirds of adults older than 70 years have significant hearing loss.[2] For children, incidence of permanent hearing loss is approximately 1.7 in 1000 live births annually, and untreated hearing loss is associated with suboptimal speech, language, academic, and social outcomes.[3,4] Approximately 88% of adult hearing loss cases go untreated,[5] and hearing loss has independent associations with incident dementia,[6] falls,[7] and increases in health care costs and hospitalizations.[8] The economic impacts of hearing loss are significant and pervasive, affecting more than 13% of US workers, with lost productivity costs estimated at $615 billion in 2013.[9]

Hearing aids are largely underutilized in the United States, despite being a highly efficacious treatment of hearing loss associated with improvements in speech understanding and socialization and higher quality of life.[10–12] High out-of-pocket costs are a barrier for many who would benefit from hearing aids.[12,13] A recent survey of audiologists and hearing aid dispensers reported a median hearing aid unit price of $2000 ($4000 for a set), with costs reaching up to $3000 per unit ($6000 for a set), which makes hearing aids unaffordable for most adults with hearing loss living in the United States.[14,15]

Despite the benefits of hearing aids, traditional Medicare Parts A and B do not cover hearing aids or related services for beneficiaries. Medicare benefits are federally regulated; thus, individual states cannot modify Medicare coverage or mandates. The lack of hearing aid coverage by traditional Medicare is especially problematic given higher rates of hearing loss among older adults and associated comorbidities such as Alzheimer's disease and related dementias, falls, and increased hospitalizations.[6–8] In the absence of federal action, many states have adopted private insurance hearing aid mandates that apply to fully insured private health plans covered by a commercial insurance carrier.

Private employer self-insured group health plans regulated by the Employee Retirement Income Security Act of 1974 (Pub L No. 93-406) are not required to adhere to state mandates, which significantly hinders state efforts to expand coverage, as these plans were estimated to cover 58% of privately insured workers in 2021.[16] An additional limitation is that in the absence of a federal mandate, states' legislation for private health insurance varies. One previous study found high variability in hearing aid coverage through state Medicaid programs,[17] but little is known about policy variability in state private insurance hearing aid mandates.

We used health-related policy surveillance methods[18] to create a database of private insurance hearing aid mandates and summarize salient features of legislation across time. Policy surveillance, which is the ongoing, systematic identification, collection, interpretation, and dissemination of laws, focuses on published, enacted legislation and involves a coding process that allows the quantification of features of the law.[18,19] Several such policy surveillance databases are available that describe variations in statutes for important health issues, including the regulation of tobacco and e-cigarettes,[20] cytomegalovirus screening and treatment,[21] and diabetes treatment.[22] These databases can be easily incorporated into relevant health outcomes research.

In addition to building a database that can be used by researchers and other key stakeholders, we used a subset of our collected information combined with population-level insurance data from American Community Survey (ACS) and Medical Expenditure Panel Survey (MEPS) to quantify national yearly averages of the share of privately insured youths 18 years and younger and adults aged 19 to 64 years covered by a private insurance hearing aid mandate. We demonstrate how mandate exceptions potentially affect coverage and identify strategies to expand coverage.

## METHODS

Using consensus guidelines for legal epidemiology methods from Temple University Center for Public Health Law Research,[19,23] we conducted longitudinal policy surveillance of state statutes to compile a database of private insurance hearing aid coverage mandates. Three individuals were responsible for the systematic retrieval, review, and coding process: an expert in hearing health care and public policy (M. L. A.), an expert in clinical hearing health care (M. D.), and an expert in health ethics and law (B. J. H.).

### Data Sources

We collected the data from June 2022 to January 2023. Primary data sources were published statutes retrieved using Westlaw Campus and Lexis Uni legal search engines and state legislature Web sites. We consulted the American Speech–Language-Hearing Association Web site compilation of hearing health care coverage data as a secondary source.[24]

### Inclusion and Exclusion Criteria

We included statutes and amendments in the data if they were published and effective between January 1, 1997, and December 31, 2022, and described private insurance requirements for covering hearing aids. We excluded statutes if they described only coverage for diagnosis of hearing loss; the scope of practice for audiologists and hearing instrument dispensers; price transparency of devices and services; or receipt, packaging, disclaimers, and return policies related to hearing aid sales.

We retrieved statutes using the terms "hearing aid/instrument/device," "audiologist," "hearing aid/instrument dispenser/specialist," "cochlear implant," "bone-anchored hearing aid," "osseointegrated/implantable device/aid," "hearing loss treatment/rehabilitation," "aural rehabilitation," and "hearing rehabilitation."

## Data Retrieval and Coding

We collected data from 50 US states, the District of Columbia, and the unincorporated territories of American Samoa, Guam, Puerto Rico, and the US Virgin Islands, for a total of 55 jurisdictions. We were interested in whether a jurisdiction had enacted a hearing aid coverage mandate, when the mandate was effective, amendments to the mandate during the period coded, and the comprehensiveness of coverage based on best practices for hearing aid provision.[25,26] We coded effective start dates of coverage directly from the statutory language when available; otherwise, we used individual jurisdiction standard effective dates. In addition to details about allowable costs and exemptions, we coded coverage for hearing devices, supplies and batteries, allowable frequency of benefit use, and follow-up programming and rehabilitation. A list of variables coded, cited statutes, and statutory language coded can be found online (Table A, available as a supplement to the online version of this article at http://www.ajph.org).

M. L. Arnold coded data from an initial subset of 2 states (IL and CT), which M. Dowdy and B. J. Heslin then replicated. Once the search strategy and coding scheme were replicable, we coded remaining jurisdictions, with 80% of jurisdictions redundantly coded to ensure continued consistency between coders. We resolved differences in coding with input from health law expert S. P. Kershner.

## Data Analysis

We estimated the annual national share of the population of privately insured youths aged 18 years and younger and adults aged 19 to 64 years living in states or territories with private insurance hearing aid mandates with and without exceptions from 2008 to 2022, including all 50 states and the District of Columbia. Mandates we considered to have exceptions were those only requiring optional coverage, only covering government employees, or having carve outs for small employers or cost-prohibitive benefits (exception details are listed in Table 1).

We used effective start dates of coverage at the month level to calculate the fraction of each year that a hearing aid mandate was in place for each state and age group. We downloaded individual-level 2008 to 2020 ACS survey data—containing age, state, and private insurance coverage status—from Integrated Public Use Microdata Series USA.[27] We did not have ACS individual-level private insurance information from earlier than 2008, even though our policy surveillance started with 1997. We also obtained annual state-level proportions of private sector enrollees with self-insured plans at establishments offering health insurance (i.e., those not subject to state hearing aid mandates) from the MEPS Insurance Component data,[16] and we set the proportion enrolled in fully insured plans (i.e., those subject to mandates) to be the remaining individuals. Because ACS data were available through 2020 and MEPS were available through 2021 at the time of analysis, we imputed through the end of our policy data collection period in 2022 using values from the final data years available.

We linked the hearing aid policy, MEPS, and ACS data by state and year, so we considered privately insured individuals in the ACS data residing in a state with a mandate covering their age to be covered for the fraction of the year that the relevant mandate was in place. Because plan type information is not available in the ACS data, we multiplied the hearing aid mandate status variable by the MEPS-derived state percentage of fully insured enrollees to account for differences in applicability of mandates for self- versus fully insured plans. We then used ACS survey weights to calculate weighted means by age group and year to obtain nationally representative estimates of the percentage of the privately insured covered by hearing aid mandates in the United States, creating separate estimates for all mandates and mandates excluding those with exceptions as previously defined.

# RESULTS

We identified 26 states and 1 US territory (US Virgin Islands) with private health insurance hearing aid mandates effective as of January 2023. Summaries of key current mandate features are displayed in Table 1. Three states (CT, IL, and ME) had earlier versions of mandates that predate the status shown in Table 1. This historical information and additional mandate features not shown in Table 1 are available as part of Table A.

A number of states have current mandates that are weakened by 1 or more exceptions: requirement to offer optional hearing aid coverage (n = 2), exemptions for small employers (n = 3), coverage for state employees only (n = 2), and allowing insurers to drop the benefit if the costs exceed 1% of premiums (n = 3). Texas additionally has a trigger provision that will cause the mandate to dissolve if the Centers for Medicare & Medicaid Services determine that the hearing aid mandate exceeds federal essential health

AJPH April 2024, Vol. 114, No. 4

## TABLE 1— Status of Private Insurance Hearing Aid Coverage Mandates as of January 1, 2023: United States

| States and Territories | Date Coverage Effective | Age Maximum | Frequency of Use, Mo | Total Coverage Amount, $ | Supplies and Repairs | Follow-Up or Rehabilitation[a] | OOP Cost Limits/Cost Sharing Allowed | Coverage Exceptions |
|---|---|---|---|---|---|---|---|---|
| AR | Jan 1, 2010 | ≥ 99 | NS | 2800 | NS | NS | No | No |
| CO | Aug 5, 2009 | 18 | 60 | NS | NS | Yes | Yes | No |
| CT | Jan 1, 2020[b] | ≥ 99 | 24 | NS | NS | NS | NS | No |
| DE | Jun 18, 2008 | 24 | 36 | 2000 | NS | NS | Yes | No |
| GA | Jun 1, 2018 | 18 | 48 | 6000 | Yes | Yes | Yes | Yes[c,d] |
| IL | Aug 22, 2018[a] | ≥ 99 | 24 | 5000 | Yes | Yes | Yes | Yes[c,d,e] |
| KY | Jul 15, 2002 | 18 | 36 | 2800 | Yes | Yes | Yes | No |
| LA | Jan 1, 2004 | 18 | 36 | 2800 | NS | NS | NS | No |
| ME | Sep 20, 2007[a] | ≥ 99 | 36 | 6000 | Yes | NS | Yes | No |
| MD | Oct 1, 2001 | 18 | 36 | 2800 | NS | NS | NS | No |
| MA | Nov 4, 2012 | 21 | 36 | 4000 | Yes | Yes | Yes | No |
| MN | Aug 1, 2007 | 18 | 36 | NS | NS | NS | Yes | No |
| MO | Aug 1, 2021 | 18 | 48 | NS | Yes | Yes | NS | No |
| MT | Jan 1, 2022 | 18 | 36 | NS | Yes | NS | Yes | No |
| NE | Jan 1, 2020 | 18 | 48 | 6000 | Yes | Yes | Yes | Yes[d] |
| NH | Jan 1, 2011 | ≥ 99 | 60 | 3000 | Yes | No | Yes | No |
| NJ | Mar 30, 2009 | 15 | 24 | 2000 | NS | NS | Yes | No |
| NM | Jul 1, 2007 | 21 | 36 | 4400 | NS | Yes | Yes | No |
| NC | Jan 1, 2011 | 22 | 36 | 5000 | Yes | Yes | Yes | No |
| OK | Nov 1, 2010 | 18 | 48 | NS | NS | NS | NS | No |
| OR | Jan 1, 2010 | 25 | 36 | NS | Yes | Yes | Yes | No |
| RI | Jan 1, 2006 | 99 | 36 | 1400 | Yes | NS | NS | Yes[c,e] |
| TN | Jan 1, 2012 | 18 | 36 | 2000 | Yes | Yes | Yes | No |
| TX | Sep 1, 2017 | 18 | 36 | NS | NS | Yes | Yes | No |
| WA | Jan 1, 2019 | ≥ 99 | 60 | NS | Yes | Yes | NS | Yes[f] |
| WI | Jan 1, 2010 | 18 | 36 | NS | Yes | Yes | Yes | Yes[f] |
| US Virgin Islands | May 16, 2004 | 18[g] | 36 | 4400 | NS | Yes | Yes | No |

*Note.* NS = not stated; OOP = out of pocket. ≥ 99 indicates no maximum age limit on benefits coverage.
[a]Equals "yes" if rehabilitation (general) or rehabilitation. Fittings columns are "yes" in Table A (available as a supplement to the online version of this article at http://www.ajph.org).
[b]CT, IL, and ME changed coverage between first adoption and the current status as reported in the table. A database providing more detailed information on these mandates and changes over time is available online.
[c]Small employer benefit plans are exempt from providing coverage.
[d]Health insurance plan is exempt from providing coverage if benefit costs exceed 1% of annual premiums.
[e]Coverage offered as an optional rider.
[f]Hearing aid coverage mandated for state employees and their dependents.
[g]Virgin Islands mandate covers up to age 21 years if beneficiary still attends high school.

benefits (thus otherwise forcing the state to make payments to provide the benefit).[28] We did not count Texas's provision as an exception in our coding because it did not affect subgroups in the state.

Most states with current mandates (n = 18/26) allowed but curtailed the use of cost sharing, for example, by allowing hearing aids to apply to the deductible or allowing coinsurance at a rate equal to other medical equipment. Only Arkansas explicitly prohibited cost sharing in its statute. Seven states (CT, LA, MD, MO, OK, RI, WA) did not specifically restrict cost sharing in any way; thus, health insurance companies in these states could provide coverage to fulfill their legal obligation but with high coinsurance rates to reduce use.

Allowable frequency of benefit use, or how often an insured beneficiary was eligible for new hearing aids, varied from 24 (n = 3; CT, IL, NJ) to 60 months (n = 3; CO, NH, WA), with a mode of 36 months (n = 15 states). One state (AR) did not specify the allowable frequency of benefit use in its published statute. Of the 26 states with mandates, 16 statutes defined maximum total coverage amounts per period of benefit use, ranging from $1400 (n = 1; RI) to $6000 (n = 3; GA, ME, NE) for 2 hearing aids. The statutes of 10 states (CO, CT, MN, MO, MT, OK, OR, TX, WA, WI) did not specify coverage amounts. An independent samples *t* test revealed no differences in coverage amounts between states with mandates focused on hearing aid provision for youths compared with states with no age limits ($t[15] = 0.051$; $P = .59$).

Age eligibility cutoffs were included in 19 of 26 states with current mandates. For states with eligibility cutoffs, the ages ranged from 15 to 25 years, and the mode maximum age cutoff was 18 years (n = 13). Seven states (AR, CT, IL, ME, NH, RI, WA) had no maximum age limits.

Some states included statutory language addressing coverage of supplies and repairs (e.g., earmolds and replacement parts; n = 15/26) and follow-up or rehabilitation (e.g., hearing aid adjustments and self-management skills training services; n = 14/26). Otherwise, states did not address this coverage, except for New Hampshire, which defined the "practice of fitting, dispensing, servicing, or sale of hearing instruments" as only those that involved use of a calibrated audiometer to test hearing and make selection and fitting recommendations. Note that for most individuals, hearing aids require multiple adjustments as well as self-management skills training over an acclimatization period to optimize outcomes.

Table 2 shows that between 2008 and 2022 the national share of private sector enrollees in fully insured plans ranged from 39.9% to 44.6%, with state-level minimums and maximums ranging from 24.0% to 29.7% and 60.3% to 72.1%, respectively. Figure 1 shows that between 2008 and 2022, the proportion of privately insured youths in the 50 US states and the District of Columbia living under a private insurance hearing aid mandate increased by approximately 5 times, from 3.4% to 18.7%. Meanwhile, for privately insured adults aged 19 to 64 years, this

**TABLE 2— Percentage of Private Sector Enrollees in Fully Insured Plans at Establishments That Offer Health Insurance, by Year: United States**

| Year | States and DC, No. | State Level | | | National Level, Mean % |
|---|---|---|---|---|---|
| | | Mean % | Minimum % | Maximum % | |
| 2008 | 51 | 44.2 | 29.0 | 62.1 | 44.6 |
| 2009 | 51 | 43.4 | 29.5 | 71.1 | 43.8 |
| 2010 | 51 | 42.2 | 26.2 | 72.1 | 42.4 |
| 2011 | 51 | 41.0 | 26.2 | 69.5 | 41.6 |
| 2012 | 51 | 39.6 | 26.0 | 62.9 | 39.9 |
| 2013 | 51 | 40.9 | 26.5 | 64.5 | 41.8 |
| 2014 | 51 | 40.0 | 27.7 | 68.4 | 40.4 |
| 2015 | 51 | 39.3 | 24.0 | 60.3 | 39.9 |
| 2016 | 51 | 41.0 | 28.2 | 62.4 | 42.3 |
| 2017 | 51 | 40.4 | 27.6 | 68.8 | 40.6 |
| 2018 | 51 | 40.0 | 27.3 | 68.6 | 41.3 |
| 2019 | 51 | 41.1 | 29.7 | 71.1 | 41.5 |
| 2020 | 51 | 40.7 | 26.8 | 65.2 | 42.3 |
| 2021 | 51 | 41.2 | 24.5 | 66.4 | 42.1 |
| 2022 | 51 | 41.2 | 24.5 | 66.4 | 42.1 |

*Note.* Fully insured plans are expected to be affected by hearing aid mandates. The firm-level data are drawn from the Medical Expenditure Panel Survey (MEPS) Insurance Component. The table includes all 50 states and the District of Columbia; it does not include US territories. We imputed values for 2022 from 2021, the last available year of MEPS data at the time of analysis. We derived national values by weighting state-level values by state populations obtained from the Surveillance, Epidemiology, and End Results Program (2008–2020), with population values for most recent years imputed from 2020.

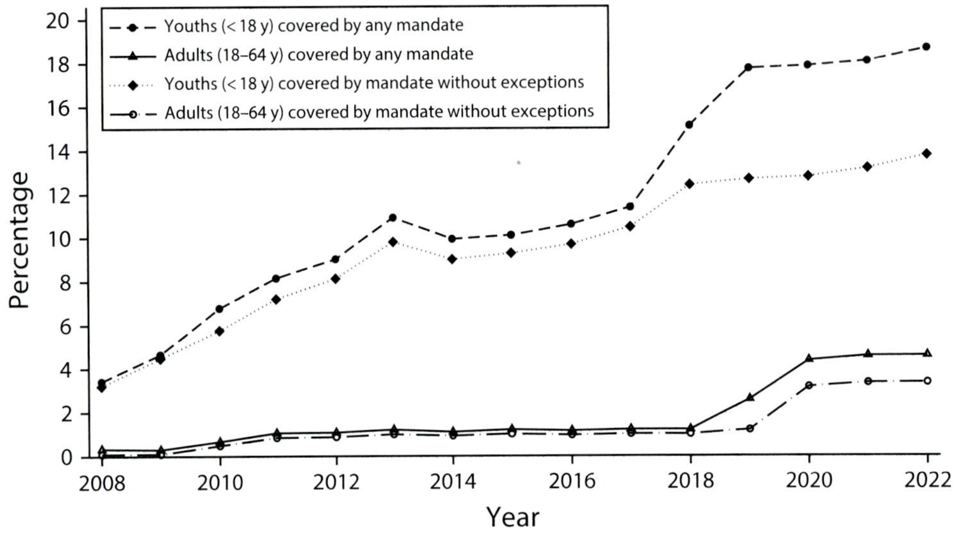


**FIGURE 1— Annual Share of Privately Insured Youths (≤ 18 Years) and Adults (19–64 Years) Covered by Private Insurance Hearing Aid Mandates From 2008 to 2022 With and Without Exceptions: United States**

*Note.* The figure includes all 50 states and the District of Columbia and does not include US territories. This graph starts in 2008, despite longitudinal policy surveillance starting in 1997, because American Community Survey individual-level private insurance coverage data are only available starting in 2008.



proportion increased from 0.3% in 2008 to 4.6% in 2022. When we excluded mandates with exceptions, these shares of youths (aged ≤ 18 years) and adults (aged 19–64 years) in 2022 decreased to 13.8% and 3.3%, respectively.

## DISCUSSION

To our knowledge, this study is the first to examine US private insurance mandates for hearing aids using a detailed policy surveillance approach. Results of our policy surveillance and coding methodologies revealed measurable variability between state mandates for private insurance coverage of hearing aids, consistent with previous work that documented meaningful differences in the generosity of state Medicaid coverage of hearing aids.[17] Policy surveillance of private insurance mandates for, for example, autism[29] and mental health care, for adolescents[30] demonstrated variability similar to this analysis in the areas of age limits, maximum allowable costs, and covered treatments.

Our research revealed substantial gaps in current (as of January 2023) effective statutes. Many states limit the total coverage amount, and only 1 state prohibits cost sharing. Nine states have coverage limits that were less than $4000, which is lower than the median cost of a pair of hearing aids.[15] Furthermore, most mandates pertain to individuals younger than 25 years and do not address access to hearing aids for older adults, who have a higher prevalence of hearing loss. Reflecting these limitations, we estimated that in 2022 only 18.7% of privately insured youth aged 18 years and younger and 4.6% of privately insured adults aged 19 to 64 years were covered by a mandate. Although these shares are likely to grow in the future as additional states implement coverage mandates, we are aware of only 1 state (VT) that has enacted a hearing aid coverage statute since the conclusion of our policy surveillance time horizon in 2022. Like many existing mandates, Vermont's law applies to beneficiaries up to 25 years of age and allows a maximum hearing aid benefit reimbursement of $4000 every 48 months.

Although the share of privately insured children covered by a mandate remains low, the fact that more states have opted to cover more children than adults is consistent with the prioritization of children's health in other policy contexts. For example, Medicaid eligibility limits are higher for children than for adults,[31] and the early and periodic screening, diagnostic and treatment benefit requires that all states cover hearing aids and other preventive services for children enrolled in Medicaid.[32] Providing hearing aid coverage is likely to be less costly for children than for adults given the lower prevalence of hearing loss at younger ages.[4] Finally, access to sound during childhood is crucial for language and speech development.[3] Policymakers may be more likely to invest in children's hearing health for these reasons.

Our review also found a lack of statutory language regarding coverage of aural rehabilitation services. Although hearing aids are an efficacious treatment, devices alone do not address the self-management skills training necessary to optimize treatment benefits for adults.[25] For youth, aural rehabilitation is a crucial aspect of normal speech, language, and academic ability, without which children are at significant risk for delays in these areas.[33] Given that coverage limits were lower than the median cost of entry-level hearing aids in 9 states and never exceeded $6000 in any of the 16 states with a specified limit, it is unlikely that providers in these states would be able to deliver appropriate aural rehabilitation in addition to devices without high out-of-pocket expenditures.

Federal and state policymakers have recently focused on improving hearing health care access and utilization, including by finalizing the Over-the-Counter Hearing Aid Act in August 2022.[34] Although the availability of over-the-counter hearing aids is likely to increase access and affordability, there is no over-the-counter option for severe hearing loss. The National Academies also prioritized addressing the affordability of hearing health care, with recommendations for mandated coverage of hearing loss treatment, highlighting hearing aids as primary treatment options.[12] The Medicare Audiologist Access and Services Act of 2021 (MAASA; S.1731) proposed amendments to the Social Security Act to address statutory barriers to accessing hearing health care for Medicare beneficiaries. However, MAASA only proposes to mandate coverage for services that would otherwise be provided by a physician instead of allowing a licensed audiologist to bill for these services. Databases such as the one we developed will inform future initiatives to broaden access to hearing aids for all US residents.

Our research identifies other legislative strategies to expand coverage. The most beneficial would be a federal mandate, as this would bring coverage to 100% of privately insured individuals and is the only strategy to guarantee this benefit to the approximately 58% of privately insured workers in self-insured plans in 2021. In the absence of a federal mandate, 2 states (WA and WI) do use a strategy to incentivize self-insured plans to offer hearing aid benefits by requiring that governments select insurance offerings for their employees that include these benefits. States that wish to maximize coverage could do so by passing a mandate that government employees be provided health insurance with hearing aid coverage. This is an opportunity for states wishing to expand coverage against the constraints of self-insured plans.

Our analysis had limitations. Our findings were based on coding legislatively enacted mandates and do not include actions such as administrative agency regulations or policies. Our estimates of the percentage of privately insured children and adults covered by a mandate could also underestimate the proportion of people with hearing aid benefits to the extent that self-insured group health plans voluntarily provide coverage or that coverage is available through another source. Self-insured plans may offer some coverage for hearing aids; however, benefit allowances may be capped or offered as discount programs or an optional benefit for recipients with additional out-of-pocket costs.[35] Additional research is needed to determine whether self-insured plans may be influenced by state mandates to cover hearing aids even though these plans are not subject to state mandates.

In summary, extensive variability exists across states with laws mandating private insurance hearing aid coverage. Hearing aid mandates cover a small but growing share of US residents. Future work is needed to understand the effects of these mandates and their provisions on hearing aid utilization and out-of-pocket payments. AJPH

## ABOUT THE AUTHORS

Michelle L. Arnold and Madison Dowdy are with the Department of Communication Sciences & Disorders, University of South Florida, Tampa. Brianna J. Heslin and Stacie P. Kershner are with the Center for Law, Health & Society, Georgia State University College of Law, Atlanta. Serena Phillips and Michael F. Pesko are with the Department of Economics, College of Arts and Science, University of Missouri, Columbia. Brandy Lipton is with the Program in Public Health, University of California, Irvine.

## CORRESONDENCE

Correspondence should be sent to Michelle L. Arnold, AuD, PhD, University of South Florida, Department of Communication Sciences & Disorders, 4202 E. Fowler Ave, PCD 1017, Tampa, FL 33620 (e-mail: mlarnold@usf.edu). Reprints can be ordered at http://www.ajph.org by clicking the "Reprints" link.

## PUBLICATION INFORMATION

Full Citation: Arnold ML, Heslin BJ, Dowdy M, et al. Longitudinal policy surveillance of private insurance hearing aid mandates in the United States: 1997–2022. *Am J Public Health*. 2024;114(4): 407–414.

Acceptance Date: November 26, 2023.

DOI: https://doi.org/10.2105/AJPH.2023.307551

ORCID iDs:

Michelle L. Arnold https://orcid.org/0000-0002-5633-3715

Serena Phillips https://orcid.org/0000-0002-7100-9710

Michael F. Pesko https://orcid.org/0000-0002-9247-9703

## CONTRIBUTORS

M. L. Arnold led the writing of the original draft, editing, and revisions of the article. M. L. Arnold led and B. J. Heslin and M. Dowdy contributed to the curation of the legislative data. M. L. Arnold, B. J. Heslin, M. Dowdy, S. P. Kershner, S. Phillips, and M. F. Pesko analyzed the data. M. L. Arnold, S. P. Kershner, and M. F. Pesko administered and supervised the research activities. M. L. Arnold and B. Lipton contributed to and M. F. Pesko led the conceptualization of the study goals, aims, and design. M. F. Pesko led funding acquisition. All authors contributed to the writing of the original draft, editing, and revisions of the article.

## ACKNOWLEDGMENTS

Research reported in this publication was supported by the National Institute on Deafness and Other Communication Disorders, National Institutes of Health (NIH; grant R01 DC019661-01A1).

**Note.** The content of this article is solely the responsibility of the authors and does not necessarily represent the official views of the NIH.

## CONFLICTS OF INTEREST

The authors have no conflicts of interest from funding or affiliation activities to declare.

## HUMAN PARTICIPANT PROTECTION

The study was deemed exempt from Human Participants Protection by the institutional review board at the University of South Florida because no human participants took part.

## REFERENCES

1. GBD 2019 Hearing Loss Collaborators. Hearing loss prevalence and years lived with disability, 1990–2019: findings from the Global Burden of Disease Study 2019. *Lancet.* 2021;397(10278): 996–1009. https://doi.org/10.1016/S0140-6736(21)00516-X
2. Goman AM, Lin FR. Prevalence of hearing loss by severity in the United States. *Am J Public Health.* 2016;106(10):1820–1822. https://doi.org/10.2105/AJPH.2016.303299
3. Lieu JEC, Kenna M, Anne S, Davidson L. Hearing loss in children: a review. *JAMA.* 2020;324(21):2195–2205. https://doi.org/10.1001/jama.2020.17647
4. National Institute on Deafness and Other Communication Disorders. Quick statistics about hearing. 2016. Available at: https://www.nidcd.nih.gov/health/statistics/quick-statistics-hearing#5. Accessed July 21, 2016.
5. Mamo SK, Nieman CL, Lin FR. Prevalence of untreated hearing loss by income among older adults in the United States. *J Health Care Poor Underserved.* 2016;27(4):1812–1818. https://doi.org/10.1353/hpu.2016.0164
6. Lin FR, Metter J, O'Brien RJ, Resnick SM, Zonderman AB, Ferrucci L. Hearing loss and incident dementia. *Arch Neurol.* 2011;68(2):214–220. https://doi.org/10.1001/archneurol.2010.362
7. Lin FR, Ferrucci L. Hearing loss and falls among older adults in the United States. *Arch Intern Med (Chic).* 2012;172(4):369–371. https://doi.org/10.1001/archinternmed.2011.728
8. Reed NS, Altan A, Deal JA, et al. Trends in health care costs and utilization associated with untreated hearing loss over 10 years. *JAMA Otolaryngol Head Neck Surg.* 2019;145(1):27–34. https://doi.org/10.10January jamaoto.2018.2875
9. Neitzel RL, Swinburn TK, Hammer MS, Eisenberg D. Economic impact of hearing loss and reduction of noise-induced hearing loss in the United States. *J Speech Lang Hear Res.* 2017;60(1):182–189. https://doi.org/10.1044/2016_JSLHR-H-15-0365
10. Cox RM, Johnson JA, Xu J. Impact of hearing aid technology on outcomes in daily life I: the patients' perspective. *Ear Hear.* 2016;37(4): e224–e237. https://doi.org/10.1097/AUD.0000000000000277
11. Ferguson M, Kitterick PT, Chong L, Edmundson-Jones M, Barker F, Hoare DJ. Hearing aids for mild to moderate hearing loss in adults. *Cochrane Database Syst Rev.* 2017;9(9):CD012023. https://doi.org/10.1002/14651858.CD012023.pub2
12. National Academies of Sciences Engineering and Medicine. *Hearing Health Care for Adults: Priorities for Improving Access and Affordability.* Washington, DC: National Academies Press; 2016. https://doi.org/10.17226/23446
13. Wallhagen MI. Access to care for hearing loss: policies and stakeholders. *J Gerontol Nurs.* 2014; 40(3):15–19. https://doi.org/10.3928/00989134-20140131-01
14. Jilla AM, Johnson CE, Huntington-Klein N. Hearing aid affordability in the United States. *Disabil Rehabil Assist Technol.* 2023;18(3):246–252. https://doi.org/10.1080/17483107.2020.1822449
15. Strom KE. *Hearing Review* survey of RIC pricing in 2017. *Hearing Review.* 2018;25(3):28–38.
16. Agency for Healthcare Research and Quality Medical Expenditure Panel Survey (MEPS) Insurance Component (IC). Available at: https://datatools.ahrq.gov/meps-ic?type=tab&tab=mepsich3ntl. Accessed January 5, 2023.
17. Arnold ML, Hyer K, Chisolm TH. Medicaid hearing aid coverage for older adult beneficiaries: a state-by-state comparison. *Health Aff (Millwood).* 2017;36(8):1476–1484. https://doi.org/10.1377/hlthaff.2016.1610
18. Chiriqui JF, O'Connor JC, Chaloupka F. What gets measured, gets changed: evaluating law and policy for maximum impact. *J Law Med Ethics.* 2011; 39(supp 1):21–26. https://doi.org/10.1111/j.1748-720X.2011.00559.x
19. Burris SC. A technical guide for policy surveillance. Temple University Legal Studies research paper no. 2014-34. July 23, 2014. Available at: https://papers.ssrn.com/sol3/papers.cfm?abstract_id=2469895. Accessed May 8, 2022. https://doi.org/10.2139/ssrn.2469895.
20. Policy Surveillance Program. Electronic cigarette laws. 2017. Available at: https://lawatlas.org/datasets/electronic-nicotine-delivery-systems. Accessed January 12, 2023.
21. Yassine B, Hulkower R, Dollard S, Cahill E, Lanzieri T. A legal mapping assessment of cytomegalovirus-related laws in the United States. *J Public Health Manag Pract.* 2022;28(8):E624–E629. https://doi.org/10.1097/PHH.0000000000001401
22. Carr D, Kappagoda M, Boseman L, Could L, Croom B. Advancing diabetes-related equity through diabetes self-management education and training: existing coverage requirements and considerations for increased participation. *J Public Health Manag Pract.* 2020;26(suppl 2):S37–S44. https://doi.org/10.1097/PHH.0000000000001109
23. Presley D, Reinstein T, Webb-Barr D, Burris S. Creating legal data for public health monitoring and evaluation: Delphi standards for policy surveillance. *J Law Med Ethics.* 2021;43(suppl 1): 27–31. https://doi.org/10.1111/jlme.12210
24. American Speech-Language-Hearing Association. State insurance mandates for hearing aids. Available at: https://www.asha.org/advocacy/state/issues/ha_reimbursement/#:~:text=Requires%20insurers%20to%20provide%20coverage,in%20the%20insured's%20hearing%20status. Accessed September 3, 2020.
25. Basura G, Cienkowski KM, Hamlin L, et al. American Speech-Language-Hearing Association clinical practice guideline on aural rehabilitation for adults with hearing loss. *Am J Audiol.* 2023;32(1):1–51. https://doi.org/10.1044/2022_AJA-21-00252
26. Valente M, Abrams HB, Benson D, et al. Guidelines for the audiological management of adult hearing impairment. *Audiology Today.* 2006;18(5): 32–38. Available at: https://audiology-web.s3.amazonaws.com/migrated/haguidelines.pdf_53994876e92e42.70908344.pdf. Accessed February 10, 2024.
27. Ruggles S, Flood S, Goeken R, Schouweiler M, Sobek M. *IPUMS USA: Version 12.0* [dataset]. Minneapolis, MN: IPUMS; 2022. Available at: https://www.ipums.org/projects/ipums-usa/d010.v12.0. Accessed February 10, 2024.
28. S.B. 2016. Bill analysis. Available at: https://capitol.texas.gov/tlodocs/87R/analysis/html/SB02016I.htm. Accessed March 7, 2023.
29. Douglas MD, Benevides T, Carretta H. Analyzing state autism private insurance mandates for allied health services: a pilot study. *OTJR (Thorofare, NJ).* 2017;37(4):218–226. https://doi.org/10.1177/1539449217730355
30. Douglas MD, Weber SB, Bass C, et al. Creation of a longitudinal legal data set to support legal epidemiology studies of mental health insurance legislation. *Psychiatr Serv.* 2022;73(3):265–270. https://doi.org/10.1176/appi.ps.202100019
31. Kaiser Family Foundation. Medicaid and CHIP income eligibility limits for children as a percent of the federal poverty level. 2023. Available at: https://www.kff.org/health-reform/state-indicator/medicaid-and-chip-income-eligibility-limits-for-children-as-a-percent-of-the-federal-poverty-level/?currentTimeframe=0&sortModel=%7B%22colId%22:%22Location%22,%22sort%22:%22asc%22%7D. Accessed August 21, 2023.
32. Centers for Medicare & Medicaid Services. Vision and hearing screening services for children and adolescents. 2014. Available at: https://www.medicaid.gov/medicaid/benefits/early-and-periodic-screening-diagnostic-and-treatment/vision-and-hearing-screening-services-children-and-adolescents/index.html#:~:text=EPSDT%20requires%20Medicaid%20coverage%20of,are%20not%20covered%20for%20adults. Accessed August 21, 2023.
33. American Academy of Audiology. American Academy of Audiology clinical practice guidelines: pediatric amplification. 2013. Available at: https://apps.asha.org/EvidenceMaps/Articles/ArticleSummary/ecbfe2a5-c85d-4836-a629-f4454e43844b. Accessed February 10, 2024.
34. Over-the-Counter Hearing Aid Act of 2017. Pub L No. 115-263 (2017).
35. Whelan C. Insurance and financial assistance for hearing aids. 2023. Available at: https://www.healthyhearing.com/help/hearing-aids/insurance-financial-assistance. Accessed August 15, 2023.

# County-Level Factors Associated With Influenza and COVID-19 Vaccination in Indiana, 2020–2022

Monica L. Kasting, PhD, Alfu Laily, BNutr, Heather N. Burney, MS, Katharine J. Head, PhD, MA, Joanne K. Daggy, PhD, MS, Gregory D. Zimet, PhD, MA, and Laura M. Schwab-Reese, PhD, MA

See also Bednarczyk, p. 359.

**Objectives.** To assess COVID-19 and influenza vaccination rates across Indiana's 92 counties and identify county-level factors associated with vaccination.

**Methods.** We analyzed county-level data on adult COVID-19 vaccination from the Indiana vaccine registry and 2021 adult influenza vaccination from the Centers for Disease Control and Prevention. We used multiple linear regression (MLR) to determine county-level predictors of vaccinations.

**Results.** COVID-19 vaccination ranged from 31.2% to 87.6% (mean = 58.0%); influenza vaccination ranged from 33.7% to 53.1% (mean = 42.9%). In MLR, COVID-19 vaccination was significantly associated with primary care providers per capita (b = 0.04; 95% confidence interval [CI] = 0.02, 0.05), median household income (b = 0.23; 95% CI = 0.12, 0.34), percentage Medicare enrollees with a mammogram (b = 0.29; 95% CI = 0.08, 0.51), percentage uninsured (b = −1.22; 95% CI = −1.57, −0.87), percentage African American (b = 0.31; 95% CI = 0.19, 0.42), percentage female (b = −0.97; 95% CI = −1.79, –0.15), and percentage who smoke (b = −0.75; 95% CI = −1.26, −0.23). Influenza vaccination was significantly associated with percentage uninsured (b = 0.71; 95% CI = 0.22, 1.21), percentage African American (b = −0.07; 95% CI = −0.13, −0.01), percentage Hispanic (b = −0.28; 95% CI = −0.40, −0.17), percentage who smoke (b = −0.85; 95% CI = −1.06, −0.64), and percentage who completed high school (b = 0.54; 95% CI = 0.21, 0.87). The MLR models explained 86.7% (COVID-19) and 70.2% (influenza) of the variance.

**Conclusions.** Factors associated with COVID-19 and influenza vaccinations varied. Variables reflecting access to care (e.g., insurance) and higher risk of severe disease (e.g., smoking) are notable. Programs to improve access and target high-risk populations may improve vaccination rates. (*Am J Public Health*. 2024;114(4):415–423. https://doi.org/10.2105/AJPH.2023.307553)

AJPH April 2024, Vol. 114, No. 4

The COVID-19 pandemic, caused by the novel severe acute respiratory syndrome coronavirus 2 (SARS-CoV-2),[1] represents an unprecedented public health crisis in modern times. While initial pandemic hotspots centered in densely populated urban areas, infections in rural areas began to rise as the pandemic progressed.[2] This rise in rural infections highlighted rural disparities in access to health care as well as differences in health beliefs, resistance to preventive health behaviors (e.g., mask wearing and social distancing), and higher vaccine hesitancy and lower vaccine confidence.[3] Vaccine hesitancy, which involves distrust or concern about vaccination, is predictive of, but distinct from, vaccine uptake.[4,5] Rural–urban differences in vaccine hesitancy, confidence, and health beliefs are being seen both with new COVID-19 vaccines and more established adult vaccinations, including human papillomavirus and influenza.[6,7] Nationally, there is a significant urban–rural vaccination coverage disparity. This disparity encompasses different age ranges, including child, adolescent, and adult vaccination, and different vaccines, ranging from influenza to pneumococcal to human papillomavirus.[6,8–10]

Addressing these disparities must begin with an understanding of the unique context of rural areas. Furthermore, effective interventions must account for the "triad" of local culture, geographic location, and economics of the region.[11] For example, in addition to higher vaccine hesitancy rates,[12,13] rural residents also face more logistical barriers such as access to, and quality of, health care.[14] Importantly, rural individuals' health care providers play a crucial role in vaccination. Interventions that partner with clinics and health care providers show more vaccine improvement than interventions without these components.[15] In addition, rural individuals must depend more on traditional clinical settings (e.g., their provider's office) for vaccination versus their urban counterparts with more access to alternative vaccine sites (e.g., pharmacies, health fairs), which may contribute to disparities in uptake.[7] Most relevant interventions have focused on improving provider communication,[16] practice-based strategies (e.g., provider prompts, standing orders),[17,18] and shifting individual attitudes and intent.[19] Although these approaches have shown some success, the typical effect size is small to moderate, and these approaches have not often targeted those who live in rural areas. In sum, continued work is needed to investigate rural–urban disparities in vaccination and identify factors associated with these disparities within specific geographic areas, especially during a complex vaccine rollout like the COVID-19 vaccine.

Therefore, this study aimed to assess existing differences among adults in both COVID-19 and influenza vaccinations by county in Indiana and determine what county-level factors are associated with those vaccination rates. We chose to focus on these 2 vaccines as they both involve respiratory viruses, both have generated greater hesitancy than other adult vaccines, and both are routinely recommended for all adults.

## METHODS

In this study, we examined COVID-19 and influenza vaccination rates across Indiana's 92 counties among adults aged 18 years and older from December 2020 through March 2022. We extracted the data for COVID-19 vaccinations from the Indiana State Department of Health, Children and Hoosier Immunization Registry Program (CHIRP). We extracted influenza rates from the Centers for Disease Control and Prevention (CDC) US Influenza Surveillance Dashboard (FluVaxView),[20] which reports weekly national influenza vaccination data by county.

### Measures

***Vaccination data.*** The Indiana CHIRP database is a secure, Web-based immunization registry program that permanently stores immunization records. CHIRP provided county-level data on the number of first and second doses of Pfizer and Moderna COVID-19 vaccinations given as well as single-dose Johnson & Johnson vaccination, consistent with vaccine recommendations at the time of data collection, from December 2020 through March 2022. While CHIRP was designed to track pediatric vaccinations, the state uses CHIRP to track all COVID-19 vaccinations, regardless of age. These data are publicly available through a data request with the Indiana State Department of Health. In addition, CHIRP also provided information on county-level vaccination rates by age group, race/ethnicity, and sex. All data were aggregate, and no individual-level data were available.

Because CHIRP does not track influenza vaccinations for adults, we obtained county-level influenza vaccination in 2021 from the FluVaxView database, administered by the CDC.[20] From the database, we downloaded a comma-separated values–format report, and we extracted influenza vaccination rates by using the Federal Information Processing Standard codes—unique codes assigned to identify each county in the United States. We used codes 18001 through 18183 to filter down to only Indiana counties.

***County-level data.*** We derived county-level population estimates from the US Census to determine COVID-19 vaccination rates. We derived county-specific socio-demographic and health data from the County Health Rankings Report, a program supported by the Robert Wood Johnson Foundation and the University of Wisconsin Population Health Institute.[21] Lastly, because we aimed to investigate county-level factors associated with vaccination rates, we gathered information on number of primary care providers per 100 000 individuals, as reported by the County Health Rankings Report, and the existence of a community paramedicine program that incorporates vaccination services. Information on community paramedicine programs was available, by request, from the Indiana Department of Homeland Security. Recently, the Department of Homeland Security released updated information on these programs.[22] The latter practice has increased in use across the country to improve vaccination rates[23–29] and was therefore included as a potential predictor variable.

## Statistical Analyses

Descriptive statistics were presented using mean ±SD and median (minimum–maximum) and reported for all county-level variables and COVID-19 and influenza vaccination rates at the county level. COVID-19 vaccination rates were calculated by determining the percentage of individuals in each county aged 18 years and older who received either their second dose of the Pfizer or Moderna COVID-19 vaccinations or a single dose of the Johnson & Johnson COVID-19 vaccination.

We modeled county-level vaccination rates by using linear regression weighted by the total adult population of each county. We conducted model selection by using forward, backward, and stepwise selection to determine the best multiple linear regression model for each vaccination rate. The forward and stepwise selection methods used a .05 significance level for entry criterion, and the backward and stepwise selection methods used a .05 significance level for staying in the model. We selected the best model based on the adjusted $R^2$ value. We examined tolerance values for variables in each final model to ensure issues with multicollinearity were negligible, and we assessed residuals for normality. The full model for each vaccination rate is reported along with the selected reduced model. Estimated model coefficients and associated 95% confidence intervals (CIs) are reported. The squared semipartial correlation coefficient for each variable is also reported as a measure of effect size. We considered a *P* value less than .05 to be statistically significant. We conducted statistical analyses with SAS version 9.4 (SAS Institute, Cary, NC).

# RESULTS

The mean COVID-19 vaccination rate across the 92 counties in Indiana was 58% and ranged from 31.2% to 87.6% (Table 1). The mean influenza vaccination rate was 42.9% and ranged from 33.7% to 53.1%. Figure 1 displays the variability in COVID-19 (panel a) and influenza (panel b) vaccination rates across Indiana counties with darker color indicating a higher vaccination rate.

## County-Level Factors and COVID-19 Vaccination

Although the univariable regression results between county factors and COVID-19 or influenza vaccination (Table A, available as a supplement to the online version of this article at https://ajph.org) were generally similar, differences were evident in the multiple linear regression models (Table 2). The final selected model for COVID-19 vaccination, which was obtained by both forward and stepwise selection, contained 7 explanatory variables with an

**TABLE 1— Summary Statistics for County-Level Demographic and Health Care Variables: Indiana**

| Variable | Mean ± SD | Median (Min–Max) |
|---|---|---|
| Total primary care providers per 100 000 individuals[a] | 124.0 ± 63.3 | 116.5 (18.8–321.9) |
| Median household income, $[b] | 60 637.4 ± 10 163.5 | 59 269 (42 504–96 359) |
| % of the county that is rural[c] | 54.5 ± 26.9 | 53.6 (0.6–100) |
| % of Medicare enrollees with influenza vaccine[a] | 50.5 ± 6.6 | 52.0 (31.0–62.0) |
| % of Medicare enrollees with mammography screening[a,d] | 42.7 ± 5.0 | 43.0 (31.0–54.0) |
| % of all county residents | | |
| Uninsured[a] | 10.4 ± 2.7 | 10.0 (6.0–27.9) |
| Food insecure[a] | 12.5 ± 1.9 | 12.5 (7.5–16.6) |
| Aged ≥ 65 years[b] | 18.6 ± 2.3 | 18.8 (12.2–25.7) |
| African American[b] | 3.0 ± 4.5 | 0.9 (0.2–28.7) |
| Hispanic[b] | 4.5 ± 3.8 | 3.1 (1.3–20.0) |
| Female[b] | 50.1 ± 1.2 | 50.2 (45.3–52.9) |
| % of adult county residents | | |
| Smoke[a] | 22.0 ± 2.4 | 22.3 (12.5–26.9) |
| Obesity[a] | 36.0 ± 2.3 | 36.2 (26.3–39.8) |
| Unemployed[b] | 6.7 ± 1.3 | 6.5 (3.8–11.1) |
| Completed high school[e] | 88.6 ± 4.4 | 89.2 (61.1–97.1) |
| Fully vaccinated against COVID-19 | 58.0 ± 8.4 | 57.1 (31.2–87.6) |
| Vaccinated against influenza[f] | 42.9 ± 3.5 | 42.5 (33.7–53.1) |

*Note.* n = 92.
[a]Data from 2019.
[b]Data from 2020.
[c]Data from 2010.
[d]Defined as the percentage of female Medicare enrollees aged 65–74 years that received annual mammography screening.
[e]Data from 2016–2020.
[f]Data from 2021.

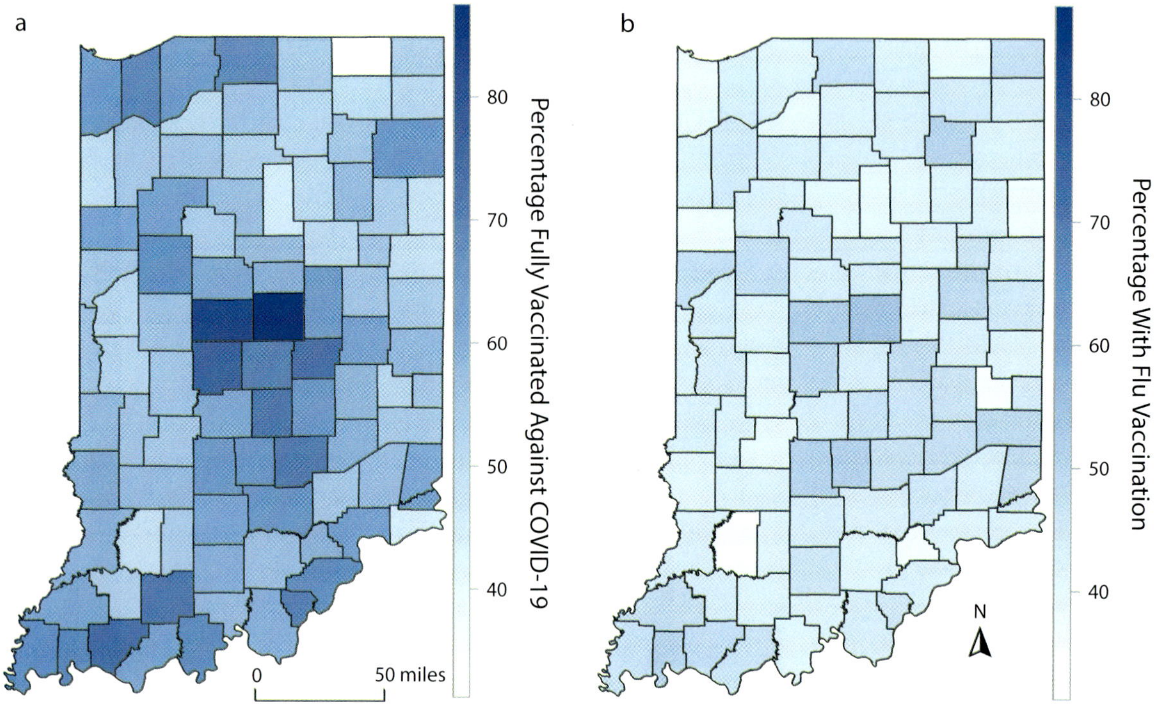


**FIGURE 1—** **Heatmap of Vaccination Rates by Indiana County for (a) COVID-19 (December 2020–March 2022) and (b) Influenza (2021)**

adjusted $R^2 = 0.867$. The unit of the outcome of the model is percentage with COVID-19 vaccination with a 0-to-100 range. Based on this model, 1 additional primary care provider per 100 000 individuals was associated with an increase of 0.04 (b = 0.04; 95% CI = 0.02, 0.05) in the percentage with COVID-19 vaccination after adjusting for other factors in the model. An increase in median household income of $1000 is associated with an increase in

**TABLE 2—** **Association of County-Level Factors and COVID-19 (December 2020–March 2022) or Influenza (2021) Vaccination: Indiana**

| | COVID-19 (Forward/Stepwise) | | Influenza (Backward) | |
|---|---|---|---|---|
| **Variable** | **b (95% CI)** | **Effect Size** | **b (95% CI)** | **Effect Size** |
| Total primary care providers per 100 000 individuals | 0.04 (0.02, 0.05) | 0.040 | . . . | . . . |
| Median household income (thousands) | 0.23 (0.12, 0.34) | 0.027 | . . . | . . . |
| % of Medicare enrollees with mammography screening | 0.29 (0.08, 0.51) | 0.011 | . . . | . . . |
| % of all county residents | | | | |
| Uninsured | −1.22 (−1.57, −0.87) | 0.071 | 0.71 (0.22, 1.21) | 0.027 |
| African American | 0.31 (0.19, 0.42) | 0.041 | −0.07 (−0.13, −0.01) | 0.016 |
| Female | −0.97 (−1.79, −0.15) | 0.008 | . . . | . . . |
| Hispanic | . . . | . . . | −0.28 (−0.40, −0.17) | 0.079 |
| % of adult county residents | | | | |
| Smoke | −0.75 (−1.26, −0.23) | 0.012 | −0.85 (−1.06, −0.64) | 0.216 |
| Completed high school | . . . | . . . | 0.54 (0.21, 0.87) | 0.035 |
| Adjusted $R^2$ | 0.867 | | 0.702 | |

*Note.* CI = confidence interval. This table shows multiple linear regression results—selected reduced models.

the percentage with COVID-19 vaccination of 0.23 (b = 0.23; 95% CI = 0.12, 0.34). All other explanatory variables are in percentages; thus, interpretations are similar for each.

A 1-percentage-point increase in Medicare enrollees with mammography screening was associated with an increase of 0.29 in the percentage with COVID-19 vaccination (b = 0.29; 95% CI = 0.08, 0.51); a 1-percentage-point increase of uninsured residents was associated with a decrease of 1.22 in the percentage with COVID-19 vaccination (b = −1.22; 95% CI = -1.57, −0.87); a 1-percentage-point increase of African American residents was associated with an increase of 0.31 in the percentage with COVID-19 vaccination (b = 0.31; 95% CI = 0.19, 0.42); a 1-percentage-point increase of female residents was associated with a decrease of 0.97 in the percentage with COVID-19 vaccination (b = −0.97; 95% CI = -1.79, −0.15); and a 1-percentage-point increase of adult smokers was associated with a decrease of 0.75 in the percentage with COVID-19 vaccination (b = −0.75; 95% CI = -1.26, −0.23).

The percentage of uninsured residents had the largest effect size with 7.1% of the total variation in COVID-19 vaccination rates being explained by this covariate. Overall, this model explained 86.7% of the variation in COVID-19 vaccination rates across Indiana counties.

## County-Level Factors and Influenza Vaccination

The final multiple linear regression model for influenza vaccination rates contained 5 explanatory variables, was obtained by backward selection, and provided an adjusted $R^2$ = 0.702 (Table 2). Similar to the COVID-19 model, the unit of outcome was the percentage. Based on this model, a 1-percentage-point increase of uninsured residents (b = 0.71; 95% CI = 0.22, 1.21) and adults who completed high school (b = 0.54; 95% CI = 0.21, 0.87) was associated with a higher influenza vaccination rate, whereas a 1-percentage-point increase of African American residents (b = −0.07; 95% CI = -0.13, −0.01), Hispanic residents (b = −0.28; 95% CI = -0.40, −0.17), and adults who smoke (b = −0.85; 95% CI = -1.06, −0.64) was associated with a lower influenza vaccination rate.

The percentage of adults who smoke had the largest effect size with 21.6% of the total variation in influenza vaccination rates being explained by this covariate. Overall, this model explained 70.2% of the variation in influenza vaccination rates across Indiana counties. For each vaccination rate, the full model with all candidate variables for model selection is presented in Table B (available as a supplement to the online version of this article at https://ajph.org).

In sum, different county-level factors were associated with COVID-19 vaccination rates and influenza vaccination rates. Greater access to health care (e.g., primary care providers per capita, percentage of uninsured residents, household income, percentage of Medicare enrollees with mammography screening) was associated with COVID-19 vaccination rates, as were the percentage of residents who were African American or female, or who smoked. For influenza vaccination, mostly demographic factors (i.e., percentage Hispanic, percentage African American, percentage who completed high school) had a significant association. The percentages of uninsured residents and African American residents were associated with both but were in opposite directions for each vaccine. Percentage of adults in the county who smoke was the only variable that was significant for each vaccine in the same direction (a higher percentage of smokers was associated with lower vaccination rates).

# DISCUSSION

In this study, we examined county-level factors associated with adult influenza and COVID-19 vaccination rates. While both vaccinations are recommended for adults, adjusted models showed that county-level factors associated with each vaccination varied greatly. Specifically, the reduced model for COVID-19 vaccination explained a slightly higher percentage of the variance (86.7%) than the model for influenza vaccination (70.2%). This may reflect greater polarization surrounding COVID-19 vaccination, leading to a greater influence of sociodemographic factors with COVID-19 vaccination as compared with influenza vaccination. Of note were variables reflecting access to care (e.g., number of primary care providers per capita), which were significant for COVID-19 vaccination rates but not for influenza vaccination rates.

One finding of interest was that the percentage of uninsured residents in the county was associated with each vaccination, but in opposite directions. Higher COVID-19 vaccination rates were associated with a decrease in the percentage of uninsured residents, whereas higher influenza vaccination rates were associated with an increase in uninsured residents, although this effect size was small (0.016). In addition, the number of primary care providers per capita was associated with COVID-19 vaccination rates but was not significant for influenza.

People wishing to obtain the COVID-19 vaccine should have faced fewer barriers than perhaps any other vaccination in recent decades. A combination of federal, state, and local programs including Operation Warp Speed,[30] the American Rescue Plan Act of 2021,[31] and Section 317 of the Public Health Service Act,[32] among others, eliminated copays for the vaccine and ensured it was available at community locations beyond traditional health care provider offices. Therefore, structural barriers for COVID-19 vaccination should have been minimal.

Furthermore, research shows that structural inequities (e.g., health insurance, lack of access to primary care) are associated with influenza vaccination rates.[33] Thus, the findings from this study that structural inequities were associated with COVID-19 vaccination rates, but not influenza vaccination rates, were surprising and point to the need for more research. One possible explanation is the unique way in which the COVID-19 vaccine was rolled out, which involved different dates when people were eligible (based on age, for instance), the need to sign up for vaccination online, and difficulties, particularly early on, in finding available appointments, all of which may have increased logistical barriers.

Another finding of interest was the association between each vaccination and county-level racial/ethnic distribution. The percentage of Hispanic residents in the county was associated with influenza vaccination but not COVID-19 vaccination. Furthermore, the percentage of African American residents in a county was negatively associated with influenza vaccination but positively associated with COVID-19 vaccination.

Similar differences across the 2 types of vaccination were demonstrated in other studies. Adult COVID-19 vaccination rates were not significantly different between non-Hispanic Black, Hispanic, and non-Hispanic White adults at the end of 2021,[34] whereas non-Hispanic White adults had higher influenza vaccination rates than either non-Hispanic Black and Hispanic adults during the same timeframe.[35] One possible explanation for the differing associations for the 2 vaccinations is that there was significant outreach to the Hispanic and Latinx community to promote vaccine equity for COVID-19 vaccination, and similar efforts have not been implemented for influenza vaccination. Specifically, 1 systematic review found that in the 2021 calendar year, there were coordinated efforts to understand the nuances of vaccine hesitancy, access issues, and structural inequities experienced by Latinx communities with regard to the COVID-19 vaccination.[36] Furthermore, disparities in influenza vaccination persist, even among Hispanic adults who report a recent medical checkup, suggesting that missed opportunities for vaccination occurred at these clinic visits.[37]

Lastly, an additional study found racial/ethnic disparities for influenza vaccination among adults aged 50 years and older with lower vaccination rates for Hispanics and non-Hispanic Black adults compared with non-Hispanic White adults.[38] However, there was not a disparity for those aged 18 to 49 years, when controlling for patient characteristics. Given these results, it is possible the differing findings by Hispanic population may be better explained if we controlled for individual patient characteristics. However, this was not possible with our county-level aggregate data, and future research should explore these racial/ethnic disparities while taking individual patient characteristics into account.

We found that smoking was strongly negatively associated with vaccination rates for both COVID-19 and influenza. While this may seem counterintuitive, given that smoking is a risk factor for severe COVID-19 disease,[39] it is consistent with the literature. Research has consistently shown that preventive health behaviors cluster together, and people who engage in one healthy (or unhealthy) behavior, are more likely to engage in another.[40] Likewise, research has shown that people who smoke are less likely to receive routine preventive services, which may reduce the opportunity to get vaccinated.[41] Another study, conducted before the COVID-19 pandemic, showed lower rates of influenza and pneumococcal vaccination among smokers,[42] and the authors highlighted the importance of providers facilitating smoking cessation and promoting vaccinations for people who smoke. As we continue to see hospitalizations and deaths from COVID-19 and seasonal influenza, it is important to raise awareness of the factors associated with severe disease and improve public health messaging to target groups who are disproportionately affected and should be targeted for vaccination efforts.

Finally, while the percentage of the county that was rural was significantly associated with both COVID-19 and influenza vaccination in univariable linear regression analyses, these associations were no longer significant when other variables were included in the model. This is consistent with other recent research that has found no rural–urban differences in influenza vaccination rates using data from the Behavioral Risk Factor Surveillance System.[43]
It is possible that the rural–urban differences were accounted for with other county-level factors, including income

or smoking status. Indeed, another study examining rural–urban differences in COVID-19 vaccination rates found that the differences were explained by a combination of educational attainment, health care infrastructure, and political ideology.[44] Reasons for rural–urban disparities across a multitude of health indicators are multifaceted and are likely a complex combination of access, infrastructure, attitudes, and beliefs.

## Strengths and Limitations

In this study, we examined county-level factors associated with adult influenza and COVID-19 vaccination uptake. While it had numerous strengths, including using a population-based data set and incorporating county-level variables, results should be interpreted in light of several limitations. First, the data are cross-sectional, and a causal relationship between county-level variables and vaccination rates cannot be established. Second, the data are aggregate and are subject to ecological fallacy (i.e., erroneously inferring characteristics to an individual based on characteristics of a group). Third, this cross-sectional study cannot determine the sequence of events between exposure and outcome, which may lead to temporal ambiguity.

Fourth, this study focused only on Indiana, and, therefore, the findings may not be applicable to other states or jurisdictions. Indiana, as a state, has more non-Hispanic White residents and fewer Hispanic or non-Hispanic Black residents than the overall United States.[45] Furthermore, per-capita income tends to be lower, resulting in higher percentages of people living in poverty.[45] Indiana also has a higher percentage of its population living in rural areas[46] and fewer primary care providers.[47] As these factors emerged as having a significant relationship with vaccination rates, our findings may generalize most to other Midwestern states. Additional research is needed to identify how these findings may differ in other regions.

Fifth, influenza and COVID-19 vaccinations have differing numbers of vaccinations to be considered fully vaccinated. While we examined recommended series completion at the time of data collection (1 dose of influenza vaccine and 2 doses of COVID-19 vaccine), it is possible that there are differing barriers to receiving 1 influenza vaccination than there are to completing 2 COVID-19 vaccinations. Lastly, because CHIRP does not track adult influenza vaccination, we used 2 different data sources to examine the 2 vaccination rates. Therefore, it is possible that the 2 data sources differ in their accuracy and reporting. Results of this study should be interpreted with caution, and further studies are needed to understand the complex association between the systems-level factors we examined and vaccination rates.

## Conclusions

In this study, we explored county-level factors associated with rates of vaccination for 2 adult vaccines: COVID-19 and influenza. While both of these vaccines protect against respiratory viruses and are recommended for all adults, the factors associated with uptake of each varied. Variables reflecting access to care (e.g., number of primary care providers per capita, median household income) were significant for COVID-19 vaccination rates but not influenza vaccination rates. In addition, the percentage of uninsured residents in the county was significant for both vaccines, but in opposite directions. The rate was negatively associated with COVID-19 vaccination and positively associated with influenza vaccination. The polarization surrounding COVID-19 vaccination may have led to a greater influence of sociodemographic factors with COVID-19 vaccination as compared with influenza vaccination. Further research, including patient-level data, is needed to better understand these associations and develop effective interventions to address county-level factors and improve vaccine uptake. AJPH

### ABOUT THE AUTHORS

Monica L. Kasting, Alfu Laily, and Laura M. Schwab-Reese are with the Department of Public Health at Purdue University, West Lafayette, IN. Heather N. Burney and Joanne K. Daggy are with the Department of Biostatistics and Health Data Science at the Indiana University School of Medicine, Indianapolis. Katharine J. Head is with the Department of Communication Studies at Indiana University–Purdue University, Indianapolis. Gregory D. Zimet is professor emeritus of Pediatrics and Psychiatry at the Indiana University School of Medicine, Indianapolis.

### CORRESPONDENCE

Correspondence should be sent to Monica L. Kasting, PhD, Department of Public Health, Purdue University, 812 W State St, Suite 223, West Lafayette, IN 47907 (e-mail: mlkastin@purdue.edu). Reprints can be ordered at https://ajph.org by clicking the "Reprints" link.

### PUBLICATION INFORMATION

Full Citation: Kasting ML, Laily A, Burney HN, et al. County-level factors associated with influenza and COVID-19 vaccination in Indiana, 2020–2022. *Am J Public Health.* 2024;114(4):415–423.

Acceptance Date: November 28, 2023.

DOI: https://doi.org/10.2105/AJPH.2023.307553

ORCID iD:
Monica L. Kasting https://orcid.org/0000-0002-9879-7235

### CONTRIBUTORS

M. L Kasting, L. M. Schwab-Reese, K. J. Head, and G. D. Zimet originated the study and designed the analysis. A. Laily collected the data. H. N. Burney and J. K. Daggy performed the analysis. M. L. Kasting drafted the article. All of the authors interpreted the data, critically revised the article, and approved the final version.

## ACKNOWLEDGMENTS

This project was supported in part by a research grant from the Investigator-Initiated Studies Program of Merck Sharp & Dohme Corp. M. L. Kasting was supported by grants KL2TR002530 (B. Tucker Edmonds, principal investigator [PI]) and UL1TR002529 (S. Moe and S. Wiehe, co-PIs) from the National Institutes of Health, National Center for Advancing Translational Sciences, Clinical and Translational Sciences Award.

Findings from this study were presented at the American Public Health Association 2023 Annual Meeting and Expo in Atlanta, GA.

**Note.** The opinions expressed in this article are those of the authors and do not necessarily represent those of Merck Sharp & Dohme Corp. The funding agencies had no role in designing the study, interpreting the data, writing the article, or making the decision to submit the article for publication.

## CONFLICTS OF INTEREST

G. D. Zimet has served as an external advisory board member for Pfizer and Moderna, and as a consultant to Merck. G. D. Zimet, K. J. Head, and M. L. Kasting have received investigator-initiated research funding from Merck administered through Indiana University and Purdue University, respectively.

## HUMAN PARTICIPANT PROTECTION

This study was reviewed by the institutional review board at Purdue University and was determined not to be human participant research.

## REFERENCES

1. World Health Organization. WHO timeline—COVID-19. April 2020. Available at: https://www.who.int/news/item/29-06-2020-covidtimeline. Accessed January 27, 2024.
2. Paul R, Arif AA, Adeyemi O, Ghosh S, Han D. Progression of COVID-19 from urban to rural areas in the United States: a spatiotemporal analysis of prevalence rates. *J Rural Health.* 2020;36(4):591–601. https://doi.org/10.1111/jrh.12486
3. Kasting ML, Head KJ, Hartsock JA, Sturm L, Zimet GD. Public perceptions of the effectiveness of recommended non-pharmaceutical intervention behaviors to mitigate the spread of SARS-CoV-2. *PLoS One.* 2020;15(11):e0241662. https://doi.org/10.1371/journal.pone.0241662
4. Larson HJ, Gakidou E, Murray CJL. The vaccine-hesitant moment. *N Engl J Med.* 2022;387(1):58–65. https://doi.org/10.1056/NEJMra2106441
5. Baldwin AS, Tiro JA, Zimet GD. Broad perspectives in understanding vaccine hesitancy and vaccine confidence: an introduction to the special issue. *J Behav Med.* 2023;46(1-2):1–8. https://doi.org/10.1007/s10865-023-00397-8
6. Zhai Y, Santibanez TA, Kahn KE, Srivastav A, Walker TY, Singleton JA. Rural, urban, and suburban differences in influenza vaccination coverage among children. *Vaccine.* 2020;38(48):7596–7602. https://doi.org/10.1016/j.vaccine.2020.10.030
7. Bennett KJ, Pumkam C, Probst JC. Rural–urban differences in the location of influenza vaccine administration. *Vaccine.* 2011;29(35):5970–5977. https://doi.org/10.1016/j.vaccine.2011.06.038
8. Center for Medicare and Medicaid Services Office of Minority Health. Data snapshot August 2020: Annual influenza vaccination disparities in Medicare beneficiaries. Available at: https://www.cms.gov/files/document/data-snapshot-annual-influenza-vaccination.pdf. Accessed February 8, 2021.
9. McLaughlin JM, Swerdlow DL, Khan F, et al. Disparities in uptake of 13-valent pneumococcal conjugate vaccine among older adults in the United States. *Hum Vaccin Immunother.* 2019;15(4):841–849. https://doi.org/10.1080/21645515.2018.1564434
10. Swiecki-Sikora AL, Henry KA, Kepka D. HPV vaccination coverage among US teens across the rural–urban continuum. *J Rural Health.* 2019;35(4):506–517. https://doi.org/10.1111/jrh.12353
11. Thomas TL, DiClemente R, Snell S. Overcoming the triad of rural health disparities: how local culture, lack of economic opportunity, and geographic location instigate health disparities. *Health Educ J.* 2014;73(3):285–294. https://doi.org/10.1177/0017896912471049
12. Santibanez TA, Nguyen KH, Greby SM, et al. Parental vaccine hesitancy and childhood influenza vaccination. *Pediatrics.* 2020;146(6):e2020007609. https://doi.org/10.1542/peds.2020-007609
13. Khubchandani J, Sharma S, Price JH, Wiblishauser MJ, Sharma M, Webb FJ. COVID-19 vaccination hesitancy in the United States: a rapid national assessment. *J Community Health.* 2021;46(2):270–277. https://doi.org/10.1007/s10900-020-00958-x
14. Purnell TS, Calhoun EA, Golden SH, et al. Achieving health equity: closing the gaps in health care disparities, interventions, and research. *Health Aff (Millwood).* 2016;35(8):1410–1415. https://doi.org/10.1377/hlthaff.2016.0158
15. Brandt HM, Vanderpool RC, Pilar M, Zubizarreta M, Stradtman LR. A narrative review of HPV vaccination interventions in rural US communities. *Prev Med.* 2021;145:106407. https://doi.org/10.1016/j.ypmed.2020.106407
16. Gilkey MB, Dayton AM, Moss JL, et al. Increasing provision of adolescent vaccines in primary care: a randomized controlled trial. *Pediatrics.* 2014;134(2):e346–e353. https://doi.org/10.1542/peds.2013-4257
17. Gilkey MB, Moss JL, Roberts AJ, Dayton AM, Grimshaw AH, Brewer NT. Comparing in-person and webinar delivery of an immunization quality improvement program: a process evaluation of the adolescent AFIX trial. *Implement Sci.* 2014;9(1):21. https://doi.org/10.1186/1748-5908-9-21
18. Dixon BE, Kasting ML, Wilson S, Kulkarni A, Zimet GD, Downs SM. Health care providers' perceptions of use and influence of clinical decision support reminders: qualitative study following a randomized trial to improve HPV vaccination rates. *BMC Medical Inform Decis Mak.* 2017;17(1):119. https://doi.org/10.1186/s12911-017-0521-6
19. Kennedy A, Sapsis KF, Stokley S, Curtis CR, Gust D. Parental attitudes toward human papillomavirus vaccination: evaluation of an educational intervention, 2008. *J Health Commun.* 2011;16(3):300–313. https://doi.org/10.1080/10810730.2010.532296
20. Centers for Disease Control and Prevention. FluVaxView Interactive! Available at: https://www.cdc.gov/flu/fluvaxview/index.htm. Accessed January 17, 2023.
21. County Health Rankings and Roadmaps. About us. Available at: https://www.countyhealthrankings.org/about-us. Accessed February 9, 2021.
22. Indiana Department of Homeland Security. Mobile Integrated Health: Indiana MIH Dashboard. Available at: https://www.in.gov/dhs/ems/mobile-integrated-health/#MIHDash. Accessed October 9, 2023.
23. Drennan IR, Dainty KN, Hoogeveen P, et al. Expanding Paramedicine in the Community (EPIC): study protocol for a randomized controlled trial. *Trials.* 2014;15(1):473. https://doi.org/10.1186/1745-6215-15-473
24. O'Meara P, Ruest M, Stirling C. Community paramedicine: higher education as an enabling factor. *Australasian J Paramedicine.* 2014;11(2):1–9. https://doi.org/10.33151/ajp.11.2.22
25. Rasku T, Kaunonen M, Thyer E, Paavilainen E, Joronen K. The core components of community paramedicine–integrated care in primary care setting: a scoping review. *Scand J Caring Sci.* 2019;33(3):508–521. https://doi.org/10.1111/scs.12659
26. Bigham BL, Kennedy SM, Drennan I, Morrison LJ. Expanding paramedic scope of practice in the community: a systematic review of the literature. *Prehosp Emerg Care.* 2013;17(3):361–372. https://doi.org/10.3109/10903127.2013.792890
27. Chan J, Griffith LE, Costa AP, Leyenaar MS, Agarwal G. Community paramedicine: a systematic review of program descriptions and training. *CJEM.* 2019;21(6):749–761. https://doi.org/10.1017/cem.2019.14
28. Gregg A, Tutek J, Leatherwood MD, et al. Systematic review of community paramedicine and EMS mobile integrated health care interventions in the United States. *Popul Health Manag.* 2019;22(3):213–222. https://doi.org/10.1089/pop.2018.0114
29. Pang PS, Litzau M, Liao M, et al. Limited data to support improved outcomes after community paramedicine intervention: a systematic review. *Am J Emerg Med.* 2019;37(5):960–964. https://doi.org/10.1016/j.ajem.2019.02.036
30. Slaoui M, Hepburn M. Developing safe and effective Covid vaccines—Operation Warp Speed's strategy and approach. *N Engl J Med.* 2020;383(18):1701–1703. https://doi.org/10.1056/NEJMp2027405
31. Library of Congress. H.R.1319 - American Rescue Plan Act of 2021. 2021. Available at: https://www.congress.gov/bill/117th-congress/house-bill/1319/text. Accessed March 9, 2023.
32. National Vaccine Advisory Committee. Protecting the public's health: critical functions of the Section 317 Immunization Program—a report of the National Vaccine Advisory Committee. *Public Health Rep.* 2013;128(2):78–95. https://doi.org/10.1177/003335491312800203
33. Brewer LI, Ommerborn MJ, Nguyen AL, Clark CR. Structural inequities in seasonal influenza vaccination rates. *BMC Public Health.* 2021;21(1):1166. https://doi.org/10.1186/s12889-021-11179-9
34. Kriss JL, Hung MC, Srivastav A, et al. COVID-19 vaccination coverage, by race and ethnicity—National Immunization Survey Adult COVID Module, United States, December 2020–November 2021. *MMWR Morb Mortal Wkly Rep.* 2022;71(23):757–763. https://doi.org/10.15585/mmwr.mm7123a2
35. Centers for Disease Control and Prevention. Flu vaccination coverage, United States, 2021–22

influenza season. 2022. Available at: https://www.cdc.gov/flu/fluvaxview/coverage-2022estimates.htm. Accessed March 9, 2023.

36. Demeke J, Ramos SR, McFadden SM, et al. Strategies that promote equity in COVID-19 vaccine uptake for Latinx communities: a review. *J Racial Ethn Health Disparities.* 2023;10(3):1349–1357. https://doi.org/10.1007/s40615-022-01320-8

37. Black CL, O'Halloran A, Hung MC, et al. Vital signs: Influenza hospitalizations and vaccination coverage by race and ethnicity—United States, 2009–10 through 2021–22 influenza seasons. *MMWR Morb Mortal Wkly Rep.* 2022;71(43):1366–1373. https://doi.org/10.15585/mmwr.mm7143e1

38. Lu D, Qiao Y, Brown NE, Wang J. Racial and ethnic disparities in influenza vaccination among adults with chronic medical conditions vary by age in the United States. *PLoS One.* 2017;12(1):e0169679. https://doi.org/10.1371/journal.pone.0169679

39. Poudel R, Daniels LB, DeFilippis AP, et al. Smoking is associated with increased risk of cardiovascular events, disease severity, and mortality among patients hospitalized for SARS-CoV-2 infections. *PLoS One.* 2022;17(7):e0270763. https://doi.org/10.1371/journal.pone.0270763

40. Fortenberry JD, Costa FM, Jessor R, Donovan JE. Contraceptive behavior and adolescent lifestyles: a structural modeling approach. *J Res Adolesc.* 1997;7(3):307–329. https://doi.org/10.1207/s15327795jra0703_4

41. Vander Weg MW, Howren M, Cai X. Use of routine clinical preventive services among daily smokers, non-daily smokers, former smokers, and never-smokers. *Nicotine Tob Res.* 2012;14(2):123–130. https://doi.org/10.1093/ntr/ntr141

42. Pearson WS, Dube SR, Ford ES, Mokdad AH. Influenza and pneumococcal vaccination rates among smokers: data from the 2006 Behavioral Risk Factor Surveillance System. *Prev Med.* 2009;48(2):180–183. https://doi.org/10.1016/j.ypmed.2008.11.001

43. Alalwan AA. Influenza vaccine utilization: a comparison between urban and rural counties in Florida. *Vaccines (Basel).* 2022;10(5):669. https://doi.org/10.3390/vaccines10050669

44. Sun Y, Monnat SM. Rural-urban and within-rural differences in COVID-19 vaccination rates. *J Rural Health.* 2022;38(4):916–922. https://doi.org/10.1111/jrh.12625

45. US Census Bureau. QuickFacts: United States; Indiana. Available at: https://www.census.gov/quickfacts/fact/table/US,IN/PST045222. Accessed April 24, 2023.

46. Iowa State University. Urban percentage of the population for states, historical. Available at: https://www.icip.iastate.edu/tables/population/urban-pct-states. Accessed April 24, 2023.

47. County Health Rankings & Roadmaps. Explore health rankings: Indiana—primary care physicians. Available at: https://www.countyhealthrankings.org/explore-health-rankings/indiana?year=2023&measure=Primary+Care+Physicians. Accessed April 24, 2023.

# Inequities in Conversion Practice Exposure at the Intersection of Ethnoracial and Gender Identities

*Nguyen K. Tran, PhD, MPH, Elle Lett, PhD, MA, MBiostat, Annesa Flentje, PhD, Shalonda Ingram, Micah E. Lubensky, PhD, Zubin Dastur, MS, MPH, Juno Obedin-Maliver, MD, MPH, MAS, and Mitchell R. Lunn, MD, MAS*

**Objectives.** To examine inequities in conversion practice exposure across intersections of ethnoracial groups and gender identity in the United States.

**Methods.** Data were obtained from The Population Research in Identity and Disparities for Equality Study of sexual and gender minority people from 2019 to 2021 (n = 9274). We considered 3 outcomes: lifetime exposure, age of first exposure, and period between first and last exposure among those exposed to conversion practices. We used log-binomial, Cox proportional hazards, and negative binomial models to examine inequities by ethnoracial groups and gender identity adjusting for confounders. We considered additive interaction.

**Results.** Conversion practice prevalence was highest among minoritized ethnoracial transgender and nonbinary participants (TNB; 8.6%). Compared with White cisgender participants, minoritized ethnoracial TNB participants had twice the prevalence (prevalence ratio = 2.16; 95% confidence interval [CI] = 1.62, 2.86) and risk (hazard ratio = 2.04; 95% CI = 1.51, 2.69) of conversion practice exposure. Furthermore, there was evidence of a positive additive interaction for age of first exposure.

**Conclusions.** Minoritized ethnoracial TNB participants were most likely to recall experiencing conversion practices.

**Public Health Implications.** Policies banning conversion practices may reduce the disproportionate burden experienced by minoritized ethnoracial TNB participants. (*Am J Public Health*. 2024;114(4): 424–434. https://doi.org/10.2105/AJPH.2024.307580)

AJPH April 2024, Vol. 114, No. 4

Conversion practices, also known as part of a broader set of efforts to change sexual orientation and gender identity, refer to organized attempts that seek to suppress or redirect noncisgender gender identity and expression and nonheterosexual sexual attraction.[1,2] These harmful practices—which include religious rituals, speech-based therapy, physical deprivation, aversion therapy, electroconvulsive therapy, and medication-induced emetic responses[3]—are often aimed at sexual and gender minority (SGM) individuals and have been associated with negative mental health outcomes such as distress, depression, and suicidal ideation and attempt.[4–8] While several professional bodies have denounced conversion practices given the evidence of harm,[9] only 22 states and the District of Columbia currently have laws banning conversion practices for minors, and 3 have federal injunctions preventing bans as of October 2023.[10]

Studies suggest that approximately 13% of SGM individuals in the United States have overall experienced conversion practices[4,5,8,11,12] with higher prevalence reported among transgender and nonbinary (TNB) people (4% to 31%) compared to cisgender people (2% to 21%).[5,6,13] Conceptually, conversion practices can be viewed as a manifestation of multiple forms of discrimination—including homophobia, systemic racism, and cissexism—used to uphold cisheteronormativity and White supremacy, socio-structural systems wherein cisgender heterosexual identities and Whiteness are normalized and privileged; this erases and marginalizes SGM individuals and minoritized ethnoracial groups.[1,14–16] However, previous research on conversion practices and their negative outcomes has only considered a single axis of identity, such as gender (e.g., cisgender or TNB people),[4–6] sexual orientation (e.g., sexual minority men),[8,17] or minoritized ethnoracial identity (e.g., Black, Indigenous, Asian, Pacific Islander, Hispanic, or Latina/e/o/x).[4–6] This approach obscures how interlocking systems of oppression and discrimination impact conversion practice exposure for SGM people who live their lives at the intersection of multiple minoritized identities.[18] Therefore, we applied intersectionality[19–21] to inform our research question, study design, and interpretation. We posit that the inequities to conversion practice exposure, timing, and duration experienced by TNB people from minoritized ethnoracial backgrounds will be greater than the reference intersection.

Intersectionality, a Black feminist theoretical framework rooted in social justice movements of the early 19th century and codified in a legal context in the 1980s and 1990s, posits that the experiences of individuals with multiple marginalized identities are differentially shaped by socio-structural systems that interact to provide unearned privilege for some while oppressing others of different social positions.[19–21] In this study, we were interested in 2 such systems, systemic racism and cissexism, that are proxied by self-reported ethnoracial and gender identity in The Population Research in Identity and Disparities for Equality (PRIDE) Study. By accounting for the impact of multiple forms of systemic oppression in this study,[14] we sought to better understand the inequities faced by SGM individuals with multiply marginalized identities, particularly TNB individuals from minoritized ethnoracial backgrounds.

## METHODS

We used data from 3 waves of The PRIDE Study, a longitudinal cohort of SGM adults recruited from 2019 to 2021 in the United States. Previous work has described the methods of (prospective) participant engagement, enrollment, retention, and data acquisition as well as the novel Web-based platform that The PRIDE Study uses.[22,23] The eligibility criteria for The PRIDE Study included being aged 18 years or older, being a resident of the United States or its territories, identifying as a gender or sexual minority person, and being comfortable with reading in English. Eligible participants provided electronic informed consent through an online participant portal. Upon enrollment, participants were invited to complete the lifetime and current annual health and experiences questionnaire, with future invitations to complete any subsequent annual questionnaires. Our analysis was restricted to participants who completed the lifetime and at least 1 annual questionnaire during the study period.

### Ethnoracial Identity

The PRIDE Study participants were able to self-identify their ethnoracial identity by selecting any (or multiple) of the following options: American Indian or Alaska Native; Asian; Black, African American, or African; Hispanic, Latino, or Spanish; Middle Eastern or North African; Native Hawaiian or other Pacific Islander; White; and None of these fully describe me (with a free response option). For participants who completed the free response option, we recoded them as White if they did not endorse any other ethnoracial identity and self-identified as White or of Western European descent (e.g., Irish). Because of the limited sample size within some ethnoracial groups, we collapsed ethnoracial identities into a binary variable that included White and minoritized ethnoracial groups. We use the term "minoritized ethnoracial" to highlight the context in which individuals are made to be minorities in institutions that are structured to uphold White supremacy.[14,16] Therefore, minoritized ethnoracial individuals in this analysis include participants in these ethnoracial groups: American Indian or Alaska Native; Asian; Black, African American, or African; Hispanic, Latino, or Spanish; Middle Eastern or North African; or Native Hawaiian or Pacific Islander, as they are all harmed by systemic racism in the United States.

### Gender Identity and Sex Assigned at Birth

Participants were asked to report their current gender identity with the option to select multiple responses (agender, cisgender man, cisgender woman, genderqueer, man, nonbinary, questioning, transgender man, transgender woman, Two-Spirit, woman, and another gender identity) and sex assigned at birth (female or male). To align with an Indigenous conceptualization of Two-Spirit,[24] participants who exclusively self-identified as White were not included as Two-Spirit for current gender identity in the analysis. However, it is possible that these participants may still originate from Indigenous communities; thus, we presented our results that included all participants that self-identified as

Two-Spirit in Appendix Tables A and B (available as supplements to the online version of this article at https://ajph.org).

We then used a 2-step procedure for coding items on gender identity and sex assigned at birth.[25,26] Cisgender participants were those whose gender identity was concordant with the gender commonly associated with their sex assigned at birth, or if sex assigned at birth was missing, reported their current gender identity as cisgender man or cisgender woman. TNB participants included those whose gender identity was not concordant with the gender commonly associated with their sex assigned at birth or who endorsed any of the following for their current gender identities: agender, genderqueer, nonbinary, questioning, transgender man, transgender woman, Two-Spirit, and another gender identity.

## Outcomes

We assessed lifetime exposure to conversion practices with 2 separate questions: "Have you EVER been in therapy or been part of a program or group intended to change your gender or gender identity to be consistent with the sex assigned to you at birth?" and "Have you EVER been in therapy or been part of a program or group intended to change your sexual orientation to heterosexual/straight?" Participants who answered "yes" to either question received 2 follow-up questions assessing the age of first and last exposure. For this analysis, we created a singular indicator (yes/no) for any lifetime exposure to conversion practices. To assess the age of first exposure, we used the youngest age reported by participants who experienced gender or sexual orientation conversion practice. Lastly, years between first and last exposure were quantified by calculating the difference between the latest age of last exposure and the earliest age of first exposure for gender or sexual orientation conversion practices.

## Covariates

Given that our analysis draws from intersectionality as a conceptual framework, which situates individuals within overlapping socio-structural systems that afford privilege to some people while oppressing others, we considered only the following covariates as potential confounders in our analysis: age (continuous), annual survey completion year (2019, 2020, and 2021), US Census division of residence (East North Central, East South Central, Mid-Atlantic, Mountain, New England, Pacific, South Atlantic, West North Central, West South Central, and unknown), and religious upbringing (yes/no). We did not adjust for socioeconomic position (i.e., education level and individual annual income) because these measures are potentially mediators or descendants of recall history of conversion practices. However, education level and annual income, along with ethnoracial groups, gender identity, and sexual orientation, are included in Table 1 for the purpose of describing the sample. Similar to current gender, participants who exclusively self-reported White were excluded as Two-Spirit for sexual orientation.

## Statistical Analysis

Our analysis drew on McCall's framework for intersectional complexity[27] and used a descriptive intercategorical intersectional approach to evaluate the association between the axes of cissexism and systemic racism (as proxied by gender and ethnoracial identities) on measures of conversion practices. We first defined 4 cross-stratified groups based on ethnoracial identity and current gender identity: minoritized ethnoracial cisgender sexual minority individuals, minoritized ethnoracial TNB individuals of any sexual orientation, White cisgender sexual minority individuals, and White TNB individuals of any sexual orientation. We then summarized key sample characteristics and measures of conversion practices using descriptive statistics for the overall sample and by cross-stratified groups. While these categories were selected to encompass groups that are harmed by the interlocking impact of systemic racism and cissexism and are analogous to other intersectional analyses across ethnoracial and gender groups,[28] we acknowledge that this approach may obscure meaningful within-group differences and conducted a secondary descriptive analysis that further disaggregated the sample by ethnoracial identities for cisgender and TNB participants.

We used log-binomial models to estimate prevalence ratios (PRs) of lifetime exposure recall, Cox proportional hazards models to estimate hazard ratios (HRs) for age of first exposure, and negative binomial models to estimate count ratios for period from first to last exposure among participants who reported conversion practice exposure. All models adjusted for age, survey year, division of residence, and religious upbringing. For each model, we selected White cisgender participants as the reference group to reflect our theoretical understanding of how White supremacy and cissexism confer certain social advantages that may reduce exposure to conversion practices.

In our survival analysis, we used age (in years) as the time scale.

## TABLE 1— Participant Sociodemographic Characteristics, Religious Upbringing, and Experiences With Conversion Practices: United States, 2019 to 2021

| | Total (n = 9274), No. (%), or Mean, Median ± SD | Minoritized Ethnoracial Transgender and Nonbinary (n = 888), No. (%) or Mean, Median ± SD | Minoritized Ethnoracial Cisgender (n = 970), No. (%) or Mean, Median ± SD | White Transgender and Nonbinary (n = 3280), No. (%) or Mean, Median ± SD | White Cisgender (n = 4136), No. (%) or Mean, Median ± SD |
|---|---|---|---|---|---|
| Age | 35.5, 31.0 ± 14.1 | 29.9, 26.3 ± 11.4 | 35.8, 31.2 ± 13.8 | 32.1, 28.6 ± 12.0 | 39.4, 35.0 ± 15.2 |
| Ethnoracial identity[a] | | | | | |
| American Indian or Alaska Native | 312 (3.4) | 184 (20.7) | 128 (13.2) | 0 (0.0) | 0 (0.0) |
| Asian | 484 (5.2) | 228 (25.7) | 256 (26.4) | 0 (0.0) | 0 (0.0) |
| Black, African American, or African | 400 (4.3) | 178 (20.0) | 222 (22.9) | 0 (0.0) | 0 (0.0) |
| Hispanic, Latino, or Spanish | 689 (7.4) | 312 (35.1) | 377 (38.9) | 0 (0.0) | 0 (0.0) |
| Middle Eastern or North African | 137 (1.5) | 78 (8.8) | 59 (6.1) | 0 (0.0) | 0 (0.0) |
| Native Hawaiian or Pacific Islander | 27 (0.3) | 14 (1.6) | 13 (1.3) | 0 (0.0) | 0 (0.0) |
| White | 8333 (89.9) | 498 (56.1) | 427 (44.0) | 3274 (99.8) | 4134 (100.0) |
| Another ethnoracial identity | 134 (1.4) | 47 (5.3) | 31 (3.2) | 37 (1.1) | 19 (0.5) |
| Gender identity[a] | | | | | |
| Agender | 455 (4.9) | 95 (10.7) | 0 (0.0) | 360 (11.0) | 0 (0.0) |
| Cisgender man | 1217 (13.1) | 17 (1.9) | 255 (26.3) | 48 (1.5) | 897 (21.7) |
| Cisgender woman | 2271 (24.5) | 40 (4.5) | 384 (39.6) | 168 (5.1) | 1679 (40.6) |
| Genderqueer | 1259 (13.6) | 228 (25.7) | 0 (0.0) | 1031 (31.4) | 0 (0.0) |
| Man | 2037 (22.0) | 139 (15.7) | 267 (27.5) | 453 (13.8) | 1178 (28.5) |
| Nonbinary | 2054 (22.1) | 462 (52.0) | 0 (0.0) | 1592 (48.5) | 0 (0.0) |
| Questioning | 442 (4.8) | 111 (12.5) | 0 (0.0) | 331 (10.1) | 0 (0.0) |
| Transgender man | 1183 (12.8) | 237 (26.7) | 0 (0.0) | 946 (28.8) | 0 (0.0) |
| Transgender woman | 523 (5.6) | 96 (10.8) | 0 (0.0) | 427 (13.0) | 0 (0.0) |
| Two-Spirit | 49 (0.5) | 49 (5.5) | 0 (0.0) | 0 (0.0) | 0 (0.0) |
| Woman | 2231 (24.1) | 148 (16.7) | 271 (27.9) | 559 (17.0) | 1253 (30.3) |
| Another gender identity | 556 (6.0) | 142 (16.0) | 0 (0.0) | 414 (12.6) | 0 (0.0) |
| Sexual orientation[a] | | | | | |
| Asexual | 955 (10.3) | 151 (17.0) | 59 (6.1) | 547 (16.7) | 198 (4.8) |
| Bisexual | 2826 (30.5) | 304 (34.2) | 294 (30.3) | 1127 (34.4) | 1101 (26.6) |
| Gay | 2985 (32.2) | 162 (18.2) | 419 (43.2) | 552 (16.8) | 1852 (44.8) |
| Lesbian | 2139 (23.1) | 146 (16.4) | 215 (22.2) | 618 (18.8) | 1160 (28.0) |
| Pansexual | 1514 (16.3) | 220 (24.8) | 101 (10.4) | 770 (23.5) | 423 (10.2) |
| Queer | 3682 (39.7) | 452 (50.9) | 248 (25.6) | 1821 (55.5) | 1161 (28.1) |
| Questioning | 273 (2.9) | 55 (6.2) | 14 (1.4) | 148 (4.5) | 56 (1.4) |
| Same-gender loving | 479 (5.2) | 75 (8.4) | 53 (5.5) | 193 (5.9) | 158 (3.8) |
| Straight/heterosexual | 176 (1.9) | 42 (4.7) | 2 (0.2) | 114 (3.5) | 18 (0.4) |
| Two-Spirit | 24 (0.3) | 23 (2.6) | 1 (0.1) | 0 (0.0) | 0 (0.0) |
| Another sexual orientation | 354 (3.8) | 56 (6.3) | 20 (2.1) | 204 (6.2) | 74 (1.8) |
| Education level | | | | | |
| High school or less | 509 (5.5) | 84 (9.5) | 37 (3.8) | 241 (7.3) | 147 (3.6) |
| Some college | 2089 (22.5) | 278 (31.3) | 190 (19.6) | 926 (28.2) | 695 (16.8) |
| 4-y college graduate | 2850 (30.7) | 269 (30.3) | 290 (29.9) | 1040 (31.7) | 1251 (30.2) |

*Continued*

## TABLE 1— Continued

| | Total (n = 9274), No. (%), or Mean, Median ± SD | Minoritized Ethnoracial Transgender and Nonbinary (n = 888), No. (%) or Mean, Median ± SD | Minoritized Ethnoracial Cisgender (n = 970), No. (%) or Mean, Median ± SD | White Transgender and Nonbinary (n = 3280), No. (%) or Mean, Median ± SD | White Cisgender (n = 4136), No. (%) or Mean, Median ± SD |
|---|---|---|---|---|---|
| Advanced degree | 2958 (31.9) | 150 (16.9) | 353 (36.4) | 793 (24.2) | 1662 (40.2) |
| Missing | 868 (9.4) | 107 (12.0) | 100 (10.3) | 280 (8.5) | 381 (9.2) |
| Individual income, $ | | | | | |
| 0–20 000 | 3129 (33.7) | 440 (49.5) | 289 (29.8) | 1426 (43.5) | 974 (23.5) |
| 20 001–50 000 | 2411 (26.0) | 209 (23.5) | 247 (25.5) | 853 (26.0) | 1102 (26.6) |
| 50 001–100 000 | 1871 (20.2) | 99 (11.1) | 216 (22.3) | 511 (15.6) | 1045 (25.3) |
| > 100 000 | 950 (10.2) | 25 (2.8) | 112 (11.5) | 199 (6.1) | 614 (14.8) |
| Missing | 913 (9.8) | 115 (13.0) | 106 (10.9) | 291 (8.9) | 401 (9.7) |
| Survey year | | | | | |
| 2019 | 5341 (57.6) | 419 (47.2) | 530 (54.6) | 1801 (54.9) | 2591 (62.6) |
| 2020 | 2553 (27.5) | 327 (36.8) | 298 (30.7) | 939 (28.6) | 989 (23.9) |
| 2021 | 1380 (14.9) | 142 (16.0) | 142 (14.6) | 540 (16.5) | 556 (13.4) |
| US Census division of residence | | | | | |
| East North Central | 742 (8.0) | 72 (8.1) | 66 (6.8) | 297 (9.1) | 307 (7.4) |
| East South Central | 1106 (11.9) | 102 (11.5) | 123 (12.7) | 399 (12.2) | 482 (11.7) |
| Mid-Atlantic | 1199 (12.9) | 114 (12.8) | 83 (8.6) | 450 (13.7) | 552 (13.3) |
| Mountain | 642 (6.9) | 37 (4.2) | 35 (3.6) | 258 (7.9) | 312 (7.5) |
| New England | 1460 (15.7) | 125 (14.1) | 156 (16.1) | 478 (14.6) | 701 (16.9) |
| Pacific | 302 (3.3) | 22 (2.5) | 14 (1.4) | 126 (3.8) | 140 (3.4) |
| South Atlantic | 657 (7.1) | 79 (8.9) | 84 (8.7) | 212 (6.5) | 282 (6.8) |
| West North Central | 639 (6.9) | 46 (5.2) | 61 (6.3) | 232 (7.1) | 300 (7.3) |
| West South Central | 2194 (23.7) | 241 (27.1) | 310 (32.0) | 703 (21.4) | 940 (22.7) |
| Missing | 333 (3.6) | 50 (5.6) | 38 (3.9) | 125 (3.8) | 120 (2.9) |
| Religious upbringing | 7169 (77.3) | 678 (76.4) | 759 (78.2) | 2429 (74.1) | 3303 (79.9) |
| Lifetime exposure | 533 (5.7) | 76 (8.6) | 44 (4.5) | 207 (6.3) | 206 (5.0) |
| Age of first exposure[b] | 18.4, 16.0 ± 8.2 | 16.8, 16.0 ± 8.2 | 18.3, 16.0 ± 6.4 | 18.5, 16.0 ± 10.0 | 18.9, 17.5 ± 6.4 |
| Age of last exposure[b] | 21.4, 18.0 ± 9.6 | 20.5, 18.0 ± 9.7 | 22.6, 18.0 ± 10.9 | 21.8, 18.0 ± 10.8 | 21.2, 19.0 ± 8.0 |
| Years between first and last exposure[b] | 3.1, 1.0 ± 6.1 | 3.7, 2.0 ± 6.9 | 4.3, 1.0 ± 8.8 | 3.3, 1.0 ± 6.2 | 2.4, 1.0 ± 4.7 |

[a]Participants may select multiple options; thus, the sum of percentages will be greater than 100%.
[b]Among participants who reported lifetime exposure to conversion practices (n = 533).

Cohort entry was defined based on participants' date of birth, while cohort exit was based on the age of the first event (conversion practice) or the age when participants completed their first annual questionnaire (end of observation period). Since the use of age as the time scale adjusts for age, we did not include age as a covariate in the Cox proportional hazard model. Furthermore, the assessment of the proportional hazard assumptions indicated that religious upbringing was not consistent over age (Appendix Table C); therefore, we conducted time-dependent Cox models to account for the dependencies between age and religious upbringing. Specifically, we allowed for the baseline hazard function to differ between 2 age groups (< 24 and ≥ 24 years); this was defined based on an exploratory assessment of Schoenfeld residuals (Appendix Figure A). Additional information regarding model specification is presented in

AJPH April 2024, Vol. 114, No. 4

the "Model Specifications" section of the Appendix.

We evaluated additive interaction for each outcome by using the estimated coefficients to calculate the relative excess risk due to interaction (RERI) that tested whether minoritized ethnoracial TNB experienced a disproportionate increase in risk of conversion practices (i.e., "excess risk").[29] RERI values range from negative to positive infinity, and estimates greater than 0 indicate the presence of a positive additive interaction. We obtained confidence intervals (CIs) for all estimates by bootstrapping more than 1000 resamples. We conducted all analyses in R version 4.2.2,[30] and we fitted the models by using the *stat*, *survival*,[31] and *MASS*[32] packages.

## RESULTS

In this study, we analyzed data from 9310 participants who completed lifetime and annual questionnaires between 2019 and 2021. Participants with missing data on age (n = 2), conversion practice recall (n = 22), gender identity (n = 1), and religious upbringing (n = 4) were excluded. Additionally, 7 participants were excluded who exclusively identified as White and Two-Spirit. This resulted in a final sample of 9274 participants (Table 1). Among the sample, 10.5% (n = 970) were minoritized ethnoracial cisgender, 9.6% (n = 888) were minoritized ethnoracial TNB, 44.5% (n = 4136) were White cisgender, and 35.4% (n = 3280) were White TNB.

Overall, 5.7% (n = 533) of participants recalled lifetime exposure to conversion practices, and 77.3% (n = 7169) reported a religious upbringing. Conversion practices prevalence was highest among minoritized ethnoracial TNB participants (8.6%; n = 76), followed by White TNB (6.3%; n = 207), White cisgender (5.0%; n = 206), and minoritized ethnoracial cisgender (4.5%; n = 44). The mean age of first exposure to conversion practices was 18.4 years (SD = 8.2), and the mean time from first to last episode was 3.1 years (SD = 6.1). Minoritized ethnoracial TNB participants experienced conversion practices at the youngest age (mean = 16.8 years; SD = 8.2), while minoritized ethnoracial cisgender participants experienced conversion practices for the longest period between the first and last exposure (mean = 4.3 years; SD = 8.8).

Among minoritized ethnoracial groups, lifetime recall to conversion practices ranged from 0% to 6.7% for cisgender participants and 5.4% to 19.0% for TNB participants (Table 2). The highest prevalence was among American Indian or Alaska Native TNB participants (19.0%). Multiracial cisgender and Middle Eastern or North African TNB participants were exposed to conversion practices at the youngest age, whereas American Indian or Alaska Native TNB participants had the longest period between their first and last exposure.

Adjusted log-binomial models indicated that minoritized ethnoracial TNB (PR = 2.16; 95% CI = 1.62, 2.86) and White TNB (PR = 1.57; 95% CI = 1.30, 1.92) participants had a higher conversion practice prevalence compared with White cisgender participants (Table 3). However, there was no significant difference between White cisgender and minoritized ethnoracial cisgender participants. Within the gender identity strata, minoritized ethnoracial participants had a higher conversion practice prevalence compared with White participants (PR = 1.38; 95% CI = 1.04, 1.75). Similarly, within the ethnoracial strata, TNB participants had a higher conversion practice prevalence compared with cisgender participants (PR = 2.14; 95% CI = 1.51, 3.19). There was also a positive additive interaction (RERI = 0.58; 95% CI = −0.04, 1.20), indicating that the joint effect of gender and ethnoracial identity is greater than the sum of their individual effects.

Kaplan-Meier curves are depicted in Figure 1, illustrating the unadjusted probability of not recalling exposure to conversion practices across each intersectional group. By age 18 years, the estimated probability was highest for minoritized ethnoracial cisgender (97.2%) and White cisgender (97.1%) individuals, followed by White TNB (95.6%) and minoritized ethnoracial TNB (93.5%) participants (log-rank $P < .001$). Adjusted Cox proportional hazard models indicated significant differences in the age to first exposure to conversion practices across intersectional groups. Both minoritized ethnoracial (HR = 2.04; 95% CI = 1.51, 2.69) and White (HR = 1.48; 95% CI = 1.20, 1.82) TNB participants had increased risk of conversion practices compared with White cisgender participants. There was no significant difference between White cisgender and minoritized ethnoracial cisgender participants. Furthermore, within the gender identity strata, minoritized ethnoracial participants had increased risk of conversion practices compared with White participants (HR = 1.38; 95% CI = 1.04, 1.78). Within the ethnoracial strata, TNB participants had increased risk of conversion practices compared with cisgender participants (HR = 2.13; 95% CI = 1.47, 3.21). Minoritized ethnoracial TNB participants experienced an "excess" increase in risk of conversion practices attributable to the intersection of gender and ethnoracial identity (RERI = 0.60; 95% CI = 0.02, 1.21).

In the adjusted negative binomial model among participants exposed to

**TABLE 2—** Conversion Practice Prevalence, Age of First and Last Exposure, and Time Between First and Last Exposure Among Cisgender and Transgender or Nonbinary Participants From Minoritized Ethnoracial Backgrounds: United States, 2019 to 2021

| | No. | Lifetime Exposure, No. (%) | Age of First Exposure, Mean, Median ± SD[a] | Age of Last Exposure, Mean, Median ± SD[a] | Years Between First and Last Exposure, Mean, Median ± SD[a] |
|---|---|---|---|---|---|
| Cisgender | | | | | |
| American Indian or Alaska Native | 9 | 0 (0.0) | NA | NA | NA |
| Asian, Native Hawaiian, or Pacific Islander | 166 | 3 (1.8) | 20.3, 22.0 ± 5.7 | 21.3, 22.0 ± 4.0 | 1.0, 0 ± 1.7 |
| Black, African American, or African | 142 | 9 (6.3) | 19.6, 18.0 ± 9.5 | 23.2, 21.0 ± 10.2 | 3.7, 2.0 ± 3.9 |
| Hispanic, Latino, or Spanish | 377 | 19 (5.0) | 19.5, 17.5 ± 6.2 | 22.4, 19.0 ± 7.7 | 2.8, 1.0 ± 4.9 |
| Middle Eastern or North African | 15 | 1 (6.7) | NA | NA | NA |
| Multiracial | 261 | 12 (4.6) | 15.3, 15.0 ± 2.7 | 19.5, 16.0 ± 9.5 | 4.2, 1.0 ± 7.6 |
| Transgender and nonbinary | | | | | |
| American Indian or Alaska Native | 21 | 4 (19.0) | 18.8, 13.5 ± 14.5 | 28.8, 24.5 ± 20.6 | 10.0, 9.0 ± 10.7 |
| Asian, Native Hawaiian, or Pacific Islander | 112 | 6 (5.4) | 16.4, 16.0 ± 4.6 | 18.0, 16.0 ± 6.3 | 1.6, 0 ± 2.2 |
| Black, African American, or African | 82 | 7 (8.5) | 18.3, 14.0 ± 9.2 | 20.7, 16.0 ± 8.4 | 2.4, 0 ± 4.4 |
| Hispanic, Latino, or Spanish | 312 | 25 (8.0) | 15.9, 16.0 ± 7.3 | 18.6, 17.0 ± 6.1 | 2.7, 1.5 ± 3.6 |
| Middle Eastern or North African | 16 | 3 (18.8) | 15.5, 15.5 ± 2.1 | 17.5, 17.5 ± 5.0 | 2.0, 2.0 ± 2.8 |
| Multiracial | 345 | 31 (9.0) | 16.7, 16.0 ± 8.9 | 21.0, 18.0 ± 11.3 | 3.9, 2.0 ± 8.1 |

*Notes.* NA = not applicable.
[a]Among participants who reported lifetime exposure to conversion practices (n = 533).

conversion practices, both minoritized ethnoracial TNB (count ratio = 1.92; 95% CI = 1.14, 3.00) and White TNB (count ratio = 1.80; 95% CI = 1.28, 2.46) participants experienced significantly longer periods between first and last exposure to conversion practices. We detected no significant differences between White cisgender and minoritized ethnoracial cisgender participants or within the gender identity or ethnoracial strata. Additionally, there was no evidence of an interaction on the additive scale.

## DISCUSSION

In this analysis of PRIDE participants, we found that minoritized ethnoracial TNB participants, particularly among American Indian or Alaska Native and Middle Eastern or North African participants, reported a disproportionate burden of conversion practice exposure. Specifically, living under systemic racism and cissexism, minoritized ethnoracial TNB participants had the highest conversion practice prevalence, were more likely exposed to conversion practices at a younger age, and experienced conversion practices for longer periods compared with cisgender participants and TNB participants of higher social privilege after adjusting for age, survey year, US Census division of residence, and religious upbringing. In addition, we observed heterogeneity among minoritized ethnoracial groups regarding the age of first exposure and period between first and last exposure, suggesting that gender and ethnoracial identity alone were insufficient to explain the joint disparity in conversion practices.[18,33]

Limited studies have evaluated conversion practice exposure across cross-stratified ethnoracial and gender groups; most have reported conversion practices among ethnoracial groups and gender identity separately.[4–6,8,11] For example, in the Generations study, investigators reported that the prevalence of sexual orientation change efforts among sexual minority participants was about 7% overall, which was 5.8% among White and 8.1% among Black, Latinx, and other ethnoracial groups.[4] In the US Transgender Survey, about 14% of transgender respondents reported being exposed to gender identity change efforts.[6] In our study, we found that 5.7% of PRIDE participants recalled ever experiencing conversion practices. Across cross-stratified ethnoracial and gender groups, we found that conversion

**TABLE 3— Estimated Differences in Lifetime Exposure, Age of First Exposure, and Period of Exposure for Conversion Practices by Ethnoracial Groups and Gender Identity: United States, 2019 to 2021**

| | Cisgender | Transgender and Nonbinary | Gender Identity Within Ethnoracial Strata | RERI (95% CI) |
|---|---|---|---|---|
| | Lifetime Exposure,[a,b] PR (95% CI) | | | |
| Minoritized ethnoracial | 1.01 (0.70, 1.39) | 2.16 (1.62, 2.86) | 2.14 (1.51, 3.19) | 0.58 (−0.04, 1.20) |
| White | 1 (Ref) | 1.57 (1.30, 1.92) | 1.57 (1.30, 1.92) | |
| Ethnoracial groups within gender identity strata | 1.01 (0.70, 1.39) | 1.38 (1.04, 1.75) | | |
| | Age of First Exposure,[b,c] HR (95% CI) | | | |
| Minoritized ethnoracial | 0.96 (0.65, 1.34) | 2.04 (1.51, 2.69) | 2.13 (1.47, 3.21) | 0.60 (0.02, 1.21) |
| White | 1 (Ref) | 1.48 (1.20, 1.82) | 1.48 (1.20, 1.82) | |
| Ethnoracial groups within gender identity strata | 0.96 (0.65, 1.34) | 1.38 (1.04, 1.78) | | |
| | Years Between First and Last Exposure,[a,d] CR (95% CI) | | | |
| Minoritized ethnoracial | 1.60 (0.95, 2.57) | 1.92 (1.14, 3.00) | 1.20 (0.63, 2.19) | −0.48 (−1.84, 0.67) |
| White | 1 (Ref) | 1.80 (1.28, 2.46) | 1.80 (1.28, 2.46) | |
| Ethnoracial groups within gender identity strata | 1.60 (0.95, 2.57) | 1.07 (0.64, 1.65) | | |

*Note.* CI = bootstrap confidence intervals using 1000 resamples; CR = count ratio; HR = hazard ratio; PR = prevalence ratio; RERI = relative excess risk due to interaction.

[a]Models were adjusted for age (continuous), survey year, US Census division of residence, and religious upbringing.

[b]Among all participants (n = 9281).

[c]A step function was used to divide the data into 2 epochs for < 24 y and ≥ 24 y. Additional covariates adjusted in model included survey year, US Census division of residence, and religious upbringing.

[d]Among participants who reported lifetime exposure to conversion practices (n = 533).

practice prevalence ranged between 0% and 19.0%. While these estimates are somewhat comparable to those from a recent systematic review,[12] findings from this study extend the current literature by demonstrating how intersectionality can be used to evaluate the experiences with conversion practice of individuals at the intersection of multiple social identities, which was previously overlooked. These results also emphasize the need for greater attention in future research to how structural inequities such as racism and cissexism create adverse environments and contribute to the social patterning of conversion practice exposure and its harmful health consequences.[4–6,8,11,34]

A key finding is that The PRIDE Study participants first recalled exposure to conversion practice at a mean age of 18 years, which is younger than previously reported.[34] The results further highlighted that minoritized ethnoracial TNB participants also reported the earliest age of initial exposure to conversion practice, and that there was a significant excess risk because of the intersection of racialized and gendered experiences. Further disaggregation by ethnoracial identity among cisgender and TNB participants suggested that the mean age of first exposure was 15.3 and 15.5 for multiracial cisgender and Middle Eastern or North African TNB participants, respectively, while American Indian or Alaska Native TNB participants experienced the longest average period between the age of first and last exposure. The younger age of exposure and longer duration could negatively impact the mental health and well-being of SGM participants, as conversion practice has been associated with suicidality across different age groups.[4–8,11] In addition, these findings suggest that researchers should consider the contemporary and cumulative exposure to conversion practices to fully understand the life course and cumulative disadvantage associated with exposure to conversion practices.

## Study Limitations

The results should be interpreted with consideration of several limitations. First, self-reported ethnoracial and gender identity may not fully encompass the extent of systemic racism and cissexism experienced by minoritized ethnoracial TNB participants. Second, White cisgender participants were selected as the reference group to be consistent with the theory of intersectionality; however, alternative approaches such as intersectional multilevel analysis of individual

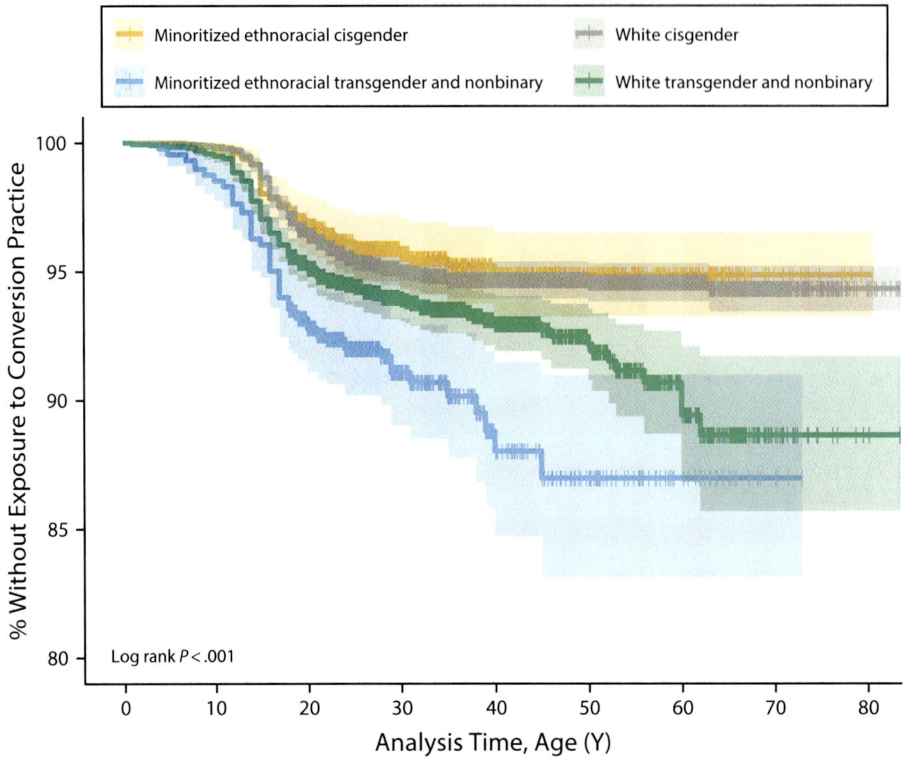


| No. at Risk for First Exposure | | | | | | | | | |
|---|---|---|---|---|---|---|---|---|---|
| Minoritized ethnoracial cisgender | 970 | 969 | 886 | 503 | 271 | 157 | 74 | 15 | 1 |
| Minoritizedx ethnoracial transgender and nonbinary | 888 | 877 | 732 | 270 | 117 | 64 | 25 | 4 | 0 |
| White cisgender | 4136 | 4131 | 3851 | 2547 | 1548 | 1011 | 515 | 144 | 14 |
| White transgender and nonbinary | 3280 | 3266 | 2855 | 1355 | 553 | 292 | 137 | 25 | 2 |

**FIGURE 1— Kaplan-Meier Curve of Age at First Exposure to Conversion Practices by Ethnoracial Groups and Gender Identity: United States, 2019 to 2021**

heterogeneity have been shown to be statistically efficient with smaller samples and do not require the selection of a reference group.[35] Third, our outcomes were broadly defined and did not differentiate between the various forms of conversion practices, including the involvement of mental health professionals and religious leaders. Relatedly, questions on frequency of conversion practice exposure were not available; thus, we could not evaluate the actual duration of conversion practices over the observation period. Fourth, the lifetime survey did not capture the age at which participants first disclosed their gender identity or sexual orientation. Younger disclosure ages may increase the duration that participants are vulnerable to experiencing conversion efforts. Fifth, we lacked additional information regarding social and cultural context of participants who identified exclusively as White and Two-Spirit; thus, we presented both sets of results. Furthermore, our analysis primarily focuses on Two-Spirit as a gender identity, which may not accurately reflect the multidimensionality and spiritual traditions of Two-Spirit identity. Last, The PRIDE Study is a convenience sample of predominately White participants that relies on self-reported data and, therefore, may be subject to sampling, recall, and social desirability bias.

## Public Health Implications

The United States has witnessed a rise in proposed and enacted antitransgender and anti-SGM legislation. This includes federal injunctions that prevent enforcement of conversion therapy bans and the absence of laws prohibiting conversion practices in 22 states.[10] Against this socio-political backdrop, our findings suggest that

TNB individuals, especially those from minoritized ethnoracial backgrounds, are more likely to experience prolonged exposure to conversion practices that occur at younger ages. This can exacerbate health disparities for individuals who face multiple forms of marginalization. Therefore, clinicians, researchers, and advocates should consider how conversion practice exposure and age of first exposure relates directly to health outcomes and differences in associations within and between intersectional groups. Finally, given the harmful effects and unethical premise of conversion practices, federal and local policies banning these practices can contribute to reducing the negative consequences of conversion practices in an equitable manner. AJPH

## ABOUT THE AUTHORS

Nguyen K. Tran, Annesa Flentje, Micah E. Lubensky, Zubin Dastur, Juno Obedin-Maliver, and Mitchell R. Lunn are with The PRIDE Study/PRIDEnet, Stanford University School of Medicine, Palo Alto, CA. Elle Lett is with the Health Systems and Population Health and the Center for Anti-Racism and Community Health, University of Washington School of Public Health, Seattle. Shalonda Ingram is with the Born Brown Institute, Washington, DC.

## CORRESPONDENCE

Correspondence should be sent to Mitchell R. Lunn, MD, MAS, Stanford University School of Medicine, 3810 Porter Dr, Ste B214, Palo Alto, CA 94304 (e-mail: lunn@stanford.edu). Reprints can be ordered at https://ajph.org by clicking the "Reprints" link.

## PUBLICATION INFORMATION

Full Citation: Tran NK, Lett E, Flentje A, et al. Inequities in conversion practice exposure at the intersection of ethnoracial and gender identities. *Am J Public Health*. 2024;114(4):424–434.

Acceptance Date: January 3, 2024.

DOI: https://doi.org/10.2105/AJPH.2024.307580

ORCID iD:

Mitchell R. Lunn https://orcid.org/0000-0002-0068-0814

## CONTRIBUTORS

N. K. Tran and E. Lett designed the study and analytic strategy. N. K. Tran completed the statistical analyses and wrote the initial draft of the article. A. Flentje, J. Obedin-Maliver, and M. R. Lunn obtained funding. S. Ingram provided community-based perspectives. M. E. Lubensky, and Z. Dastur were responsible for study operation, including participant experience and participant questions. All authors helped to interpret the findings, provided critical revisions and edits to the article, and read and approved the final version of the article.

## ACKNOWLEDGMENTS

This study was partially supported by the Gill Foundation.

The Population Research in Identity and Disparities for Equality (PRIDE) Study is a community-engaged research project that serves and is made possible by lesbian, gay, bisexual, transgender, queer, intersex, aromantic, asexual, and other sexual or gender minority community involvement at multiple points in the research process, including the dissemination of findings. We acknowledge the courage and dedication of The PRIDE Study participants for sharing their stories, the careful attention of the PRIDEnet Participant Advisory Committee members for reviewing and improving every study application, and the enthusiastic engagement of the PRIDEnet Ambassadors and Community Partners for bringing thoughtful perspectives and promoting enrollment and disseminating findings. For more information, visit https://pridestudy.org/pridenet.

**Note.** The funders had no role in the design and conduct of the study; collection, management, analysis, and interpretation of the data; preparation, review, or approval of the article; and decision to submit the article for publication.

## CONFLICTS OF INTEREST

J. Obedin-Maliver has consulted for Hims Inc (2019–present), Folx Inc (2020–present), and Ibis Reproductive Health (2017–present). M. R. Lunn has consulted for Hims Inc (2019–present), Folx Inc (2020), and Otsuka Pharmaceutical Development and Commercialization Inc (2023).

## HUMAN PARTICIPANT PROTECTION

The study was approved by the University of California San Francisco, Stanford University, and WIRB-Copernicus Group institutional review board, and now the WIRB-Copernicus Group institutional review board for ongoing analyses.

## REFERENCES

1. Kinitz DJ, Goodyear T, Dromer E, et al. "Conversion therapy" experiences in their social contexts: a qualitative study of sexual orientation and gender identity and expression change efforts in Canada. *Can J Psychiatry*. 2022;67(6):441–451. https://doi.org/10.1177/07067437211030498
2. Ashley F. *Banning Transgender Conversion Practices: A Legal and Policy Analysis*. Vancouver, BC: University of British Columbia Press; 2022. https://doi.org/10.59962/9780774866941
3. Hein LC, Matthews AK. Reparative therapy: the adolescent, the psych nurse, and the issues. *J Child Adolesc Psychiatr Nurs*. 2010;23(1):29–35. https://doi.org/10.1111/j.1744-6171.2009.00214.x
4. Blosnich JR, Henderson ER, Coulter RWS, Goldbach JT, Meyer IH. Sexual orientation change efforts, adverse childhood experiences, and suicide ideation and attempt among sexual minority adults, United States, 2016–2018. *Am J Public Health*. 2020;110(7):e1–e7. https://doi.org/10.2105/AJPH.2020.305637
5. Green AE, Price-Feeney M, Dorison SH, Pick CJ. Self-reported conversion efforts and suicidality among US LGBTQ youths and young adults, 2018. *Am J Public Health*. 2020;110(8):1221–1227. https://doi.org/10.2105/AJPH.2020.305701
6. Turban JL, Beckwith N, Reisner SL, Keuroghlian AS. Association between recalled exposure to gender identity conversion efforts and psychological distress and suicide attempts among transgender adults. *JAMA Psychiatry*. 2020;77(1):68–76. https://doi.org/10.1001/jamapsychiatry.2019.2285
7. Flentje A, Heck NC, Cochran BN. Sexual reorientation therapy interventions: perspectives of ex-ex-gay individuals. *J Gay Lesbian Ment Health*. 2013;17(3):256–277. https://doi.org/10.1080/19359705.2013.773268
8. Meanley S, Haberlen SA, Okafor CN, et al. Lifetime exposure to conversion therapy and psychosocial health among midlife and older adult men who have sex with men. *Gerontologist*. 2020;60(7):1291–1302. https://doi.org/10.1093/geront/gnaa069
9. The United States Joint Statement. United States joint statement against conversion efforts. August 23, 2023. Available at: https://usjs.org/usjs-final-version. Accessed September 18, 2023.
10. Movement Advancement Project. Equality maps: conversion "therapy" laws. Available at: https://www.lgbtmap.org/equality-maps/conversion_therapy. Accessed August 14, 2023.
11. Higbee M, Wright ER, Roemerman RM. Conversion therapy in the Southern United States: prevalence and experiences of the survivors. *J Homosex*. 2022;69(4):612–631. https://doi.org/10.1080/00918369.2020.1840213
12. Salway T, Kinitz DJ, Kia H, et al. A systematic review of the prevalence of lifetime experience with 'conversion' practices among sexual and gender minority populations. *PLoS One*. 2023;18(10):e0291768. https://doi.org/10.1371/journal.pone.0291768
13. The Trevor Project. 2022 National Survey on LGBTQ Youth Mental Health. Available at: https://www.thetrevorproject.org/survey-2022. Accessed October 7, 2022.
14. Lett E, Asabor E, Beltrán S, Cannon AM, Arah OA. Conceptualizing, contextualizing, and operationalizing race in quantitative health sciences research. *Ann Fam Med*. 2022;20(2):157–163. https://doi.org/10.1370/afm.2792
15. Wesp LM, Malcoe LH, Elliott A, Poteat T. Intersectionality research for transgender health justice: a theory-driven conceptual framework for structural analysis of transgender health inequities. *Transgend Health*. 2019;4(1):287–296. https://doi.org/10.1089/trgh.2019.0039
16. Harris CI. Whiteness as property. *Harv Law Rev*. 1993;106(8):1707–1791. https://doi.org/10.2307/1341787
17. Salway T, Juwono S, Klassen B, et al. Experiences with sexual orientation and gender identity conversion therapy practices among sexual minority men in Canada, 2019–2020. *PLoS One*. 2021;

16(6):e0252539. https://doi.org/10.1371/journal.pone.0252539

18. Hancock AM. When multiplication doesn't equal quick addition: examining intersectionality as a research paradigm. *Perspect Polit.* 2007;5(1):63–79. https://doi.org/10.1017/S1537592707070065
19. Crenshaw K. Demarginalizing the intersection of race and sex: a Black feminist critique of antidiscrimination doctrine, feminist theory and antiracist politics. *Univ Chic Leg Forum.* 1989;1989(1):139–167. Available at: http://chicagounbound.uchicago.edu/uclf/vol1989/iss1/8. Accessed February 27, 2024.
20. Crenshaw K. Mapping the margins: intersectionality, identity politics, and violence against women of color. *Stanford Law Rev.* 1991;43(6):1241–1299. https://doi.org/10.2307/1229039
21. Collins PH. *Intersectionality as Critical Social Theory.* Durham, NC: Duke University Press; 2019.
22. Lunn MR, Lubensky M, Hunt C, et al. A digital health research platform for community engagement, recruitment, and retention of sexual and gender minority adults in a national longitudinal cohort study—The PRIDE Study. *J Am Med Inform Assoc.* 2019;26(8-9):737–748. https://doi.org/10.1093/jamia/ocz082
23. Lunn MR, Capriotti MR, Flentje A, et al. Using mobile technology to engage sexual and gender minorities in clinical research. *PLoS One.* 2019;14(5):e0216282. https://doi.org/10.1371/journal.pone.0216282
24. Morgensen SL. Conversations on Berdache: anthropology, counterculturism, Two-Spirit organizing. In: Morgensen SL, ed. *Spaces Between Us: Queer Settler Colonialism and Indigenous Decolonization.* Minneapolis, MN: University of Minnesota Press; 2011. https://doi.org/10.5749/minnesota/9780816656325.003.0003
25. Bauer GR, Braimoh J, Scheim AI, Dharma C. Transgender-inclusive measures of sex/gender for population surveys: mixed-methods evaluation and recommendations. *PLoS One.* 2017;12(5):e0178043. https://doi.org/10.1371/journal.pone.0178043
26. Tate CC, Ledbetter JN, Youssef CP. A two-question method for assessing gender categories in the social and medical sciences. *J Sex Res.* 2013;50(8):767–776. https://doi.org/10.1080/00224499.2012.690110
27. McCall L. The complexity of intersectionality. *Signs (Chic Ill).* 2005;30(3):1771–1800. https://doi.org/10.1086/426800
28. Cicero EC, Lett E, Flatt JD, Perusi Benson G, Epps F. Transgender adults from minoritized ethnoracial groups in the US report greater subjective cognitive decline. *J Gerontol B Psychol Sci Soc Sci.* 2023;78(6):1051–1059. https://doi.org/10.1093/geronb/gbad012
29. Knol MJ, VanderWeele TJ, Groenwold RHH, Klungel OH, Rovers MM, Grobbee DE. Estimating measures of interaction on an additive scale for preventive exposures. *Eur J Epidemiol.* 2011;26(6):433–438. https://doi.org/10.1007/s10654-011-9554-9
30. R Core Team. R: A language and environment for statistical computing. Vienna, Austria: R Foundation for Statistical Computing; 2023.
31. Therneau TM. A package for survival analysis in R, version 3.5.5. 2023. Available at: https://CRAN.R-project.org/package=survival. Accessed April 20, 2023.
32. Venables WN, Ripley BD. *Modern Applied Statistics With S.* 4th ed. New York, NY: Springer; 2002.
33. Bauer GR. Incorporating intersectionality theory into population health research methodology: challenges and the potential to advance health equity. *Soc Sci Med.* 2014;110:10–17. https://doi.org/10.1016/j.socscimed.2014.03.022
34. Forsythe A, Pick C, Tremblay G, Malaviya S, Green A, Sandman K. Humanistic and economic burden of conversion therapy among LGBTQ youths in the United States. *JAMA Pediatr.* 2022;176(5):493–501. https://doi.org/10.1001/jamapediatrics.2022.0042
35. Evans CR, Williams DR, Onnela JP, Subramanian SV. A multilevel approach to modeling health inequalities at the intersection of multiple social identities. *Soc Sci Med.* 2018;203:64–73. https://doi.org/10.1016/j.socscimed.2017.11.011

# Funding and Delivery of Syringe Services Programs in the United States, 2022

Shelley N. Facente, PhD, MPH, Jamie L. Humphrey, PhD, MPH, Christopher Akiba, PhD, MPH, Sheila V. Patel, PhD, Lynn D. Wenger, MPH, MSW, Hansel Tookes, MD, MPH, Ricky N. Bluthenthal, PhD, Paul LaKosky, PhD, Stephanie Prohaska, Terry Morris, Alex H. Kral, PhD, and Barrot H. Lambdin, PhD, MPH

**Objectives.** To describe the current financial health of syringe services programs (SSPs) in the United States and to assess the predictors of SSP budget levels and associations with delivery of public health interventions.

**Methods.** We surveyed all known SSPs operating in the United States from February to June 2022 (n = 456), of which 68% responded (n = 311). We used general estimating equations to assess factors influencing SSP budget size and estimated the effects of budget size on multiple measures of SSP services.

**Results.** The median SSP annual budget was $100 000 (interquartile range = $20 159–$290 000). SSPs operating in urban counties and counties with higher levels of opioid overdose mortality had significantly higher budget levels, while SSPs located in counties with higher levels of Republican voting in 2020 had significantly lower budget levels. SSP budget levels were significantly and positively associated with syringe and naloxone distribution coverage.

**Conclusions.** Current SSP funding levels do not meet minimum benchmarks. Increased funding would help SSPs meet community health needs.

**Public Health Implications.** Federal, state, and local initiatives should prioritize sustained SSP funding to optimize their potential in addressing multiple public health crises. (*Am J Public Health*. 2024;114(4): 435–443. https://doi.org/10.2105/AJPH.2024.307583)

Over the past decade, morbidity and mortality among people who inject drugs (PWID) has steadily increased throughout the United States. A total of 106 699 unintentional drug overdose deaths occurred in the United States in 2021,[1] with a 30% increase from 2019 to 2020[2] and another 14% increase from 2020 to 2021.[1] Viral infections such as HIV and hepatitis C[3] as well as skin and soft tissue infections[4] remain prevalent among PWID. Syringe services programs (SSPs) are an evidence-based, low-threshold public health intervention designed to reduce the risk of infections and fatal overdose for PWID, if supported adequately.[5]

SSPs were first implemented in the 1980s as a direct response to spread of viral hepatitis and HIV among PWID and, over time, have become recognized as one of the most cost-effective HIV prevention interventions.[6] Over the years, many US-based SSPs have broadened their delivery to include provision of equipment for safer snorting or smoking of drugs, naloxone kits and training to identify and reverse opioid overdoses, drug checking services, wound care, and education on safer drug use and infection prevention. Many SSPs also provide basic medical care, infectious disease screening and treatment, and linkage to psychosocial care and support for basic needs such as food and housing. SSPs are the most common place for PWID to seek substance use disorder treatment or basic medical care.[7,8] During the COVID-19 pandemic, the US federal government loosened regulations to

AJPH April 2024, Vol. 114, No. 4

allow buprenorphine treatment inductions via telehealth, which many SSPs implemented.[9]

SSPs provide services at no cost to their participants and are not-for-profit entities. As such, SSPs require funding from individual donations, foundations, or governmental agencies to operate; many are set up as mutual aid collaboratives, and many are volunteer-based before formally receiving funding. When first implemented in the United States, SSPs were often illegal and depended solely on private funding.[10] Some local health departments started funding SSPs in the 1990s as they gained legal status, and some state health departments started funding SSPs in the late 1990s.[11] US federal funding for SSPs was not available until the past decade, has been limited, and until the 2020s has included many restrictions.[12]

In 2018, even before the COVID-19 pandemic led to costly supply chain disruptions and severe staffing challenges, Teshale et al. at the Centers for Disease Control and Prevention (CDC) estimated the minimum costs of running a comprehensive SSP.[13] They did this accounting for costs of personnel (including a program director, part-time accountant, peer navigators, part-time nurse, and counselors), operational costs (i.e., lease or rent, insurance, utilities, mail, and janitorial), prevention services (i.e., syringes, injection equipment, naloxone, sharps containers, and hazardous waste management), onsite medical or testing services (i.e., point-of care testing for HIV and hepatitis C, hepatitis A and B vaccination, wound care, and pregnancy tests), and a mobile van unit to serve people who cannot or will not come to a fixed site (i.e., van leasing, maintenance, registration, gas, storage, and insurance). The estimated costs for running a comprehensive SSP ranged from US $400 000 for a small rural SSP (serving 250 clients) to US $1.8 million for a large urban SSP (serving 2500 clients).

Because governmental funding of SSPs has been sparse and varies greatly by geography, broader development of SSP organizational structures and staff is often not properly optimized. In turn, the public health benefits that SSPs can confer are geographically disparate, fluctuate over time, and do not typically deliver the full continuum of services that can improve the health and well-being of PWID.[14]

After decades of SSPs operating underground because of prohibitive laws and lack of public support, since 2020, the US government has officially supported SSPs as a critical public health intervention.[5] In December 2021, the Substance Abuse and Mental Health Services Administration announced it would provide $30 million in grant awards to harm reduction programs through the American Rescue Plan,[15] and, in 2022, the Biden administration awarded another $1.5 billion in funding for states and territories to address the opioid epidemic.[16] These shifts have made it increasingly more common for state and local governments to provide funding for SSPs in their jurisdictions. Most of the states that fund SSPs have Democratic legislatures. Among states with Republican legislatures, existing laws often prevent operation of SSPs.[17]

To better understand the current funding environment of SSPs in the United States, we analyzed data from the 2022 National Survey of Syringe Services Programs (NSSSP) to (1) describe current funding levels, (2) assess the factors related to annual SSP budgets, and (3) understand how funding levels are associated with the amount and types of public health interventions that SSPs provide.

## METHODS

As part of a larger effort supported by Arnold Ventures to understand the impact of state-level policy initiatives on service delivery from SSPs, RTI International conducted a study of all known SSPs operating in the United States from February to July 2022, which included an online, cross-sectional survey about the services the organization provided in 2021. The survey was administered using the Voxco platform (Voxco, Montreal, Canada). Referred to as the NSSSP, this survey has been repeated annually since 2019, following consistent procedures previously described.[18]

To recruit SSPs to participate, the North American Syringe Exchange Network (NASEN) emailed SSP contacts from a database of SSPs operating in the United States, continuously maintained for the last 30 years. To build this SSP database, we proactively contacted, searched, and followed up with SSPs from a variety of different sources, including NASEN's online directory, NASEN's Buyers Club, state and county public health department Web sites, social media platforms, regional and national networks of SSPs, webinars, and conferences. SSP organizational directors were e-mailed up to 3 times asking them to participate, and for those who did not respond, we conducted additional follow-up with individual programs via e-mail, phone calls, or both. SSPs were offered a $75 honorarium if they completed the survey. Our target population was the total number of known SSPs at the time of the 2022 NSSSP (n = 456), of which 311 (68%) completed our survey.

## Measures

The NSSSP included questions about distribution of syringes, naloxone, fentanyl test strips, and buprenorphine treatment initiation, as well as other organizational characteristics, including annual budgets, funding sources, and organizational types. We identified 2 types of dependent variables. First was the SSP's 2021 annual budget, treated as a continuous variable with budgets rounded to the nearest US dollar. Each SSP's annual budget was ascertained with the following question: "What was your syringe services program's annual budget last fiscal or calendar year? (Please estimate if records are not easily available.)" No specific instructions were provided regarding the inclusion or exclusion of in-kind costs. We also asked SSPs "What were your syringe services program's sources of funding for the last fiscal or calendar year?" and SSPs could select funded or not from a list of different funding sources.

For a separate set of analyses, we examined dependent variables from a series of questions about the (1) quantity of equipment or services provided in 2021, including the number of syringes distributed, the number of participant contacts for syringe distribution, the number of naloxone doses distributed, and the number of participant contacts for naloxone distribution, and (2) whether the program offered fentanyl test strips or buprenorphine to their participants, either in person or via telehealth.

For independent variables, we classified SSPs as being operated by a city, county, or state department of public health (DPH-SSP) or as their own community-based organization (CBO-SSP), defined as a standalone community-based, nonprofit organization with or without a fiscal sponsor or a program within a larger community-based, nonprofit organization. Some CBO-SSPs received partial funding from public health departments but were still considered CBO-SSPs if they were independently managed and operated.

We also constructed a 3-tier, county-level measure of urbanicity from the National Center for Health Statistics (NCHS) Urban-Rural Classification Scheme, following guidance from the Pew Research Center.[19] Urban counties are located in 53 metropolitan areas with at least a million people. In the NCHS classification system, they are called "large central metro" counties, where about 31% of Americans live. Suburban and smaller metropolitan counties, where about half of Americans (55%) live, include those outside the core cities of the largest metro areas, as well as the entirety of other metropolitan areas. This group includes "large fringe metro," "medium metro," and "small metro" counties in the NCHS classification system. Rural counties are located in nonmetropolitan areas. With a median population size of 16 535, only 14% of Americans live in rural counties.[19]

Next, we assessed opioid overdose mortality rates per 100 000 population as a standardized continuous measure with a mean = 0 and standard deviation = 1. We used opioid mortality rates from 2020,[20] the year before NSSSP data, as a proxy for the level of need in the community at the time funding was allocated in 2021. We obtained these data through the National Vital Statistics System, following details described previously.[21]

Finally, county-level data on percentage that voted for the Republican presidential candidate in the 2020 presidential election was obtained from the Massachusetts Institute of Technology Election Data and Science Lab County Presidential Election Return 2000–2020[22] and represented as a continuous variable.

## Data Analysis

We first summarized the data with descriptive statistics, with missing responses handled using listwise deletion. We then assessed how the annual budget of SSPs compared with minimum benchmarks established by Teshale et al. for small SSPs of 250 clients per year, as this was the most conservative (lowest-cost) benchmark against which to compare.[13] We omitted the start-up costs used by Teshale et al. to compare annual operating costs of SSPs that completed the NSSSP with budget benchmarks for annual operating costs of small SSPs. In addition, we ranked SSP funding sources from most common to least common. To better understand the characteristics associated with SSP budget size, we then used generalized estimating equations with SSPs nested within counties, and an exchangeable correlation structure.[23] The outcome variable was SSP annual budget in 2021. Independent variables were the smoothed opioid-related mortality rate per 100 000 population for that SSP's county in 2020, urbanicity, SSP type, and the percentage of voters who voted Republican in the 2020 election.

We then examined the effect of SSP annual budget (scaled per $100 000), smoothed opioid-related mortality in 2020, urbanicity, SSP type, percentage of voters who voted Republican in the 2020 election, and population obtained from the American Community Survey 5-year estimates (2016–2020, scaled to 100 000)[24] on the number of participant encounters where syringes were distributed, number of syringes distributed, number of participant encounters where naloxone was distributed, and number of naloxone doses distributed, all scaled per 1000, using a negative binomial generalized estimating equation with SSPs nested within counties and an exchangeable correlation structure. We then used a logit generalized estimating equation in a similar way to look at the effect of the same independent variables on whether the SSP offered fentanyl test strips or offered buprenorphine either in person or via telehealth. We conducted sensitivity analyses to assess the impact of nesting SSPs within states rather than counties; we observed no substantive differences.

In the regression analyses, we considered all variables with $P < .05$ statistically significant. We conducted data preparation and analyses in SAS Enterprise Guide version 7.15 (SAS Institute Inc, Cary, NC).



## RESULTS

The median SSP annual budget was $100 000 (interquartile range [IQR] = $20 159–$290 000). One hundred thirteen responding organizations (36.3%) were DPH-SSPs, either local or state, and 198 (63.7%) were CBO-SSPs (Table 1). The median budget for DPH-SSPs was $50 000 (IQR = $9336–$150 000) and for CBO-SSPs was $149 000 (IQR = $42 000–$359 890). Data were missing for key variables (annual budget, % voted Republican in the 2020 presidential election) for 32 SSPs, creating an analytic sample of n = 279 SSPs. Sensitivity analyses found that variables in Table 1 were not meaningfully different between the full (n = 311) and analytic sample (n = 279).

**TABLE 1— Descriptive Characteristics of the 2022 National Survey of Syringe Services Programs: United States**

| Characteristic | No. (%) or Median (IQR) |
|---|---|
| Urbanicity | |
| Rural | 74 (24) |
| Suburban | 154 (50) |
| Urban | 81 (26) |
| Syringe services program (SSP) type | |
| Department of public health run | 113 (36) |
| Community-based organization run | 198 (64) |
| Supplemental services offered at SSP | |
| Fentanyl test strips | 201 (65) |
| Buprenorphine | 107 (34) |
| Annual budget, $ | 100 000 (24 000–296 583) |
| No. of syringe contacts | 1 432 (306–5 000) |
| No. of syringes distributed | 125 000 (32 741–457 963) |
| No. of naloxone contacts | 500 (150–1 873) |
| No. of naloxone kits distributed | 1 500 (396–4 585) |
| Opioid-related mortality (per 100 000 population; smoothed), 2020 | 21 (13–32) |
| % of voters in the SSP catchment area who voted Republican during the presidential election, 2020 | 40 (25–51) |

*Note.* IQR = interquartile range; SSP = syringe services program. The sample size was n = 311.

We observed the following ranking of most-to-least-common funding sources: state health department (63%); fundraising or donations from individuals (42%); private foundations (29%); city or county health department (25%); other sources, including national networks and coalitions (20%); out of pocket, including staff donations (19%); and federal government (11%). Funding levels for SSPs also varied by urbanicity, yet most SSPs operating in rural, suburban, and urban environments had an annual budget that met 5%, 23%, and 46%, respectively, of the minimum benchmarks established by Teshale et al. for a small-scale program[13] (Figure 1).

SSPs operating in areas with higher levels of opioid-related overdose mortality in the previous year had higher budget levels (adjusted mean difference [AMD] = $77 949; 95% confidence interval [CI] = $7216, $146 681; Table 2). SSPs in urban environments also reported significantly higher budget levels compared with SSPs operating in rural environments (AMD = $241 965; 95% CI = $89 664, $394 265). SSPs operating in suburban environments had similar budget levels to those operating in rural environments. SSPs operating in counties with a higher percentage of voters who voted Republican in the 2020 presidential election reported significantly smaller SSP budget levels (AMD = –$80 890; 95% CI = –$153 821, $7958). While, on average, CBO-SSPs had higher budget levels than DPH-SSPs, these differences were not statistically significant.

When adjusting for the opioid-related mortality rate per 100 000 population in 2020, urbanicity, total population (per 100 000), and percentage of voters who voted Republican in 2020, the total

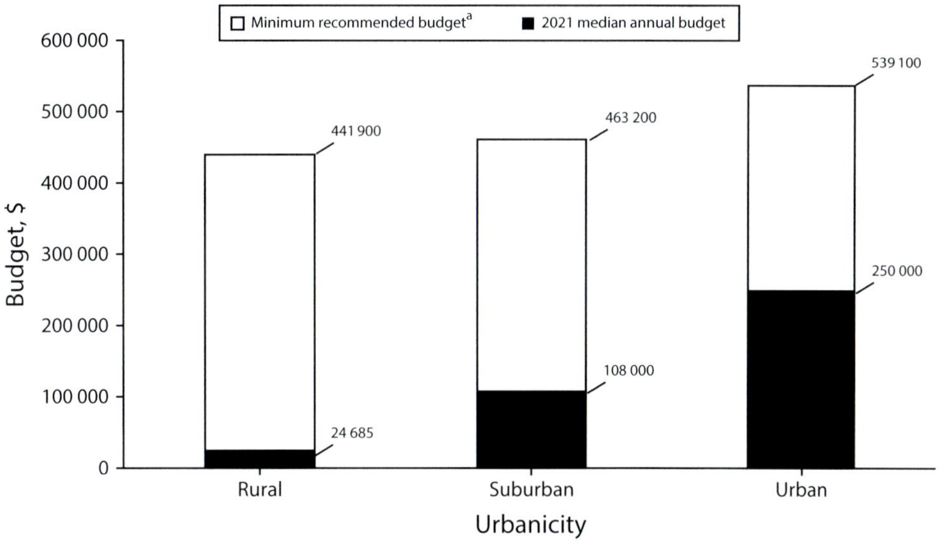


**FIGURE 1— Minimum Benchmark and Median Actual Annual Budgets in 2021 for Syringe Services Programs in United States, by Urbanicity**

[a]Benchmarks were taken from Teshale et al.[13] omitting start-up costs and based on a small (250 clients per year) syringe services program using 2016 US dollars.

SSP budget had a statistically significant association with the number of participant encounters where syringes were distributed (incidence rate ratio [IRR] = 1.16 per $100 000 budget increase; 95% CI = 1.13, 1.20), the number of syringes distributed (IRR = 1.21; 95% CI = 1.18, 1.24), the number of participant encounters where naloxone was distributed (IRR = 1.09; 95% CI = 1.06, 1.12), and the number of naloxone doses distributed (IRR = 1.09; 95% CI = 1.06, 1.12; Figure 2). SSP budget also had a positive association with the offering of fentanyl test strips and buprenorphine treatment, though those adjusted odds ratios (AORs) were not statistically significant (AOR = 1.27; 95% CI = 0.85, 1.92 and AOR = 1.13; 95% CI = 1.00, 1.29, respectively).

**TABLE 2— Association of Community and Organizational Characteristics With Syringe Services Program (SSP) Budget Size in the United States, 2021**

| | AMD, $ (95% CI) | P |
|---|---|---|
| Opioid-related mortality per 100 000 population (smoothed), 2020 | 77 949[a] (7 216, 148 681) | .031 |
| Urbanicity (Ref = rural) | | |
| Suburban | 10 856 (−75 694, 97 406) | .81 |
| Urban | 241 965 (89 664, 394 265) | .002 |
| CBO-SSP (Ref = DPH-SSP) | 64 146 (−10 136, 138 428) | .09 |
| % of voters in the SSP catchment area who voted Republican during the presidential election, 2020 | −80 890[a] (−153 821, 7 958) | .03 |

*Note.* AMD = adjusted mean difference; CBO-SSP = community-based organization–run SSP; CI = confidence interval; DPH-SSP = department of public health–run SSP.
[a]In the case of continuous variables (which were standardized with mean = 0 and SD = 1), the AMD is presented for a 1-SD increase.

## DISCUSSION

One of our most striking findings was that the majority of SSPs' actual annual budget levels were far below minimum benchmarks for a small-scale SSP. This funding gap was even more evident with decreasing levels of urbanicity. This is particularly alarming given the potential that SSPs hold for reaching PWID and delivering evidence-based public health interventions that can prevent infectious diseases and overdose deaths. The unrealized potential of SSPs is substantial; even though the federal government has recently begun funding these organizations, SSPs require substantially greater sustained resources from local, state, and federal sources to be optimally effective.

In our analysis, we found that most SSPs had diverse funding sources, with fundraising or donations from

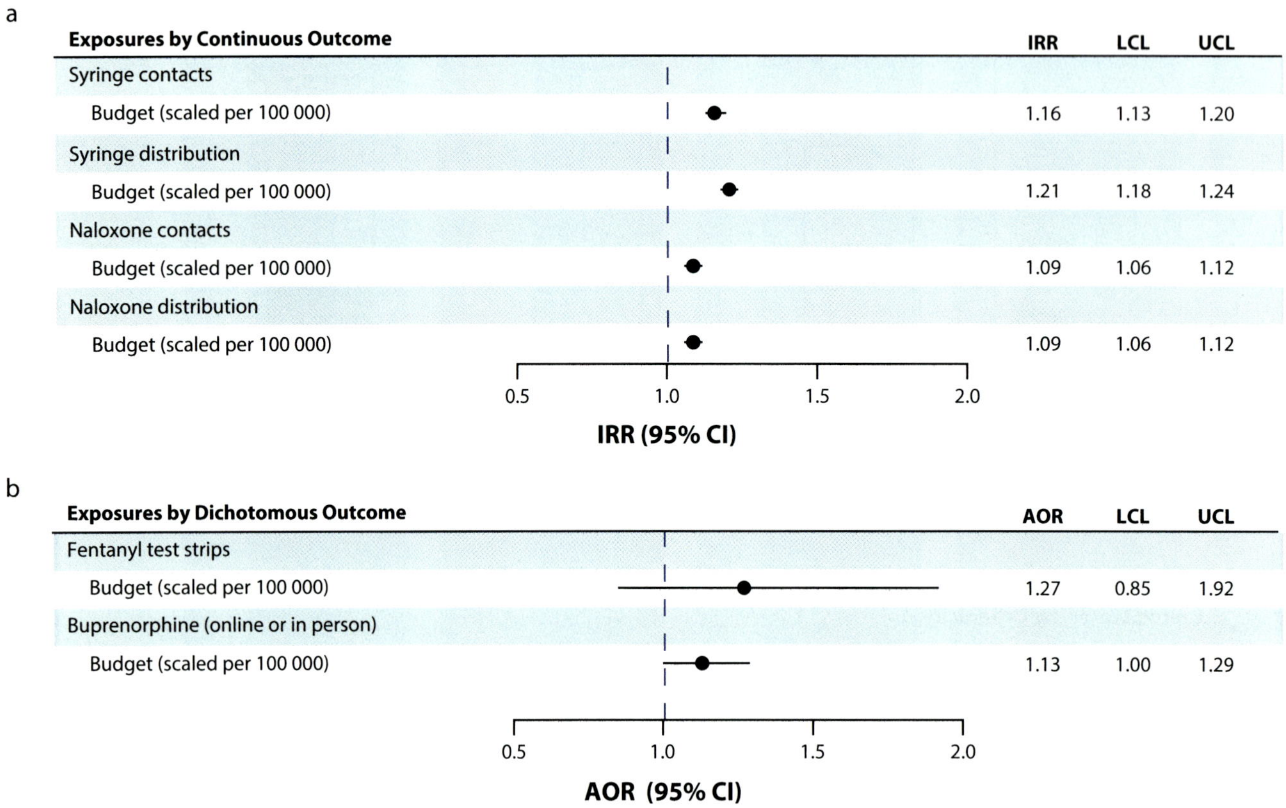


**FIGURE 2—** **Relationship of Syringe Services Program (SSP) Budget Level and Service Scale, by (a) Continuous Outcomes and (b) Dichotomous Outcome: United States, 2021**

*Note.* AOR = adjusted odds ratio; CI = confidence interval; IRR = incidence rate ratio; LCL = lower confidence limit; UCL = upper confidence limit. The vertical, blue dotted line represents 1.0, or the null. Outcomes are shaded in green. IRR and AOR point estimates for each exposure's association with the outcome above it are represented with black dots, and the 95% CI is demonstrated by the horizontal line. All models were adjusted for SSP annual budget (scaled per $100 000), smoothed opioid-related mortality in 2020, urbanicity, SSP type, percentage of voters who voted Republican in the 2020 election, and population (scaled per 100 000).

individuals the second-most-common source of funding. Individual donations, while beneficial, are typically not in amounts comparable to large government contracts and are typically inconsistent over time, creating an uncertain climate in which to build staffing and broader organizational structures. Previous research has shown that limited, fragmented funding can be detrimental to implementation of evidence-based interventions.[25] Many SSPs with small budgets rely heavily on volunteer labor, especially CBO-SSPs. While volunteer support is welcomed, it increases instability for these underresourced programs, and civil society should not rely on volunteerism to provide essential public health interventions.

We also found that higher levels of SSP funding led to greater distribution of a variety of SSP services, regardless of underlying community or organizational characteristics. SSPs have repeatedly been shown to be cost-effective, life-saving public health interventions,[26–28] and public health departments have a responsibility to make data-informed funding decisions. Throughout the United States, we need more institutional structures for people with substance use disorders to receive culturally sensitive treatment services that aid recovery from problematic use.[29,30] As SSPs are a trusted, culturally sensitive source of care for many PWID, they are ideal settings for building infrastructure to improve access to treatment. Without increasing funding for SSPs, it will be difficult for public health institutions to meet the emerging and changing needs of PWID.[14]

We found many variables that were significantly associated with SSP budget size. SSP budget size was significantly greater in counties with higher opioid-related mortality in the previous year, and, while encouraging, the level of funding remains inadequate. Urban SSPs had higher budgets than suburban and rural SSPs, even after accounting for opioid-related mortality rates and voting history; as more than two thirds of the US population live in suburban and rural areas,[19] there is a clear need to improve SSP funding in less densely populated areas.

Finally, while we found significantly lower budget levels for SSPs in areas where a higher percentage of voters voted Republican in the 2020 presidential election, it remains unclear whether the driving factors for less-resourced programs in Republican districts are unique to SSPs. For example, it could also be that similar underlying factors are driving findings from other recent research showing Republican-dominated districts in the United States have had the lowest COVID-19 vaccine uptake[31] and the highest COVID-19 mortality rates.[32] As long as the United States remains highly politically polarized, funding for SSPs among states with Republican-dominant governments may have little chance of increased support despite the evidence supporting implementation. Further work is needed to untangle and address partisan differences with regard to individual autonomy, use of public resources, science-based approaches, and morality-based decision-making specific to SSP support.

One case study that highlights the importance of adequate funding is the California Harm Reduction Initiative, or CHRI.[33] CHRI was a state government--funded initiative that began in August 2020 and provided more than $15 million to SSPs over 3 years through direct funding and technical assistance from the National Harm Reduction Coalition. CHRI-supported SSPs in our study had a median total annual budget of $245 000, which was $151 080 more than the median annual budget across non-CHRI SSPs.[33] Though CHRI represents the largest single investment in harm reduction ever made by the State of California before 2023, the median annual budget provided to California SSPs through CHRI was $112 500, which still remains far below benchmarks set by Teshale et al. SSPs that were funded by CHRI had significantly more participant encounters than non–CHRI-funded SSPs, and provided significantly more syringes, naloxone, fentanyl test strips, and buprenorphine treatment than those not funded through this initiative. Moving forward, this type of evidence-based investment in harm reduction service provision is one that other states can look to as a model to increase funding levels for their programs. Future work should investigate the impact of state-level funding initiatives on SSP operations in states other than California.

## Limitations

There are a number of potential limitations to this analysis. First, we had a survey response rate of 68%, which may have contributed to some selection bias in the sample. It remains possible that other SSPs exist that are unknown to us and that our findings do not represent those SSPs that did not respond. Previous surveys have suggested that SSPs that do not respond to surveys like this one tend to be small programs.[34] This is unsurprising, as smaller programs would likely have less staff time available to fill out a survey. If this were true for the 2022 NSSSP, our study could be overestimating actual budget levels for SSPs in the United States.

Second, program budgets can be complex, and while we estimated the association of variables with budget size, other unmeasured factors driving annual SSP budgets in various communities could exist. This could vary by region, which we did not attempt to address in this analysis. Furthermore, while this analysis used the number of syringes distributed as 1 outcome, many jurisdictions face legal barriers to syringe distribution that limit distribution to a 1:1 ratio (only 1 sterile syringe can be provided in exchange for every used syringe returned). These and similar legal barriers were likely unmeasured confounders on the association between SSP budget and number of syringes distributed, and do not reflect CDC recommendations.[35]

Third, we used county-level, smoothed opioid mortality rates in the previous year as a proxy for underlying need in a community. Smoothed estimates may over- or underestimate actual opioid overdose death rates, may not match drug overdose death rates obtained from NCHS, and do not fully represent community need, which would ideally also include measures of substance use disorder treatment accessibility and viral infection rates.

Fourth, this analysis was not designed for a detailed budget comparison of actual budget levels for specific services versus benchmarks for that service as put forward by Teshale et al. No data were available to differentiate budget and service outcomes for SSPs embedded within organizations that provide clinical services and those that are nonclinical. In addition, we did not capture information about SSP affiliations with other organizations whose mission includes delivery of clinical or other types of billable services, nor did we capture information about in-kind contributions. Future work should assess allocation of SSP budget levels to different services within SSPs.

## Public Health Implications

SSPs are well positioned to have an impact on the health of PWID in ways beyond prevention of HIV and hepatitis C if they are funded and supported to distribute naloxone, integrate fentanyl test strips, and offer buprenorphine to those who are interested. Higher funding levels could yield greater staffing and supplies, better partnerships and integration throughout the community, improved workplace culture, and ability for SSPs to reach those who are most vulnerable to drug-related (and other) harms. Increased local, state, and federal funding must come with low administrative burden to ensure that SSPs retain organizational autonomy to adapt as needed. Otherwise, SSPs will need to carefully consider the trade-offs of accepting funding from specific sources.[36]

With financial and political support, SSPs will be able to provide more services to a population at high risk of morbidity and mortality. Federal, state, and local health departments must issue more funding for SSPs—to at least benchmarks described by Teshale et al. and CDC colleagues—and provide political support for them to do this life-saving work. AJPH

### ABOUT THE AUTHORS

Shelley N. Facente is with the School of Public Health, University of California Berkeley. Jamie L. Humphrey, Christopher Akiba, Sheila V. Patel, Lynn D. Wenger, Terry Morris, Alex H. Kral, and Barrot H. Lambdin are with RTI International, Berkeley. Hansel Tookes is with the University of Miami, Miami, FL. Ricky N. Bluthenthal is with University of Southern California, Los Angeles. Paul LaKosky and Stephanie Prohaska are with the North American Syringe Exchange Network, Tacoma, WA.

### CORRESPONDENCE

Correspondence should be sent to Shelley Facente, 5601 Van Fleet Ave, Richmond, CA 94804 (e-mail: shelley@facenteconsulting.com). Reprints can be ordered at https://ajph.org by clicking the "Reprints" link.

### PUBLICATION INFORMATION

Full Citation: Facente SN, Humphrey JL, Akiba C, et al. Funding and delivery of syringe services programs in the United States, 2022. *Am J Public Health*. 2024;114(4):435–443.

Acceptance Date: January 6, 2024.

DOI: https://doi.org/10.2105/AJPH.2024.307583

ORCID iD:
Shelley N. Facente https://orcid.org/0000-0002-7266-352X

### CONTRIBUTORS

S. N. Facente participated in writing and preparing the original draft of the article and in the investigation. J. L. Humphrey participated in the methodology, investigation, and visualization and in writing and preparing the original draft of the article. C. Akiba reviewed and edited the article. S. V. Patel, L. D. Wenger, H. Tookes, R. N. Bluthenthal, P. LaKosky, S. Prohaska, and T. Morris participated in data curation and reviewed and edited the article. A. H. Kral participated in conceptualization, methodology, and supervision and in writing and preparing the original draft of the article. B. H. Lambdin participated in conceptualization, methodology, investigation, and supervision and in writing and preparing the original draft of the article.

### ACKNOWLEDGMENTS

This research was supported by Arnold Ventures.

Thanks to all the staff of syringe services programs that completed surveys, which made this work possible.

### CONFLICTS OF INTEREST

The authors have no conflicts of interest to disclose.

### HUMAN PARTICIPANT PROTECTION

Our study procedures were reviewed and approved by the internal review board within the Office of Research Protection at RTI International (STUDY00021210).

### REFERENCES

1. Spencer M, Miniño A, Warner M. Drug overdose deaths in the United States, 2001–2021. Atlanta, GA: National Center for Health Statistics, Centers for Disease Control and Prevention; 2022.
2. Mattson C, Kumar S, Tanz L, Patel P, Luo Q, Davis N. Drug overdose deaths in 28 states and the District of Columbia: 2020 data from the State Unintentional Drug Overdose Reporting System (SUDORS). Atlanta, GA: Centers for Disease Control and Prevention, US Department of Health and Human Services; 2022.
3. Centers for Disease Control and Prevention. Persons who inject drugs (PWIDs): data and surveillance. 2023. Available at: https://www.cdc.gov/pwid/surveillance.html. Accessed May 13, 2023.
4. Ciccarone D, Unick GJ, Cohen JK, Mars SG, Rosenblum D. Nationwide increase in hospitalizations for heroin-related soft tissue infections: associations with structural market conditions. *Drug Alcohol Depend*. 2016;163:126–133. https://doi.org/10.1016/j.drugalcdep.2016.04.009
5. Adams JM. Making the case for syringe services programs. *Public Health Rep*. 2020;135(1, suppl): 10S–12S. https://doi.org/10.1177/0033354920936233
6. Wilson DP, Donald B, Shattock AJ, Wilson D, Fraser-Hurt N. The cost-effectiveness of harm reduction. *Int J Drug Policy*. 2015;26(suppl 1): S5–S11. https://doi.org/10.1016/j.drugpo.2014.11.007
7. Hagan H, McGough JP, Thiede H, Hopkins S, Duchin J, Alexander ER. Reduced injection frequency and increased entry and retention in drug treatment associated with needle-exchange participation in Seattle drug injectors. *J Subst Abuse Treat*. 2000;19(3):247–252. https://doi.org/10.1016/S0740-5472(00)00104-5
8. Heinzerling KG, Kral AH, Flynn NM, et al. Unmet need for recommended preventive health services among clients of California syringe exchange programs: implications for quality improvement. *Drug Alcohol Depend*. 2006;81(2): 167–178. https://doi.org/10.1016/j.drugalcdep.2005.06.008
9. Lambdin BH, Kan D, Kral AH. Improving equity and access to buprenorphine treatment through telemedicine at syringe services programs. *Subst Abuse Treat Prev Policy*. 2022;17(1):51. https://doi.org/10.1186/s13011-022-00483-1
10. Centers for Disease Control and Prevention. Syringe exchange programs—United States, 1994–1995. *MMWR Morb Mortal Wkly Rep*. 1995; 44(37):684–685, 691.
11. Bramson H, Des Jarlais DC, Arasteh K, et al. State laws, syringe exchange, and HIV among persons who inject drugs in the United States: history and effectiveness. *J Public Health Policy*. 2015; 36(2):212–230. https://doi.org/10.1057/jphp.2014.54
12. Des Jarlais DC, McKnight C, Milliken J. Public funding of US syringe exchange programs. *J Urban Health*. 2004;81(1):118–121. https://doi.org/10.1093/jurban/jth093
13. Teshale EH, Asher A, Aslam MV, et al. Estimated cost of comprehensive syringe service program in the United States. *PLoS One*. 2019;14(4): e0216205. https://doi.org/10.1371/journal.pone.0216205
14. Broz D, Carnes N, Chapin-Bardales J, et al. Syringe services programs' role in ending the HIV epidemic in the US: why we cannot do it without them. *Am J Prev Med*. 2021;61(5 suppl 1): S118–S129. https://doi.org/10.1016/j.amepre.2021.05.044
15. SAMHSA announces unprecedented $30 million harm reduction grant funding opportunity to help address the nation's substance use and overdose epidemic. Washington, DC: Substance Abuse and Mental Health Services Administration; 2021.
16. The White House. What They Are Reading in the States: Biden-Harris administration awards $1.5 billion to states and tribes to combat overdose epidemic. September 24 2022. Available at:

https://www.whitehouse.gov/briefing-room/statements-releases/2022/09/24/what-they-are-reading-in-the-states-biden-harris-administration-awards-1-5-billion-to-states-and-tribes-to-combat-overdose-epidemic. Accessed February 16, 2024.

17. Fernández-Viña MH, Prood NE, Herpolsheimer A, Waimberg J, Burris S. State laws governing syringe services programs and participant syringe possession, 2014–2019. *Public Health Rep.* 2020;135(1, suppl):128S–137S. https://doi.org/10.1177/0033354920921817

18. Lambdin BH, Bluthenthal RN, Wenger LD, et al. Overdose education and naloxone distribution within syringe service programs—United States, 2019. *MMWR Morb Mortal Wkly Rep.* 2020;69(33):1117–1121. https://doi.org/10.15585/mmwr.mm6933a2

19. Parker K, Horowitz JM, Brown A, Fry R, Cohn D, Igielnik R. What unites and divides urban, suburban and rural communities. Washington, DC: Pew Research Center; 2018.

20. Saunders ME, Humphrey JL, Lambdin BH. Spatiotemporal trends in three smoothed overdose death rates in US counties, 2012–2020. *Prev Chronic Dis.* 2023;20:E16. https://doi.org/10.5888/pcd20.220316

21. National Center for Health Statistics, Centers for Disease Control and Prevention. National Vital Statistics System. Restricted-use vital statistics data. 2022. Available at: https://www.cdc.gov/nchs/nvss/nvss-restricted-data.htm. Accessed April 27, 2022.

22. MIT Election Data Science Lab. County Presidential Election Returns 2000–2020. In: Harvard Dataverse, V11. Available at: https://dataverse.harvard.edu/dataset.xhtml?persistentId=doi:10.7910/DVN/VOQCHQ. Accessed February 16, 2024.

23. Zeger SL, Liang KY, Albert PS. Models for longitudinal data: a generalized estimating equation approach. *Biometrics.* 1988;44(4):1049–1060. https://doi.org/10.2307/2531734

24. American Community Survey 2016–2020 5-year estimates. Suitland, MD: US Census Bureau; 2021.

25. Beidas RS, Marcus S, Wolk CB, et al. A prospective examination of clinician and supervisor turnover within the context of implementation of evidence-based practices in a publicly-funded mental health system. *Adm Policy Ment Health.* 2016;43(5):640–649. https://doi.org/10.1007/s10488-015-0673-6

26. Walley AY, Xuan Z, Hackman HH, et al. Opioid overdose rates and implementation of overdose education and nasal naloxone distribution in Massachusetts: interrupted time series analysis. *BMJ.* 2013;346:f174. https://doi.org/10.1136/bmj.f174

27. Hurley SF, Jolley DJ, Kaldor JM. Effectiveness of needle-exchange programmes for prevention of HIV infection. *Lancet.* 1997;349(9068):1797–1800. https://doi.org/10.1016/S0140-6736(96)11380-5

28. Puzhko S, Eisenberg MJ, Filion KB, et al. Effectiveness of interventions for prevention of common infections among opioid users: a systematic review of systematic reviews. *Front Public Health.* 2022;10:749033. https://doi.org/10.3389/fpubh.2022.749033

29. Dickson-Gomez J, Weeks M, Green D, Boutouis S, Galletly C, Christenson E. Insurance barriers to substance use disorder treatment after passage of mental health and addiction parity laws and the affordable care act: a qualitative analysis. *Drug Alcohol Depend Rep.* 2022;3:100051. https://doi.org/10.1016/j.dadr.2022.100051

30. Lewis R, Baugher AR, Finlayson T, Wejnert C, Sionean C. Healthcare access and utilization among persons who inject drugs in Medicaid expansion and nonexpansion states: 22 United States cities, 2018. *J Infect Dis.* 2020;222(suppl 5):S420–S428. https://doi.org/10.1093/infdis/jiaa337

31. Yang TC, Matthews SA, Sun F. Multiscale dimensions of spatial process: COVID-19 fully vaccinated rates in US counties. *Am J Prev Med.* 2022;63(6):954–961. https://doi.org/10.1016/j.amepre.2022.06.006

32. Gollwitzer A, Martel C, Brady WJ, et al. Partisan differences in physical distancing are linked to health outcomes during the COVID-19 pandemic. *Nat Hum Behav.* 2020;4(11):1186–1197. https://doi.org/10.1038/s41562-020-00977-7

33. Lambdin BH, Kral AH, Wenger L, et al. Impact of the California Harm Reduction Initiative. In: *RTI Insights.* Vol 2023. Berkeley, CA: RTI International; 2023.

34. Centers for Disease Control and Prevention. Syringe service programs for persons who inject drugs in urban, suburban, and rural areas—United States, 2013. *MMWR Morb Mortal Wkly Rep.* 2015;64(48):1337–1341.

35. Javed Z, Burk K, Facente S, Pegram L, Ali A, Asher A. Syringe services programs: a technical package of effective strategies and approaches for planning, design, and implementation. Atlanta, GA: National Center for HIV/AIDS, Viral Hepatitis, STD and TB Prevention, Centers for Disease, Control and Prevention; 2020.

36. Fast D, Cunningham D. "We don't belong there": new geographies of homelessness, addiction, and social control in Vancouver's inner city. *City Soc.* 2018;30(2):237–262. https://doi.org/10.1111/ciso.12177